Hope's Daughters

Faith and Culture

Peter Humfrey

authorHOUSE®

AuthorHouse™ UK Ltd.
500 Avebury Boulevard
Central Milton Keynes, MK9 2BE
www.authorhouse.co.uk
Phone: 08001974150

First published by AuthorHouse 8/28/2009

ISBN: 978-1-4490-1852-8 (sc)

This book is printed on acid-free paper.

Hope has two beautiful daughters.
Their names are anger and courage;
anger at the way things are,
and courage to see that they change.

Augustine of Hippo.

Contents

Illustrations

Introduction

Words strain,
Crack and sometimes break, under the burden,
Under the tension, slip, slide, perish,
Decay with imprecision, will not stay in place,
Will not stay still. Shrieking voices
Scolding, mocking, or merely chattering,
Always assail them.
— T. S. Eliot, The Four Quartets, *Burnt Norton*, 19[1]

T.S. Eliot describes a world which now might be called *post-modern*. The old certainties seem insecure. What can we now rely on in this changing and changed world? "And the Word became flesh and dwelt among us, full of grace and truth" (Jn 1:14). What does this Word mean for today? How do our faith and the culture in which we live illuminate one another. The method of our quest in this book is summarised in the General Directory for Catechesis: "Availing herself of the human sciences which are always necessary, the Church seeks to discover the meaning of the present situation within the perspective of the history of salvation" (GDC 31).[2]

This book is about the foundations of faith and has its origins in the searching, questioning and discoveries of people of all ages, from cradle to grave, in over thirty years of the author's pastoral work and teaching. The author was asked, more than once: "How do you know?

That's just your opinion!" Answers to questions raised were sought and discussed with reference to wide range of sources from liturgy, theology, sociology and life experience. I have done my best to give full credit to the many authors that I have read and enjoyed and whose work has already brought help and hope to many. I apologise if I have not done justice to their intent. I have kept the spelling and the culture of the original sources (I am sorry that this means a spattering of non-English spelling and non-inclusive language). Any errors or omissions in this book are mine. This book, in which the chapters may be read in any order, is not an encyclopaedia, dictionary or text book. It simply seeks to organise some thoughts and findings in a more ordered way under the headings of formation, worship and ministry in the context of exploring the future of faith in our post-modern culture.

> Part 1 looks at modern and post-modern culture through two sociological viewpoints, one on modernism from Peter Berger and Thomas Luckmann and the other on post-modernism from Zygmunt Bauman, all of whom help us to interrogate our present reality. Chapters three, four and five consider areas which may be fruitful for a dialogue between faith and culture and include reflections on globalisation, consumerism, post-colonialism, deconstruction, loss of institutional memory and the rise of the network.

> Part 2 explores inculturation, evangelisation, lifelong learning and community.

> Part 3 opens the door on the Paschal Mystery, liturgy, initiation, imagination and sacraments.

> Part 4 examines aspects of ministry and "presence", catechesis and sacred space.

The Catholic Church itself encourages us to have recourse to the findings of modern sciences. The Second Vatican Council urged:

> The Faithful should live in the closest contact with others of their time, and should work for a perfect understanding

of their modes of thought and feelings as expressed in their culture. They should combine knowledge resulting from the new sciences and teaching, and from recent discoveries, with Christian morality and formation in Christian teaching, so that their religious worship and uprightness go hand in hand with their knowledge of the sciences and increasing technology, and they are thus able to interpret everything with full Christian awareness.[3]

Modernism

The Enlightenment of the 17th to 19th centuries was a radical break from a past in which the church had a *de facto* monopoly on philosophy, art, science and hence culture. The philosophers during the Enlightenment, such as Descartes and Locke, declared a freedom from having to define all things in terms of God. The term modernism encompasses the activities and output of those who felt the "traditional" forms of art, architecture, literature, religious faith, social organisation and daily life were becoming outdated in the new economic, social and political conditions of an emerging fully industrialised world.

Modernism includes a rationalist approach to the Bible, the evaluation of the meaning of the bible by reference to the text alone and without recourse to what the church fathers and others have historically taught about it. The ideal of secularism grew and can be summarised as holding that the best course of action in politics and other civic fields is that which flows from disparate groups' and religions' common understanding of the "good." By implication, Church and State should be separated.

One tenet of Modernism is that dogmas (what is taught by the Church and what its members are required to believe) can evolve over time, rather than being the same for all time. The Development of Doctrine, much like certain interpretations of being saved *sola fide* ("by faith alone"), allows for a constant updating (critics would say "loosening", although adherents claim that this is a misinterpretation). This aspect of thought was what made Modernism come to be considered a heresy by the Church.

Throughout the modern era, cultural, philosophical and political debates have marked out an intellectual space between the declining authority of the church on the one hand and, on the other, the economic and technical imperatives forcing the pace of change. While in some senses it has been in opposition to central ideas of the revelation and the supernatural as expressed in Christianity, modernism has also shaped Christianity by fostering an attitude of individualism, systemisation and rational apologetics.

Since Pope Paul VI, most the Church has largely dropped the term "modernism", perhaps because it is inherently ambiguous, instead preferring to identify more precise errors, such as secularism, liberalism or relativism. The term has however enjoyed a revival amongst Traditionalists and Conservative critics within the Catholic Church.

Post-modernism

Post-modernism is essentially based on socio-political theory and refers to activities from the 20th Century onwards which exhibit awareness of and reinterpret the modern. Post-modernists claim a paradigm shift from modernism seeded by two potent factors, a disenchantment with the Enlightenment and the "hegemony" of rationalism, and an emerging global culture.

Post-modern historians see the dissolution of the transparency of history and tradition. They question the representation of history and cultural identities: history as "what 'really' happened" (external to representation or mediation) opposed to history as a "narrative of what happened" with a particular point of view and cultural/ideological interests. They see a shift from universal histories, from the *long durée*, to local and explicitly contingent histories. The rise of multiculturalism sets up competing views of history and tradition.

Capitalism is now without borders. Theories and academic discourses are confronted by the wider, un-systemised, popular networks of cultural production and knowledge. The intellectual's privilege to explain and distribute knowledge is threatened. Nostalgia and retro styles abound, recycling earlier genres and styles in new contexts (not only film/TV genres, images, typography, colours, clothing styles, advertising images but even the church is not exempt with a return to old languages, old translations and old vestments). Some of these phenomenona correspond with what seems to be an effort to control time and space and create idealised representations of the past. The creation of surreal environments (from shopping malls to theme parks) and virtual tours (which bring distant objects and places to our desktop) are examples of this. The constant juxtaposition of conflicting, non-sequential information makes us willing to accept contradiction and ambiguity in other areas of life including religion. Social trends also include a distrust of institutions, authority figures and history.

As post-modernism turns away from organised, rational explanations for reality, it sometimes turns toward and embraces mystery and enchantment. This may include an interest in Medieval and ancient themes (which are pre-modern) in the form of ancient church rites, superstition, Eastern religions and New Age thinking. There is a disruptive ingression of popular culture, its aesthetics and intimate possibilities, into a previously privileged domain. Bricolage, improvisation which is primitive, unstructured and non theoretical, stands in opposition to modern thought patterns and enters the world of ritual and worship. It is seen as a welcome exercise of spontaneity; pastiche becomes an aesthetic ideal.

Faith

Post-modernism reflects a loss of modern belief in the moral progress of humankind in history, the end of a conception of reason ushering in universal agreement or certainty and the dismissal of a grand narrative account of being created human (assuming human sameness, and not differences). Post-modernism's move beyond belief is reinforced by a postcolonial insistence that the focus of this field of study would be world religions, not religion in the singular.

Theology is in danger of being marginalised and ultimately replaced by religious studies and world religions and, in certain courses of study, becomes simply philosophy and ethics, under the title of religious education. The philosophy of religion moves from the study and justification of belief in a personal God to a critical engagement with religious "practice." Belief and reason are considered western, male and cultural constructions.

Ihab Hassan, the literary theorist, avows that: "Post-modernism has become, consciously or unconsciously, for better or for worse, an interpretive category, a hermeneutic tool... More than a period, more even than a constellation of artistic trends and styles, post-modernism has become, even after its partial demise, a way we view the world."[4]

Pope John Paul II's Exhortation on Catechesis in Our Time counsels a dialogue of cultures:

> On the one hand the Gospel message cannot be purely and simply isolated from the culture in which it was first inserted (the biblical world or, more concretely, the cultural milieu in which Jesus of Nazareth lived), nor, without serious loss, from the cultures in which it has already been expressed down the centuries; it does not spring spontaneously from any cultural soil; it has always been transmitted by means of an apostolic dialogue which inevitably becomes part of a certain dialogue of cultures (CT 53).[5]

Part 1: From Modern To Post-Modern

Chapter 1
Modernity

When we consider the nature of faith in society today and the role of institutions in preserving, developing and extending this faith, it is helpful to observe the trends in recent history and to use the insights of sociology to formulate our approach to education. Richard Gaillardetz claims that: "Sociology helps us appreciate the significance of the social structures in which we are formed and nurtured, structures like the family, the school and the church. These structures exert a profound influence on our capacity for communion."[6]

Education is an intention or a function of the institution where structures and programmes and initiatives are under scrutiny. Behind the institution there is a vision of the potential of the gospel to transform not only people but their institutions, within and beyond the church and in dialogue with world faiths. Peter Berger and Thomas Luckmann in *The Social Construction of Reality* provide a seminal text for the study of and reflection on the nature of institution.[7] Their approach helps us to understand the ways in which the church might engage in education today and the assumptions that lie behind particular forms of theological education. In particular it examines the circumstances under which education can take place and develop.

The major theme of their work concerns the relationship between the structures and the action of the individual. They quote two schools

1

of thought: "The first and most fundamental rule is: consider social facts as things" (Durkheim), and "... for Sociology ... the object of cognition is the subjective meaning complex of action" (Weber). For Berger and Luckmann these two positions are not contradictory or mutually exclusive, and, further, both are correct. Throughout the book we find arguments that emphasise this dual nature of social life, the way in which social structures and individual consciousnesses are not separate but interlinked.

Here we summarise the themes of the book. As we live our lives, we tend to develop repetitive patterns of behaviour. These *habits*, as they are called, are useful to us because they allow us to handle recurring situations automatically. Our habits are also useful to other people. In face-to-face communication the participants observe and respond to each other's habits, and in this way all of us come to anticipate and depend upon the habits of others. As time goes by, some habits become shared among all of the members of the society.

An *institution* is a collection of shared expectations about such long term public habits. Institutions encourage the development of *roles*, or collections of habitual behaviours that are associated with and expected of individuals who are acting in an institutional capacity. When a person assumes a role, he or she adopts these habitual behaviours, and we interact with him or her as part of the institution rather than as a unique individual. When we interact with people in any of these institutional roles, we treat them according to our shared expectations of the role. Because they establish behavioural rules, institutions provide societal control. However, if this control is to persist over time, then each new generation of children must be trained to participate in the institutions of their parents. Thus, institutions are *legitimised* and maintained by means of tradition and education. Eventually, some institutions become *reified* – that is, the members of the society forget that the institutions are human constructions, and they begin to relate to them as if they are natural objects. In this way, we create social structures that seem as real to us as the reality the "natural" world.[8]

Origins of Institutionalisation

"How does social order arise? It is a human product or an ongoing human production. Externalisation, creating external products, is an anthropological necessity. The emergence, maintenance and transmission of social order come from institutionalisation."[9] All human activity is subject to *habitualisation*. Actions are cast into patterns which can be repeated; the important psychological gain is that choices are narrowed; habitualised activity opens up the possibility of deliberation and innovation. These processes precede institutionalisation.

How do institutions arise? Whenever people and objects are placed in categories (typification). Institution posits actions. Institutions further imply historicity (process) and control (by setting up predefined patterns of conduct). Primary social control is in the institution as such. Institutions manifest themselves in collectivities. Interaction becomes predictable. The actions which are likely to be reciprocally typified are actions that are relevant to both within their common situation – labour, sexuality, territoriality. Development and addition lead to objectivity. Although the routines, once established, carry within them a tendency to persist, the possibility of changing them or even abolishing them remains at hand in consciousness. The objectivity of the institutional world thickens and hardens. Such a world becomes real in an ever more massive way and it can no longer be changed so readily. Children have no part shaping it; it confronts them as a given reality that is opaque in places at least. The process of transmission strengthens the parents' reality. Institutions resist attempts to change or evade them. The objectivity of the institutional world is a humanly produced, constructed objectivity. It has no ontological status. The relationship between producer and the social world is dialectical. *Externalisation* and *objectivation* are moments in a continuing dialectical process; the third moment is *internalisation* which completes the process of socialisation. Only with the transmission of the social world to a new generation does the fundamental social dialectic appear in its totality. Only with the appearance of a new generation can we talk about a social world.[10]

The institutional world requires *legitimation* – that is, it can be explained and justified. Children have no memory of the original meaning of the institution. Deviance from institutionally programmed courses becomes more likely once the institutions have become realities divorced from their original relevance in the concrete social processes from which they arose. The new generation posits a problem of compliance. And socialisation requires the establishment of sanctions. The priority of institutional definitions of situations must be consistently maintained over individual temptation at redefinition. The more conduct is institutionalised, the more predictable and the more controlled it becomes.

How do institutions hang together? Some relevancies will be common. Many areas will be relevant only to certain types. The analysis of meaningful reciprocity in the process of institutionalisation shows that logic lies not in institutions but in reflection about them. The process of legitimation is built on language and integration is understood in terms of knowledge of institutional order. Primary knowledge about the institutional order is pre-theoretical. Recipe knowledge (everyday knowledge for routine activity) defines and constructs conduct and roles. Any deviance from the institutional order appears as a departure from reality. It may be seen as moral depravity, mental disease or plain ignorance. This knowledge is internalised as objectively valid truth in the course of socialisation. This body of knowledge is transmitted to the next generation. It is learned as objective truth in the course of socialisation and thus internalised as subjective reality.[11]

The Transmission of Knowledge

How is knowledge transmitted? Only a small part of the totality of human experience is retained in consciousness. These experiences are sedimented. Intersubjective *sedimentation* is social and objectivated by a sign system. Then these experiences will be transmitted to the next generation. These sedimented experiences are detached from original context of individual biographies and made generally available.

Language is the basis and instrument of the collective stock of knowledge. The objectification of experience in the language then allows its incorporation into a larger body of tradition by way of moral instruction, inspirational poetry, religious allegory and so on.

Legitimations can succeed each other from time to time bestowing new meanings on sedimented experiences of the collectivity in question. The past history of a society can be reinterpreted without necessarily upsetting the institutional order. The transmission of the meaning of an institution is based on the social recognition of that institution as a "permanent" solution to a "permanent" problem of a given collectivity. Potential actors of institutionalised actions must be systematically acquainted with these meanings. This necessitates some form of "educational" process. The formal character of institutional meanings ensures their memorability.

The authors suggest that the meanings of institutional activity are conceived of as "knowledge" and transmitted as such. Some of this "knowledge" is deemed relevant to all, some only to certain types. All transmission requires some sort of social apparatus. Certain types of "knowledge" may have to be reaffirmed through symbolic objects (fetishes, military emblems), and/or symbolic actions (religious or military ritual). All transmission of institutional meanings obviously implies control and legitimation procedures. These are attached to the institutions themselves and administered by the transmitting personnel.

Roles

All institutionalised conduct involves *roles*. These roles share in the controlling character of institutionalisation. Compliance and non-compliance with socially defined role standards cease to be optional – the severity of sanctions may vary from case to case. The roles represent institutional order. Roles make it possible for institutions to exist as a real presence in the experience of living individuals. Knowledge is socially distributed. Specialists become administrators of the sectors of knowledge that have been socially assigned to them.

If few relevance structures are shared then the scope of institutionalisation will be narrow. In that case institutional order will be highly fragmented. When the institutional order embraces the totality of social life, it resembles the continuous performance of a complex, highly stylised liturgy. Institutionalisation is not an irreversible process and secularisation occurs when the myths no longer seem plausible.

The segmentation of the institution prevents the maintenance of social experience. But competition between sub-universes makes them increasingly inaccessible to outsiders. They have become esoteric enclaves, "hermetically sealed" to all but those who are properly initiated into their mysteries. Outsiders have to be kept out through intimidation, propaganda, mystification and manipulation of prestige symbols. Insiders have to be kept in by compliance and remaining in the lay state in face of experts. Where a traditional religion is forced to cope with the popularisation of a scientific world view, the work of the legitimators becomes especially strenuous.

The basic recipe for the reification (as opposed to seeing it as a human product) of institutions is to bestow on them an ontological status, independent of human activity and signification. Roles can be reified – I have to act like this because of my role.

Legitimation

Legitimation – that is that the institutional order can be explained and justified – is a second phase of institutionalisation. Legitimation produces new meanings serving to integrate the meanings already attached to disparate institutional processes. Legitimation's main purpose is integration. First, the totality of the institution should make sense. Second, the totality of individual's life should be subjectively meaningful. The problem of legitimation arises when the institutional order is to be transmitted to a new generation, for the self-evident character of institutions can no longer be maintained by the individual's own recollection and habitualisation. The unity of history and biography is broken.

Legitimation explains the institutional order by ascribing cognitive value to its objectivated meanings, and justifies the institutional order by giving a normative dignity to its practical imperatives. There are four levels of legitimation – the first de facto, of traditional affirmations, the second is theoretical, of explaining meaning in moral terms, the third is an explanation in terms of a differentiated body of knowledge, usually entrusted to specialised personnel with formalised initiation procedures. The fourth concerns *symbolic universes* (constructed by means of social objectivations), referring to realities other than those of everyday experience. Symbolic universes follow from objectivation, sedimentation and accumulation of knowledge – they are social products with a history. The symbolic universe orders and thereby legitimates everyday roles, priorities and operating procedures. Identity is ultimately legitimated by placing it within the context of a symbolic universe. Death posits the greatest threat to the taken-for-granted realties of everyday life. The legitimation of death is one of the most important fruits of symbolic universes.

Conceptual Machineries of Universe-Maintenance

Socialisation is never completely successful in the transmission of the symbolic universe from one generation to the next. Children's questions about the symbolic universe have to be answered in a more complicated way than their questions about the institutional realities of everyday life. Heretical groups pose a theoretical threat to the symbolic order and a practical one to the institutional order legitimated by the symbolic universe in question. Repression of these groups needs to be legitimated by setting in motion of various conceptual machineries designed to maintain the official universe against the heretical challenge.

An alternative symbolic universe presented by another society must be met with the best possible reasons for the superiority of one's own. The alternative symbolic universe may have a missionary appeal. Individuals from one's own society may be tempted to emigrate from the traditional universe or, worse, change the old order into the image of the new! The winner depends on greater power, not on theoretical ingenuity, that is, those who wield the better weapons rather than those who have the better arguments. Conspicuous types of *conceptual machineries* for universe maintenance are mythology, theology, philosophy and science. Mythology as a conceptual machinery is the closest to the naive level of the symbolic universe – the level on which

7

there is the least need for theoretical universe-maintenance. More elaborate mythological systems strive to eliminate inconsistencies and maintain the mythological universe in theoretically integrated terms. Mythological thought operates within the continuity between the human world and the world of the gods. Theology has a greater degree of theoretical systematisation than its mythological predecessor.

Theological thought serves to mediate between these two worlds, precisely because their original continuity now appears broken. With the transition from mythology to theology, everyday life appears less on-goingly penetrated by sacred forces. The body of theological concepts is further removed from the naive level, from the general stock of knowledge of the society and becomes intrinsically more difficult to acquire. The populace may remain relatively unaffected by the sophisticated universe-maintaining theories concocted by the theological specialists. The coexistence of a naive mythology among the masses and a sophisticated theology among an elite of theoreticians, both serving to maintain the same symbolic universe, is a frequent historical phenomenon.

Unlike mythology, the three historically dominant conceptualisations of the cosmos, philosophy, theology and science, become the property of specialist élites whose bodies of knowledge are increasingly removed from the common knowledge of the society at large. Modern science is an extreme step in this development, and in the secularisation and sophistication of universe-maintenance, science not only completes the removal of the sacred from the world of everyday life but removes the universe-maintaining knowledge as such from the world. "Lay" members of society no longer know how their universe is to be completely maintained, although of course they still know who the specialists of universe-maintenance are presumed to be.

Therapy

At a time of rapid change there can be a tendency for the institution to engage more strenuously in maintenance. Two typical forms of *universe-maintenance* are therapy and nihilation.

Therapy entails the application of conceptual machinery to ensure that actual or potential deviants stay within the institutionalised definitions of reality, or, in other words, to prevent the "inhabitants" of a given universe from "emigrating".[12]

Every society faces the danger of individual deviance. Therapy therefore is applied by the legitimating apparatus to individual "cases". Therapy in one form or another is a global social phenomenon. Its specific institutional arrangements, from exorcism to psycho-analysis, from pastoral care to personnel counselling programmes, belong under the category of "social control". This requires a body of knowledge that includes a theory of deviance, a diagnostic apparatus, and a conceptual system for the "cure of souls". Where there is a perceived deviancy in thought or behaviour, there is a sure candidate for therapy. Therapy uses a conceptual machinery to keep everyone within the universe in question.

Nihilation

"Nihilation, in its turn, uses a similar machinery to liquidate conceptually everything *outside* the same universe." [13]

This procedure may also be described as a kind of negative legitimation. Legitimation maintains the reality of the socially constructed universe; nihilation denies the reality of whatever phenomena or interpretations of phenomena do not fit into that universe. It may be done in two ways.

First, deviant phenomena may be given a negative ontological status, with or without a therapeutic intent. This happens most often with individuals or groups foreign to the society in question and thus ineligible for therapy. The threatening neighbours are seen to be barbarians, dwellers in a hopeless cognitive darkness. They may be seen as suitable for therapy or more likely for annihilation. Sometimes circumstances force one to remain on friendly terms with barbaric neighbours. Hence the negation of one's universe is subtly changed into an affirmation of it.

Second, nihilation involves the more ambitious attempt to account for all deviant definitions of reality in terms of concepts belonging to one's own universe. In a theological frame of reference, this entails ceasing to consider the neighbours to be heretics and so to grapple with their beliefs theoretically. In this way the deviant conceptions are interpreted in terms of one's own concepts and incorporated into one's own universe. The presupposition is that they do not know what they say. Their statements are translated into more "correct" terms derived from the universe they negate. In theological terms even the atheist is really a believer.

Berger and Luckmann conclude: "The therapeutic and nihilating applications of conceptual machineries are inherent in the symbolic universe. If the symbolic universe is to comprehend all reality, nothing can be allowed to remain outside its conceptual scope. In principle, at any rate, its definitions of reality must encompass the totality of being."[14]

Social Organisation for Universe-maintenance

How does a society organise itself – what social organisation for universe-maintenance? "Because they are historical products of human activity, all socially-constructed universes change, and the change is brought about by the concrete actions of human beings."[15] Berger and Luckmann suggest that: reality is socially defined, but the definitions are always *embodied*, that is, concrete individuals and groups of individuals serve as definers of reality.

The specialisation of knowledge and the concomitant organisation of personnel for the administration of the specialised bodies of knowledge develop as a result of the division of labour. In the early stages of this development there is no competition between the different experts. As more complex forms of knowledge emerge and an economic surplus is built up, experts devote themselves full-time to the subjects of their expertise, which, with the development of conceptual machineries, may become increasingly removed from the pragmatic necessities of everyday life. Experts in rarefied bodies of knowledge lay claim to a novel status. They are not only experts in this or that sector of the societal stock of knowledge, they claim ultimate jurisdiction over that stock of knowledge in its totality. They are, literally, universal experts. This does *not* mean that they claim to know everything, but rather that they claim to know the ultimate significance of what everybody knows and does.

This stage in the development of knowledge has a number of consequences. The first is the emergence of pure theory. Because the universal experts operate on a level of considerable abstraction from the vicissitudes of everyday life, both others and they themselves may conclude that their theories have no relation whatever to the ongoing life of the society, but exist in a sort of Platonic heaven of a-historical and a-social ideation. This is, of course, an illusion, but it can have great socio-historical potency, by virtue of the relationship between the reality-defining and reality-producing process.

A second consequence is a strengthening of traditionalism in the institutionalised actions thus legitimated, that is, a strengthening of the inherent tendency of institutionalisation towards inertia. Habitualisation and institutionalisation in themselves limit the flexibility of human actions. Institutions tend to persist unless they become "problematic". Ultimate legitimations inevitably strengthen this tendency. If there is a tendency to go on as before, the tendency is obviously strengthened by having excellent reasons for doing so. This means that institutions may persist even when, to an outside observer, they have lost their original functionality or practicality. One does certain things not because they work, but because they *are right* – right, that is, in terms of the ultimate definitions of reality promulgated by the universal experts.

The emergence of full-time personnel for universe-maintaining legitimation brings with it occasions for social conflict. Some of this conflict is between experts and practitioners. The latter may come to resent the experts' grandiose pretensions and the concrete social privileges that accompany them. What is galling is the experts' claim to know the ultimate significance of the practitioners' activity better than the practitioners themselves. Another possibility of conflict is between rival coteries of experts. Some practical resolutions are possible but theory requires a theoretical and abstract argumentation. Rival definitions of reality are thus decided upon in the sphere of rival social interests whose rivalry in turn is "translated" into theoretical terms. In reverse a theory can be demonstrated to be pragmatically superior not by virtue of its intrinsic qualities but by its applicability to the social interests of the group that has become its "carrier".

In such a situation the monopolistic tradition and its expert administrators are sustained by a unified power structure. Those who occupy the decisive power positions are ready to use their power to impose the traditional definitions of reality on the population under their authority. Potentially competitive conceptualisations of the universe are liquidated as soon as they appear – either physically destroyed ("whoever does not worship the gods must die") or integrated within the tradition itself (the universal experts argue that the competing pantheon Y is "really" nothing but another aspect or nomenclature for the traditional pantheon X). In the latter case, if the experts succeed with their argument and the competition is liquidated by "merger", as it were, the tradition becomes enriched and differentiated.

The competition may also be segregated within the society and thus made innocuous as far as the traditional monopoly is concerned – for example, no member of the conquering or ruling group may worship gods of type Y, but the subjugated or lower strata may do so. The same protective segregation may be applied to foreigners or "guest peoples". The following passage provides great illumination on segregation throughout history and its relevance for today:

> Medieval Christendom (certainly not to be called primitive or archaic, but still a society with an effective symbolic mono-poly) provides excellent illustrations of all three liquidating procedures. Open heresy had to be physically destroyed, whether it was embodied in an individual (say, a witch) or a collectivity (say, the Albigensian community). At the same time, the Church, as the monopolistic guardian of the Christian tradition, was quite flexible in incorporating within that tradi-tion a variety of folk beliefs and practices so long as these did not congeal into articulate, heretical challenges to the Christian universe as such. It did not matter if the peasants took one of their old gods, "baptised" him as a Christian saint, and continued

to tell the old stories and to celebrate the old feasts associated with him. And certain competing definitions of reality at least could be segregated within Christendom without being viewed as a threat to it. The most important case of this, of course, is that of the Jews, although similar situations also arose where Christians and Muslims were forced to live close to one another in times of peace. This sort of segregation, incidentally, also protected the Jewish and Muslim universes from Christian "contamination." As long as competing definitions of reality can be conceptually and socially segregated as appropriate to strangers, and ipso facto as irrelevant to oneself, it is possible to have fairly friendly relations with these strangers. The trouble begins whenever the "strangeness" is broken through and the deviant universe appears as a possible habitat for one's own people. At that point, the traditional experts are likely to call for the fire and the sword – or, alternatively, particularly if fire and sword turn out to be unavailable, to enter into ecumenical negotiations with the competitors.[16]

Traditional definitions of reality inhibit social change. Conversely, breakdown in the taken-for-granted acceptance of the monopoly accelerates social change. In a rapidly changing world, it should not surprise us, then, that a profound affinity exists between those with an interest in maintaining established power positions and the personnel administering monopolistic traditions of universe-maintenance. In other words, conservative political forces tend to support the monopolistic claims of the universal experts, whose monopolistic organisations in turn tend to be politically conservative. Historically, of course, most of these monopolies have been religious.

It is thus possible to say that Churches, understood as monopolistic combinations of full-time experts in a religious definition of reality, are inherently conservative once they have succeeded in establishing their monopoly in a given society. Conversely, ruling groups with a stake in the maintenance of the political status quo are inherently churchly in their religious orientation and, by the same token, suspicious of all innovations in the religious tradition.[17]

It is important to bear in mind that most modern societies are pluralistic. This means that they have a shared core universe taken for granted as such, and different partial universes coexisting in a state of mutual accommodation. The latter probably have some ideological functions, but outright conflict between ideologies has been replaced by varying degrees of tolerance or even cooperation. Such a situation, brought about by a constellation of non-theoretical factors, presents the traditional experts with severe theoretical problems. Administering a tradition with age-old monopolistic pretensions, they have to find ways of theoretically legitimating the de-monopolisation that has taken place. Sometimes they take the option of continuing to voice the old totalitarian claims as if nothing had happened, but very few people are likely to take these claims seriously. Whatever the experts do, the pluralistic situation changes not only the social position of the traditional definitions of reality, but also the way in which these are held in the consciousness of individuals.

The pluralistic situation goes with conditions of rapid social change, indeed pluralism itself is an accelerating factor precisely because it helps to undermine the change-resistant efficacy of the traditional definitions of reality. Pluralism encourages both scepticism and innovation and is thus inherently subversive of the taken-for-granted reality of the traditional status quo. One can readily sympathise with the experts in the traditional definitions of reality when they think back nostalgically to the times when these definitions had a monopoly in the field.

One historically important type of expert, possible in principle in any of the situations just discussed, is "the intellectual, whom we may define as an expert whose expertise is not wanted by the society at large."[18] The intellectual is, by definition, a marginal type. Whether he was first marginal and then became an intellectual (as, for example, in the case of many Jewish intellectuals in the modern West), or whether his marginality was the direct result of his intellectual aberrations (the case of the ostracised heretic), need not concern us here. In either case, his social marginality expresses his lack of theoretical integration within the universe of his society. He appears as the counter-expert in the business of defining reality. Like the "official" expert, he has a design for society at large. But while the former's design is in tune with the institutional programmes, serving as their theoretical legitimation, the intellectual's exists in an institutional vacuum, socially objectivated at best in a sub-society of fellow-intellectuals. The extent to which such a sub-society is capable of surviving obviously depends on structural configurations in the larger society. It is safe to say that a certain degree of pluralism is a necessary condition.

Society as a Subjective Reality - Socialisation

The third part of Berger and Luckmann's work explores socialisation. Socialisation is cognitive and emotional – it is about attachment to significant others. It is a dialectical process between the individual and the world. The dialectical process is external; and internalisation occurs with identification, when a person takes on roles and attitudes which relate to fundamental identity and place in the world. Language is the most important content and the most important instrument of socialisation.

In Primary Socialisation there is no problem of identification. There is no choice of significant others. For the child, while not necessarily passive, it is the adult who sets the rules and "there is no other game around"[19] (there are no other significant others). Language must be internalised above all, through which institutionalised programmes are absorbed and the rudiments of legitimating apparatus. Primary socialisation is the world of the child in its luminous reality. Primary socialisation is constructed and has learning sequences that are socially defined. Primary socialisation ends when the concept of the generalised other has been established in the consciousness of the individual. Primary socialisation occurs with the mediation of reality; it is the world of the parents; secondary socialisation needs institutional functionaries.

Secondary socialisation is the internalisation of institutional sub-worlds, (understanding and taking part in the "division of labour" and the concomitant distribution of knowledge). Transition from primary to secondary socialisation is accomplished by rituals. To establish and maintain consistency, secondary socialisation presupposes conceptual procedures to integrate different bodies of knowledge. Secondary socialisation is not the emotionally charged identification of the child with his significant others but has only the amount of mutual identification that is necessary. In secondary socialisation the institutional context is usually apprehended. Hence social interaction e.g. between teacher and learner can be formalised. The roles of secondary socialisation carry a high degree of anonymity. But realities of home are stronger than social realities.

"Secondary relations are formal and anonymous. The primary is at home; in the secondary the lesson needs to be 'brought home' – it needs to be vivid, relevant and interesting."[20] It is rare that a language learned later in life attains the inevitable, self-evident reality of the first language learned in childhood.

Some types of learning, say Berger and Luckmann, require more attention not because of intrinsic qualities but because of a greater degree of identification and inevitability i.e. personal commitment – for example the difference between engineering and music. Sometimes the necessity for the intensifying techniques may come from both intrinsic and extrinsic factors. The socialisation of religious personnel is one example. Techniques are designed to intensify the affective charge of the socialisation process. When the process requires an actual transformation of the individual's "home" reality, it comes to replicate the character of primary socialisation. Socialising personnel take on the character of significant others. The individual then commits himself self to the new reality – gives himself to music, to faith. Religious training in a pluralistic situation posits the need for artificial techniques of reality-accentuation that are unnecessary in a situation dominated by a religious monopoly.

The Maintenance of Subjective Reality

Berger and Luckmann note the importance for reality-maintenance of routine maintenance and crisis maintenance. Everyday life maintains itself by being embodied in routines which is the essence of institutionalisation. Reality is originally internalised by a social process, so it is maintained in consciousness by social processes. The most important vehicle of reality maintenance is conversation. Conversation is engaging with the other rather than gossip/chat which is self centred. "Conversation gives firm contours to items previously apprehended in a fleeting and unclear manner."[21] Language realises a world in the double sense of apprehends and produces a world.

"In order to maintain subjective reality effectively, conversation needs to be continual and consistent. Lack of frequency can sometimes be compensated for by intensity of conversation".[22] One can maintain one's religious faith only if one retains one's significant relationship with the religious community. For example the individual Catholic, cut off from the community of those sharing his own faith, may continue to identify himself as a Catholic. Catholic reality may continue to be subjectively relevant to him. He will however become subjectively empty of "living" reality unless he is "revitalised" by social contact with other Catholics. The way to refresh these memories is to converse with those who share their relevance.

In the case of crisis maintenance, the reality-confirmations have to be explicit and intensive; society sets up specific procedures for situations recognised as involving the risk of a breakdown in reality. In a crisis, frequently ritual techniques are brought into play particularly in predefined and marginal situations e.g. death. These crises may be collective or individual. Even a person seen as a threat evokes defensive procedures. Crisis procedures can become routines.

Transformation of Subjective Reality

Can the subjective reality be transformed? There are degrees of modification of the subjective reality (subjective reality is never totally socialised therefore cannot be totally transformed by social processes) called "alternation". This is possible with a social base serving as a "laboratory" of transformation, mediated to the individual by means of significant others with whom the subject must establish affective identification: the process replicates childhood experiences of emotional dependency on significant others and guides the subject to the new reality. This is otherwise called Religious Conversion.

Significant others represent the plausibility structure. The conversion experience is maintained as plausible only within the religious community. The community provides the indispensable plausibility structure for the new reality. The relationship of conversion and community is not a peculiarly Christian phenomenon. The plausibility structures of religious conversion have been imitated by secular agencies of alternation – political indoctrination and psychotherapy. Segregation is needed from the inhabitants of the former world; disaffiliation takes place – the old reality invoked by outsiders will take form of temptation. Clergy converting from one Christian denomination to another are susceptible to this temptation. In conversation with new significant others, subjective reality is transformed. Therapeutic procedures exist to stop back-sliding.

> The old reality must be reinterpreted within the legitimating apparatus of the new reality…This reinterpretation brings about a rupture in the subjective biography of the individual in terms of "pre-Damascus" and "post-Damascus". Everything preceding the alternation is now apprehended as leading towards it (as in "Old Testament", so to speak, or as *praeparatio evangelii* [a preparation for the Gospel], and everything following it flows from the new reality. This involves a reinterpretation of past biography *in toto*, following the formula – "Then I thought…now I know"…"I already knew then, though in an unclear manner."[23]

Pre-alternation biography is typically nihilated *in toto* under a negative category occupying a strategic position in the new legitimating apparatus – "When I was still living a life of sin…" It is not that the past is forgotten but here there is a radical reinterpretation of the meaning of past events or persons in one's biography. Prophets then fail in their own town as the town does not accept their new reality. Transformations which are radical can also be defined as temporary in duration (if one joins the military for a time or spends time in hospital). The reality base for re-socialisation is the present reality; for secondary socialisation the present is interpreted so as to stand in a continuous relationship with the past.

Internalisation and Social Structure

What are the conditions and consequences of socialisation? The best success is in a society with minimal/simple division of labour and minimal distribution of knowledge: there is no problem of identity. The question: *Who am I?* is unlikely to arise in consciousness since the socially predefined answer is massively real subjectively and consistently confirmed in all significant social action.

However differences in social type in the socialising personnel (different significant others) lead to unsuccessful socialisation. Abnormality becomes a biographical possibility where choice is exercised between reality definitions. Unsuccessful socialisation requires therapy. Therapy is successful where there is no fundamental conflict between the mediated definitions of reality but only differences between versions of the same common reality. Unsuccessful socialisation leads to the question: *Who am I?* It is the same question for the socialised person facing the un-socialised!

Individualists can migrate between a numbers of available worlds. In successful socialisation where (in the post-modern world) there are discrepancies between primary and secondary socialisation, in secondary socialisation alternative realities and identities appear as subjective options; there is not necessarily a need for significant others. When discrepant worlds are available on a market basis, this entails specific constellations of subjective reality and identity. This leads to an increasing general consciousness of the relativity of all worlds. People begin to play at what they are not supposed to be and, worse, at what they are supposed to be. This arises from social division of labour and social distribution of knowledge. Social channelling of activity is the essence of institutionalisation, which is the foundation for the social construction of reality.

Berger and Luckmann's work has been a prominent resource for sociological approaches, for example, to the New Testament. David Horrell refers to the work of Margaret MacDonald who drew upon it in order to describe and understand the process of institutionalisation from the time of Paul to that of the Pastoral Epistles. MacDonald raises critical questions in relation to both Berger and Luckmann's theory and the Pastoral Epistles, in the belief that the ideologies of the theory and the texts are notably similar. The theory is in danger of reinforcing and confirming the ideology of the text, rather than penetrating it critically. A critical sociological approach, Horrell suggests, must raise the questions concerning the social interests reflected in the texts and the texts' ideological dimensions. Adopting such a critical approach, it is tentatively suggested that the Pastorals represent an ideological form of Pauline Christianity which offers religious legitimation for the domination of subordinate social groups.[24]

Horrell draws our attention to the work of Gerd Theissen, one of the earliest pioneers in the application of the principles and methods of sociology to the study of the New Testament, in an article "Legitimation and Subsistence: An Essay on the Sociology of Early Christian Missionaries," first published in 1975. Theissen opened up important questions concerning the conflict in earliest Christianity between "charismatic" and "community organiser" forms of itinerant leadership. He points out an equally significant distinction between itinerant leadership and leadership from resident members of the community. He also suggests that this change may be closely related to the development of more socially conservative patterns of instruction, such as those found in the "household codes." These forms of instruction are increasingly ideological insofar as they provide (often theological) legitimation and naturalisation of the dominant social order. In this particular trajectory – dominant at least within the New Testament itself – the transformation of leadership patterns and the development of increasingly ideological forms of instruction are inextricably interconnected.[25]

Today new approaches to and forms of leadership might need to learn some lessons from the past.

Chapter 2
Post-Modernity

Post-modernism too often seems to be an evasive body of ideas rather than a clear cut concept, mainly characterised by all embracing assertions. Yet it can be referred to as an intellectual project with specific roots and a historical development. The term post-modernity describes the social condition which emerged in the latter half of the twentieth century in the affluent countries of Europe and European descent. The term draws attention both to the continuity and discontinuity of the relationship between the present social condition and to the formation which preceded and gestated it. It confirms the bond with the soul condition of modernity which emerged in the same parts of the world in the course of the seventeenth century and took its final shape in the nineteenth century while at the same time indicating the passing of certain characteristics in whose absence one can no longer describe our present social condition as modern.[26]

Post-modernity and consumerism

Zygmunt Bauman, Emeritus Professor of Sociology at the Universities of Leeds and Warsaw, is one of the foremost sociologists in the world in recent times. In the mid and late 1990s his books began to look at two different but interrelated subjects: post-modernity and consumerism. Bauman began to develop the position that a shift had taken place in modern society in the latter half of the 20th century – it had altered from being a society of *producers* to a society of *consumers*. This switch, Bauman argued, reversed Freud's "modern" trade-off: this time security was given up in order to enjoy increased freedom, freedom to purchase, to consume and to enjoy life. In his books in the 1990s Bauman wrote of this shift as being a shift from "modernity" to "post-modernity". Since the turn of the millennium, his books have tried to avoid the confusion surrounding the term "post-modernity" by using the metaphors of "liquid" and "solid" modernity. In his books on consumerism Bauman still writes of the same uncertainties that he portrayed in his writings on "solid" modernity; but in these books he writes of these fears being more diffuse and harder to pin down. Indeed they are, to use the title of one of his books, "Liquid Fears" – fears about paedophilia, for instance, which are amorphous and which have no easily identifiable referent. Since the turn of the millennium Bauman has disposed of any form of explicit reference to "post-modern" society (preferring the phrase "liquid modern" society), but this is less to do with a rejection of his earlier ideas, where he avowedly characterised the present as "post-modern", and more to do with a recognition of the term's being "wrung dry" by misuse and overuse.

For Bauman the post-modernity has never been seen as in any way teleological (relating to a sense of design or purpose beyond the natural world), or relativistic (the suggestion that knowledge is relative to the limited nature of the mind and the conditions of knowing and that ethical truths depend on the individuals and groups holding them), but rather he characterised it as the posthumous form of modernity. That is, for Bauman's modernity, society was seen as a process of ordering and progress to a rationalised society. This however disavowed the fractal and aporetic (indeterminate) nature of human life, and thus its teleological illusions came to be deposed with the collapse of the colonial enterprise. Bauman's idea of the post-modern therefore takes two forms, firstly, as the drive to an ordered goal that is no longer recognisable, set amidst the collapsing of the "insiders" and the "outsiders"/"strangers" (a milieu in which the processes of cognitive ordering of the strange and different and the aesthetic appreciation of the strange and different are in continual conflict), and secondly, as a way of life in which such inherent human differentiation is accepted and reckoned with. His conception of social life is therefore not one of *opposing* the modern to the post-modern, but of interpolating two different logics within social life.[27]

Liquid Modernity

"Liquid Modernity" then is Bauman's term for the present condition of the world as contrasted with the "solid" modernity that preceded it. According to Bauman, the passage from "solid" to "liquid" modernity has created a new and unprecedented setting for individual life pursuits, confronting individuals with a series of challenges never before encountered. Social forms and institutions no longer have enough time to solidify and cannot serve as frames of reference for human actions and long-term life plans, so individuals have to find other ways to organise their lives. Individuals have to splice together an unending series of short-term projects and episodes that do not add up to the kind of sequence to which concepts like "career" and "progress" could be meaningfully applied. Such fragmented lives require individuals to be flexible and adaptable – to be constantly ready and willing to change tactics at short notice, to abandon commitments and loyalties without regret and to pursue opportunities according to their current availability. In liquid modernity the individual must act, plan actions and calculate the likely gains and losses of acting (or failing to act) under conditions of endemic uncertainty.[28]

Bauman sees post-modernity as modernity fully developed but without the anticipated consequences of its historical work, for its effects were produced inadvertently, rarely responsibly and by default rather than by design, as by-products often perceived as waste.[29]

> Post-modernity may be conceived of as modernity conscious of its true nature – *modernity for itself*. The most conspicuous features of the post-modern condition: institutionalised pluralism, variety, contingency and ambivalence – have been all turned out by modern society in ever increasing volumes; yet they were seen as signs of failure rather than success, as

evidence of the insufficiency of efforts so far at a time when the institutions of modernity, faithfully replicated by the modern mind, struggled for *universality, homogeneity, monotony and clarity*. The post-modern condition can be therefore described, on the one hand, as modernity emancipated from false consciousness; on the other, as a new type of social condition marked by the overt institutionalisation of the characteristics which modernity – in its designs and managerial practices – set about to eliminate and, failing that, tried to conceal.[30]

The existing models of modernity articulate a shared vision of modern history as a *movement with a direction* – but they differ only in the selection of the ultimate destination or the organising principle of the process, be it universalisation, rationalisation or systemisation. None of those principles can be upheld in the light of post-modern experience. Neither can the very master-metaphor that underlies them be sustained: that of the process with a pointer.

"Post-modernity is not a transitory departure from the 'normal state' of modernity; neither is it a diseased state of modernity, an ailment likely to be rectified, a case of 'modernity in crisis'. It is, instead, a self-reproducing, pragmatically self-sustainable and logically self-contained social condition defined by *distinctive features of its own*." [31] A theory of post-modernity therefore cannot be a modified theory of modernity. Post-modernity inhabits a cognitive space organised by a different set of assumptions; it needs its own vocabulary.

The social condition of post-modernity is essentially and perpetually a totality which is a kaleidoscopic, momentary and contingent outcome of interaction. The orderly, structured nature of totality cannot be taken for granted; all order that can be found is a local, emergent and transitory phenomenon. The post-modern condition is a site of constant mobility and change, but no clear direction of development. The post-modern condition is both *undetermined* and *undetermining*. It "unbinds" time, weakens the constraining impact of the past and effectively prevents colonisation of the future.

Bauman briefly analyses the sociological theories of modernity (which conceived of themselves as sociological theories *tout court*) which concentrated on the vehicles of homogenisation and conflict-resolution. This cognitive perspective, as we saw in the previous chapter, (shared with the one realistic referent of the concept of "society" – the national state, the only totality in history able seriously to entertain the ambition of contrived, artificially sustained and managed monotony and homogeneity) a priori disqualified any "uncertified" agency; un-patterned and unregulated spontaneity of the autonomous agent was predefined as a destabilising and, indeed, antisocial factor marked for taming and extinction in the continuous struggle for societal survival. Prime importance was assigned to the mechanisms and weapons of order-promotion and pattern-maintenance: the state and the legitimation of its authority, power, socialisation, culture, ideology, etc. – all selected for the role they played in the promotion of pattern, monotony, predictability and thus also manageability of conduct.

Habitat

The focus of post-modernity, says Bauman, must be now on the *habitat*. Unlike the system-like totalities of modern social theory the habitat neither determines the conduct of the agents nor defines its meaning; it is no more (but no less either) than the setting in which both action and meaning-assignment are possible. Its own identity is as under-determined and motile, as emergent and transitory, as those of the actions and their meanings that form it.

The habitat performs a determining (systematising, patterning) role: it sets the agenda for the "business of life" through supplying the inventory of ends and the pool of means. As the ends are offered as potentially alluring rather than obligatory, and rely for their choice on their own seductiveness rather than the supporting power of coercion, the "business of life" splits into a series of choices. The choices add up to the process of *self-constitution* which is best viewed as *self-assembly*. "The habitat, self-constitution and self-assembly should occupy in the sociological theory of post-modernity the central place that the orthodoxy of modern social theory had reserved for the categories of society, normative group (like class or community), socialisation and control."[32]

Under the post-modern condition, habitat is a *complex system*. Complex systems differ from modernistic mechanical systems in two crucial respects. First, they are unpredictable; second, they are not controlled by statistically significant factors. The consequence is that agencies active within the habitat cannot be assessed in terms of functionality or dysfunctionality.

First there is no "goal setting" agency with overall managing and co-ordinating capacities or ambitions. Second, the habitat is populated by a great number of agencies, most of them single-purpose, some of them small, some big, but none large enough to subsume or otherwise determine the behaviour of the others. Focusing on a single purpose considerably enhances the effectiveness of each agency in the field of its own operation, but prevents each area of the habitat from being controlled from a single source. Agencies are *partly* dependent on each other, but the lines of dependence cannot be fixed and thus their actions (and consequences) remain staunchly under-determined, that is autonomous.

Autonomy means that agents are only partly, if at all, constrained in their pursuit of whatever they have institutionalised as their purpose. Opportunity is what increases output in the pursuit of purpose, problems are what threatens the decrease or a halt of production. The many products of purpose-pursuing activities of numerous partly interdependent but relatively autonomous agents must yet find, ex post facto, their relevance, utility and demand-securing attractiveness. The products are bound to be created in volumes exceeding the pre-existing demand motivated by already articulated problems. They are still to seek their place and meaning as well as the problems that they may claim to be able to resolve.

For every agency, the habitat in which its action is inscribed appears therefore strikingly different from the confined space of its own autonomic, purpose-subordinated pursuits. It appears as a space of chaos and chronic indeterminacy, a territory subjected to rival and contradictory meaning-bestowing claims and hence perpetually ambivalent.

The existential modality of the agents is therefore one of insufficient determination, inconclusiveness, motility and rootlessness. The construction of identity consists of successive trials and errors. It lacks a benchmark against which its progress could be measured, and so it cannot be meaningfully described as "progressing". It is now the incessant (and non-linear) activity of self-constitution that makes the identity of the agent. In other words, the self-organisation of the agents in terms of a life-project (a concept that assumes a long-term stability, a lasting identity of the habitat, in its duration transcending, or at least commensurate with, the longevity of human life) is displaced by the process of self-constitution.

Unlike the life-project, self-constitution has no destination point in reference to which it could be evaluated and monitored. It has no visible end; not even a stable direction. Hence the self-assembly of the agency is not a cumulative process; self-constitution entails disassembling alongside the assembling, adoption of new elements as much as shedding of others, learning together with forgetting. The identity of the agency, much as it remains in a state of permanent change, cannot be therefore described as "developing."

Bauman gives as an example the attention paid to the human body:

> The only visible aspect of continuity and of the cumulative effects of self-constitutive efforts is offered by the human body. Hence the centrality of *body-cultivation* among the self-assembly concerns, and the acute attention devoted to everything "taken internally" (food, air, drugs, etc.) and to everything coming in touch with the skin. DIY operations (jogging, dieting, slimming, etc.) replace and to a large extent displace the panoptical drill of modern factory, school or the barracks; unlike their predecessors, however, they are not perceived as externally imposed, cumbersome and resented necessities, but as manifestos of the agent's freedom. Their heteronomy, once blatant through coercion, now hides behind seduction.[33]

However *freedom* of choice and *dependence* on external agents reinforce each other, and arise and grow together as products of the same process of self-assembly and of the constant demand for reliable orientation points which it cannot but generate. The growth of individually appropriated knowledge widens the range of assembly patterns which can be realistically chosen. Information becomes a major resource, and experts trusted to be the repositories and sources of valid knowledge become the crucial brokers of all self-assembly.

Post-modern politics

Modernist social theory separated theory from policy. It made a virtue out of this which was the foundation of value-free science. Post-modernity cannot follow that pattern. The politics of agents lies at the core of the habitat's existence. All description of the post-modern habitat must include politics from the beginning. The separation of theory and policy in modern *theory* could be sustained as long as there was, unchallenged or effectively immunised against challenge, a *practical* division between theoretical and political practice.

The modern national state had pretensions to and ambitions of administering a global order and of maintaining a total monopoly over rule-setting and rule-execution. The procedure for its formulations had to be made separate and independent from the procedure legitimising an acceptable theory and, more generally, intellectual work was modelled after the latter procedure. The gradual, yet relentless erosion of the national state's monopoly (undermined simultaneously from above and from below, by trans-national and sub-national agencies, and weakened by the fissures in the historical marriage between nationalism and the state, none needing the other very strongly in their mature form) ended the plausibility of theoretical segregation. With state resourcefulness and ambitions shrinking, responsibility (real or just claimed) for policy shifts away from the state/centre or is actively shed on the state's own initiative. It dissipates; it splits into a plethora of localised or partial policies pursued by localised or partial (mostly one issue) agencies.

The modern state's tendency to condensate and draw upon itself almost all social protest arising from unsatisfied re-distributional demands and expectations vanishes; it becomes vulnerable and exposed to frequent political crises (as conflicts fast turned into political protests).

In post-modern times, grievances which in the past would lead to a collective political process, stay diffuse and translate into self-reflexivity of the agents, stimulating further dissipation of policies and autonomy of post-modern agencies. Sometimes they take form of a one-issue pressure group; they bring together agents too heterogeneous in other respects to prevent the dissolution of the formation once the desired progress on the issue in question has been achieved; and even before that final outcome, the formation is unable to override the diversity of its supporters' interests and thus claim and secure their total allegiance and identification. One can speak, allegorically, of the "functionality of dissatisfaction" in a post-modern habitat.

Not all politics in post-modernity is unambiguously post-modern. Throughout the modern era, politics of inequality and hence of redistribution was by far the most dominant type of political conflict and conflict-management. With the advent of post-modernity it has been displaced from its dominant role, but remains (and in all probability will remain) a constant feature of the post-modern habitat. Indeed, there are no signs that the post-modern condition promises to alleviate the inequalities (and hence the re-distributional conflicts) proliferating in modern society. Even such an eminently modern type of politics acquires in many cases a post-modern tinge. Re-distributional vindications of our time are focused more often than not on the winning of human *rights* (a code name for the agent's autonomy, for that freedom of choice that constitutes the agency in the post-modern habitat) by categories of population heretofore denied them (this is the case of the emancipatory movements of oppressed ethnic minorities, of the black movement, of the feminist movement, as much as of the more recent rebellion against the "dictatorship over needs" practiced by the communist regimes), rather than at the express redistribution of wealth, income and other consumable values by society at large. The most conspicuous social division under post-modern conditions is one between *seduction* and *repression*: between the choice and the lack of choice, between the capacity for self-constitution and the denial of such capacity, between autonomously conceived self-definitions and imposed categorisations experienced as constraining and incapacitating. The re-distributional aims (or, more precisely, consequences) of the resulting struggle are mediated by the resistance against repression of human agency. One may as well reverse the above statement and propose that in its post-modern rendition conflicts bared their true nature, that of the drive toward freeing of human agency, which in modern times tended to be hidden behind ostensibly re-distributional battles.

Some of them are new; some others owe their new, distinctly post-modern, quality to their recent expansion and greatly increased impact. The following are the most prominent among them (the named forms are not necessarily mutually exclusive; and some act at cross-purposes). Baumann notes four areas where specifically post-modern forms of politics appear and take the centre ground.[34]

Tribal politics

This is a generic name for practices aimed at collectivisation of the agents' self-constructing efforts. Tribal politics describes the collectivisation of efforts at self-construction and the formation of imagined *communities*. Post-modern tribes symbolically manifest the commitment of their members. They rely on neither executive powers able to coerce their constituency into submission to the tribal rules (seldom do they have clearly codified rules to which submission could be demanded), nor on the strength of neighbourly bonds or intensity of reciprocal exchange (most tribes are de-territorialised, and communication between their members is hardly at any time more intense than the intercourse between members and non-members of the tribe).

Post-modern tribes are, therefore, constantly in a state of becoming *statu nascendi* rather than being *statu essendi*. Allegiance is composed of the ritually manifested support for positive tribal tokens or equally symbolically demonstrated animosity to negative (anti-tribal) tokens.

As the persistence of tribes relies solely on the deployment of the affective allegiance, one would expect an unprecedented condensation and intensity of emotive behaviour and a tendency to render the rituals as spectacular as possible – mainly through inflating their power to shock. The tribal rituals, as it were, compete for the scarce resource of public attention as the major (perhaps sole) resource of survival.

Politics of desire

This entails actions aimed at establishing the relevance of certain types of conduct (tribal tokens) for the self-constitution of the agents. If the relevance is established, the promoted conduct grows in attractiveness, its declared purposes acquire seductive power, and the probability of their choice and active pursuit increases: promoted purposes turn into agents' needs. In the field of the politics of desire, agencies vie with each other for the scarce resource of individual and collective dreams of the good life. The overall effect of the politics of desire is heteronomy of choice supported by, and in its turn sustaining, the autonomy of the choosing agents.

Politics of fear

This is aimed at drawing boundaries to heteronomy and staving off its potentially harmful effects. If the typical modern fears were related to the threat of totalitarianism perpetually ensconced in the project of rationalised and state-managed society, post-modern fears arise from uncertainty as to the soundness and reliability of advice offered through the politics of desire. More often than not, diffuse fears crystallise in the form of a suspicion that the agencies promoting desire are (for the sake of self-interest) oblivious or negligent of the damaging effects of their proposals.

In view of the centrality of body-cultivation in the activity of self-constitution, the damage most feared is one that can result in poisoning or maiming the body through penetration or contact with the skin (the most massive panics have focused recently on incidents like mad cow disease, listeria in eggs, shrimps fed on poisonous algae, dumping of toxic waste, swine flu – with the intensity of fear correlated to the importance of the body among the self-constituting concerns, rather than to the statistical significance of the event and extent of the damage). The politics of fear strengthens the position of experts in the processes of self-constitution, while ostensibly questioning their competence. Each successive instance of the suspension of trust articulates a new area of the habitat as problematic and thus leads to a call for more experts and more expertise.

Politics of certainty

This entails the vehement search for social confirmation of choice, in the face of the irredeemable pluralism of the patterns on offer and acute awareness that each formula of self-constitution, however carefully selected and tightly embraced, is ultimately one of the many, and always "until further notice". Production and distribution of certainty is the defining function and the source of power of the experts. As the pronouncements of the experts can be seldom put to the test by the recipients of their services, for most agents certainty about the soundness of their choices can be plausibly entertained only in the form of *trust*. The politics of certainty consists therefore mainly in the production and manipulation of trust; conversely, "lying", "letting down", "going back on one's words", "covering up" the unseemly deeds or just withholding information, betrayal of trust, abuse of privileged access to the facts of the case – all emerge as major threats to the already precarious and vulnerable self-identity of post-modern agents. Trustworthiness, credibility and perceived sincerity become major criteria by which merchants of certainty – experts, politicians, sellers of self-assembly identity kits – are judged, approved or rejected.

On all four stages on which the post-modern political game is played, the agent's initiative meets socially produced and sustained offers. Offers potentially available exceed as a rule the absorbing capacity of the agent. Hence the overwhelming multiplicity of choice seen in today's world. In the choice much that is on offer is seen not in its intrinsic value but simply another opportunity to choose or not. On the other hand, the reassuring potential of such offers as are in the end chosen rests almost fully on the *perceived* superiority of such offers over their competitors. This is, emphatically, a perceived superiority. The substantial value of inherited traditions carries but little weight. Its attractiveness relies on a greater volume of allocated trust. What is perceived as superiority (in the case of marketed utilities, life-styles or political teams alike) is the visible amount of public attention the offer in question seems to enjoy. Post-modern politics is mostly about the reallocation of attention. Letters from church authorities spend much energy on redirecting public attention. Public attention is the most important – coveted and struggled for – among the scarce commodities in the focus of political struggle.

Ethics

Post-modernity identifies ethics as an indispensable part of its sociological theory. Modern society could leave ethical problems aside or ascribe to them but a marginal place, in view of the fact that the moral regulation of conduct was to a large extent subsumed under the legislative and law-enforcing activity of global societal institutions, while whatever remained unregulated in such a way was "privatised" or perceived (and treated) as residual and marked for extinction in the course of full modernisation. In the post-modern situation while the church as an institution had a similar role in regulation, and doctrine was by and large accepted, in the ethical sphere moral matters gradually became for not a few privatised and matters of opinion and personal choice.

Not all ethical issues found in a post-modern habitat are new. The issues of the orthodox ethics – the rules binding short-distance, face-to-face intercourse between moral agents under conditions of physical and moral proximity – remain presently as much alive as before. In no way are they post-modern; as a matter of fact, they are not modern either. On the whole, modernity contributed little, if anything, to the enrichment of moral problematics. Its role boiled down to the substitution of legal for moral regulation and the exemption of a wide and growing sector of human actions from moral evaluation. The distinctly post-modern ethical problematic arises primarily from two crucial features of the post-modern condition: pluralism of authority, and the centrality of *choice* in the self-constitution of post-modern agents.

Pluralism of authority

Pluralism of authority, or rather the absence of an authority with globalising ambitions, has a twofold effect. First, it rules out the setting of binding norms each agency must (or could be reasonably expected to) obey. Agencies may be guided by their own purposes, paying in principle as little attention to other factors (also to the interests of other agencies) as they can afford, given their resources and degree of independence. If unmotivated by the limits of the agency's own resources, any constraint upon the agency's action has to be negotiated afresh. Rules emerge mostly as reactions to strife and consequences of ensuing negotiations; still, the already negotiated rules remain by and large precarious and under-determined, while the needs of new rules – to regulate previously unanticipated contentious issues – keep proliferating. This seems to be the current concern of governments dealing with issues of law and order. The *problem of* rules stays in the *focus of* public agenda and is unlikely to be conclusively resolved. The *negotiation of* rules assumes a distinctly *ethical* character: at stake are the principles of the non-utilitarian self-constraint of autonomous agencies – and both non-utility and autonomy define moral action as distinct from either self-interested or legally prescribed conduct.

Second, pluralism of authorities is conducive to the resumption by the agents of moral responsibility that tended to be neutralised, rescinded or ceded away as long as the agencies remained subordinated to a unified, quasi-monopolistic legislating authority. On the one hand, the agents face now point-blank the consequences of their actions. On the other, they face the evident ambiguity and controversiality of the purposes which actions were to serve, and thus the need to justify argumentatively the values that inform their activity. Purposes can no longer be substantiated *monologically*; having become perforce subjects of a *dialogue*, they must now refer to principles wide enough to command authority of the sort that belongs solely to ethical values.

Enhanced Autonomy

The enhanced autonomy of the agent has similarly a twofold ethical consequence. First, in as far as the centre of gravity shifts decisively from heteronomous control to self-determination, and autonomy turns into the defining trait of post-modern agents, self-monitoring, self-reflection and self-evaluation become principal activities of the agents, indeed the mechanisms synonymical with their self-constitution. In the absence of a universal model for self-improvement, or of a clear-cut hierarchy of models, the most excruciating choices agents face are between life-purposes and values, not between the means serving the already set, uncontroversial ends.

Supra-individual criteria of propriety in the form of technical precepts of instrumental rationality do not suffice. This circumstance, again, is potentially propitious to the sharpening up of moral self-awareness: only ethical principles may offer such criteria of value-assessment and value-choice as are at the same time supra-individual (carrying an authority admittedly superior to that of individual self-preservation), and fit to be used without surrendering the agent's autonomy. Hence the typically post-modern heightened interest in ethical debate and increased attractiveness of the agencies claiming expertise in moral values (e.g., the revival of religious and quasi-religious movements).

Second, with the autonomy of all and any agents accepted as a principle and institutionalised in the life-process composed of an unending series of choices, the limits of the agent whose autonomy is to be observed and preserved turn into a most closely guarded and hotly contested frontier. Along this borderline new issues arise which can be settled only through an ethical debate. Are the flow and the outcome of self-constitution to be tested before the agent's right to autonomy is confirmed? If so, what are the standards by which success or failure are to be judged (what about the autonomy of young and still younger children, of the indigent, of parents raising their children in unusual ways, of people choosing bizarre lifestyles, of people indulging in abnormal means of intoxication, people engaging in idiosyncratic sexual activities, individuals pronounced mentally handicapped)? And, how far are the autonomous powers of the agent to extend and at what point is their limit to be drawn (remember the notoriously inconclusive contest between "life" and "choice" principles of the abortion debate)?

All in all, in the post-modern context agents are constantly faced with moral issues and obliged to choose between equally well founded (or equally unfounded) ethical precepts. The choice always means the assumption of responsibility, and for this reason bears the character of a moral act. Under the post-modern condition, the agent is perforce not just an actor and decision-maker, but a *moral subject*. The performance of life-functions demands also that the agent be a morally competent subject.

Participation

In the modern society, it was for that reason that the proper accounting for the self-reflexive propensities of human actors proved to be so spectacularly difficult. Deliberately or against its declared wishes, sociology tended to marginalise or explain away self-reflexivity as rule-following, function performing or at best sedimentation of institutionalised learning; in each case, as an epiphenomenon of social totality, understood ultimately as "legitimate authority" capable of "principally coordinating" social space.

In a post-modern habitat sociology must conceive of itself as a participant (perhaps better informed, more systematic, more rule-conscious, yet nevertheless a participant) of this never ending, self-reflexive process of reinterpretation and devise its strategy accordingly. In practice, this will mean in all probability, replacing the ambitions of the sociologist as judge of "common beliefs", healer of prejudices and umpire of truth with those of a clarifier of interpretative rules and facilitator of communication; this will amount to the replacement of the dream of the legislator with the practice of an interpreter.

Bauman, speaking of the shift of his position on the modernity/post-modernity distinction, said:

> "Post-modernity" was but a preliminary concept – signalling that something essential has changed in modernity as we knew it and got used to describe: an important illusion – that re-making the world is a one-off job and that modern (rationally designed and problem-free) society will be the end-product of modernisation – has vanished. But that concept, being preliminary, was un-committal about the kind of realities that emerge in the wake of that vanishing act. It took me quite a few years of exploration of the various aspects of the ways we live now to replace a "negative" concept of post-modernity with the "positive" concept of liquid modernity. In a nutshell, you may say that "liquid modernity" is (to borrow Tony Giddens' term) the continuation of disembedding coupled with dis-continuation of re-embedding. The latter, once the prime goal of modernising bustle, is these days no more on offer, and shunned.[35]

In the same interview, questioned about one of the criticisms often made of his work about the emphasis he put on the individual and processes of individualisation at the expense of focusing on latter day formations of togetherness (community), Bauman responded:

> In liquid-modern society we all, and each one of us, are instructed (to paraphrase Ulrich Beck) to seek biographical exits from the socially concocted mess. So we are all individuals by (unwritten) decree – spending most of our life trying to gain an individuality de facto. This is a tall order of a task, and no wonder we tend to dream of respite. It is not true that I focus on individualisation "at the expense" of togetherness – it is my belief that, in fact, they cannot be discussed, let alone grasped, separately. I have written a little book on community with a subtitle "seeking safety in an uncertain world."[36] The more lonely we feel, the more we speak of community (which invariably stands for slowing down in the world of mind-

boggling acceleration); but community is at its strongest when it can stay silent and can do without self-adulation. The world in which community (as Raymond Williams put is) is "always has been", the gaping void is hastily filled by what I call "peg communities", "ad hoc communities", "explosive communities" and other disposable substitutes meant for an instant and one-off consumption... They quench the thirst for security, albeit briefly. None is likely to deliver on the hopes invested, since they leave the roots of insecurity unscathed.[37]

CHAPTER 3
Challenges

Globalisation and consumerism are two facets of the post-modern era which relate strongly to the dialogue between faith and culture.

Globalisation

One major consequence of the new technologies of the information network is generally called globalisation. Globalisation is not a system in itself but a way of operating. In the first place it is an economic phenomenon with effects on travel, industry, food, production. Michael Shapiro suggests that all other kinds of globalisation, cultural, legal, political, moral, educational follow from the economic.[38] Shapiro notes that as we look back over fifty years, we can see that economic growth has expanded fivefold, international trade has expanded by roughly twelve times and foreign direct investment has been expanding at two of three times the rate of trade expansion. Yet the results of these developments have been highly uneven. While economic elites and corporations have benefited tremendously the rewards have been unequally distributed, gaps between rich and poor, the haves and the have-nots, the overdeveloped and underdeveloped regions have grown exponentially. The wealthier nations continue to exploit the people, resources and land of the poorer nations, often leaving environmental degradation behind. The debt crisis in which the poorer countries owe the richer ones astronomical sums has increased dramatically since the 1970s. As Douglas Kellner observes:

> There are more poor people in the world today than ever before; violence on the local, national, and global scale has erupted throughout this century of unmitigated disaster and horror; the planet's ecosystem is under siege and the "fate of the earth" lies in immediate jeopardy. For much of the world, life is still "nasty, brutish, and short," and prosperity, health, education, and welfare remain distant dreams for much of the overpopulation of the besieged earth.[39]

Globalisation raises not only ethical and theological questions but educational too. Ethically the drive for production and profit contradicts more "ethical" forms of sociality. Global flows of capital create encounters between different worlds even as they reconfigure them. "Good will," in the sense of an ethical stance toward a cultural Other, should involve a respect for that Other's practices of singularity and a recognition that Otherness is a dynamic, inextricably related to the way capital creates identity spaces. A concern with "the ethical life" would necessitate both recognition of the contingency of one's own identity as well as of the interdependencies of global relationships as they relate to structures of inequality.

Theologically Christians have always aspired to a theology with global validity and have always explicitly recognised antagonism and resistance as constitutive of the structural demands on religious discourse. Treating what he calls "the theological challenge of globalisation," theologian Max Stackhouse, for example, calls for a "theological perspective large and supple enough truly to comprehend the social and religious pluralism of the globe," as increasing contact with other world religions "makes certainties less stable."[40] The various genres of discourse – dogmatics, apologetics and kerygmatics – are haunted. For example, a committed deconstructionist could hardly improve on this statement by a theologian Thomas O'Meara on the paradoxes and uncertainties involved in moving from the dogmas of institutionalised scriptural interpretation to the injunctions of kerygmatic discourse: "How can there be anything like dogma (which includes by definition the permanent, the lasting, the canonised in language), when historicity and linguistics have shown all language to be, despite any claim of the divine, quite human and always historical?"[41]

The drive of Christianity to create "communities of believers" or still indeed a universal community of believers leads to boundary issues treated differently by the three approaches noted above. In any case the construction of an ideal "community of faith," effectively denies an ongoing history of disagreement and schism within Christianity itself while an approach which non-Christian religious alterity as "ethnic," or (as is used later) as "cultural," effectively denies the pan-ethnic and transcultural bases of other religions, for example from the time of Constantine on.[42]

In terms of education, globalisation raises a number of issues. Mike Bottery notes that most discussion on the roles and responsibilities of educators has centred around the three core values of subject expertise, public service and the need for autonomy in exercising professional judgement. [43] These values remain essential, but in the light of the foregoing discussion, need to be supplemented. He suggests a number of areas where globalisation has had an effect on our educational discourse: environmental, cultural, demographic, political and economic. Each of these areas is also of concern to the churches in their role in education. The environmental area is already a well trodden path, so we move on to the other areas.

Bottery speaks of the "globalisation of cultural variety", where music, food and religious activities of divers origins can be experienced in one locality:

> Such variety can provide education with different windows through which new perspectives are gained on the familiar, where it can be realised that different roads are being used to pursue the same truths. Yet others may not view such experiences as opportunities for spiritual growth, seeing them instead as roads to relativity and fragmentation.[44]

Faced with too many choices, these others cease to see meaning in any choice, and only play with thoughts, ideas, meanings and values. In the process they become one of Richard Rorty's:

> ironic individuals...never quite able to take themselves seriously because [they are] always aware that the terms in which they describe themselves are subject to change, always aware of the contingency and fragility of their final vocabularies, and thus of their selves.[45]

For yet others, individuals who have used beliefs as protective structures within which to encase their lives, rather than as challenges to reflect upon and deepen themselves, such variety leads to a retreat into more rigid, fundamentalist adherences. The globalisation of cultural variety is then viewed as incursion by those who lack the truth, but who would infect you with their falsehoods. When such "incursions" are supplemented by perceptions of Western imperialist arrogance, such resistance may be translated into physical hostility.

On the other hand we can find the "globalisation of cultural standardisation". In the worlds of McDonald and Disney where the artificial and the commodified replace the real, education (and its institutions) can be a liberating experience which open up opportunities to the individual for spiritual growth or can simply make individuals fit to the standard, where the personal is constricted, the spiritual is shackled and the less secure and the more dogmatic are driven down a very different path.

A consideration of demographic globalisation reminds us of the growing tension between increasingly aging populations and those with a much younger profile. The young are less fertile and more highly taxed to support the health and financial needs of older generations. However the elderly may be a generation still interested in formal education for themselves and may develop a deeper concern for the education of generations still to come. Old age would then be a time with great potential for spiritual exploration and societal development.

Political globalisation can be initially conceptualised as the relocation of political power away from the nation state. The increasing involvement of states in global economic activity limits them in maintaining the integrity of their borders in the face of the complexity and interconnectedness of interests and power structures. Political globalisation leads to the spread of ideas, particularly those concerning democratic governance, anti-colonialism and environmental and feminist issues.

However the economic agenda shapes the political and citizenship agendas. Simple allegiances at the national level are overtaken by the call for "nested" concepts of citizenship.[46] The mediation of global forces at the national or cultural level creates a complexity which make it difficult, if not impossible, fully to comprehend, predict or control the future. Educators will probably not only experience greater control and direction of their work, but also the increasing complexity and fragmentation of the world around them; and they will have to help others make sense of this.

Economic globalisation shows different forces. One is the rapid, largely unrestricted movement of finance around the world, a process which prevents nation states from protecting welfare agendas. A second is the locking of nation states into free market agreements by supra-national organisations like the IMF, the World Trade Organisation and the World Bank, which limit the scope of nation-state activity. The third force is that of trans-national companies, who influence national government policies through their ability to relocate their capital, factories and workforces around the world, resulting in competition between nation-states to encourage these companies to do business in their country.

Capitalism's main competitors – fascism, socialism, and communism – have departed. Capitalist activity in order to succeed needs to expand not only in the private sector. Private companies take over the work of public sector companies. Private sector values – primarily those of efficiency, effectiveness and economy – become the criteria of success, whilst other values like care, trust, and equity are increasingly perceived as second order values, being used more for the pursuit of productivity objectives.

The effect of this on community is that "social virtues" are under threat, for community is about is socialisation, the shaping of people's lives and the way in which we live. Community institutions are a reflection of this spirit.[47] The logo-driven society that has become a trade mark of the globalised market system does something different; it tries to shape society in its own image to make people more receptive to its product. Christianity teaches us to love our neighbour as ourself; modern society acknowledges no neighbour. This is the product of individualism.

Margaret Thatcher famously said that: "There is no such thing as society: there are individual men and women, and there are families, and no government can do anything except through people and people look to themselves first...There is no such thing as society. There is living tapestry of men and women and people and the beauty of that tapestry and the quality of our lives will depend upon how much each of us is prepared to take responsibility for ourselves and each of us prepared to turn round and help by our own efforts those who are unfortunate."[48]

Community, be it the locality, the family, the church, the community organisations, is often seen as a threat to the opening up of the system and is more often than not recognised as the first target. The new world order seeks to destroy the traditional supports of community life and replace it with a consumerist void. The two principal victims are the church and the trade union movement – both working to give communities a support mechanism outside the unregulated market place. At the Pope Paul CAFOD lecture in London in 2003, Cardinal Oscar Rodriguez Maradiaga, the Archbishop of Tegucigalpa, Honduras, argued that the welfare state had been dismantled, and replaced by an "absolutism of capitalism...The world is becoming globalised to the rhythm of the major economic powers. Economic globalisation without the globalisation of solidarity is suicide for the poor and thus for the majority of humanity. What is morally false cannot be economically correct."[49]

The growth of globalisation has changed the nature of knowledge and the structures of educational organisations. Using a post-modern business model, we may also apply these principles to the working of the church. A critical issue in business has become the control of the points of access to consumer wants – control of access to the ideas and knowledge which generate new products, new ideas and new experiences. Now such control of access to ideas leads to the perceived need to control and "manage" knowledge, and thus to the importance of terms like "intellectual capital"[50] and the "knowledge economy".[51] May one ask what is the intellectual capital of a church or an educational organisation?

Once again, the economic attempts to commodify other areas. At the organisational level, the question becomes one of how a company's intellectual capital – the intelligence, innovation and creativity which is increasingly the wellspring of its profit base – can be better audited, managed and directed to its benefit, to become what Stewart[52] calls "packaged useful knowledge". One possible suggestion has been seen to be the development of Alpha courses which provide packaged, useful knowledge for becoming Christian. The tangible assets of a business are overtaken by intangible properties like human knowledge, imagination and creativity. Businesses which exercise control through amassing physical capital are challenged, even replaced, as market leaders by those controlling access to ideas, knowledge and expertise. The new economy, then, is a "knowledge economy"; the new capitalism is "knowledge capitalism".

Businesses – and, by implication, education – need to be able to conduct "knowledge audits", and ascertain what "workers" know, what they need to know, and how such knowledge and understanding can be transferred. Gregory Wurzburg suggests a number of strategies may help in utilising "knowledge workers" more efficiently and effectively.[53] These include:

- Doing away with hierarchies and encouraging more horizontal communication;
- Information-gathering at more levels;
- Better trained and more responsive employees;
- Multi- rather than mono-skilled employees;
- An increase in more responsible and self-managing groups.

Managements of such organisations must then differ radically from more "traditional" hierarchical ones, for the core of the knowledge-based company, the intellectual capital of its employees, is best exploited, not by top-down direction, but by multi-level collaboration. The job of leader then moves, argues Stewart,[54] from the traditional one of POEM (plan, organise, execute and measure) to that of DNA (define, nurture, allocate). Organisations must become "learning organisations" within which "responsibilised" workers flourish. They also need to develop more sensitive and flexible education and training systems for these workers. Moreover, with flattened hierarchies, better trained employees and more self-managed task groups, the organisation of the future, it is claimed, will be more empowering, more organic, more democratic, a more collaborative place to work.

People with talent – those who have intellectual capital – will be highly prized and paid, and a critical function of such organisations will be to ensure that those who lack the intellectual capital are given the opportunities to develop it which requires extensive programmes of training and education. Such a knowledge economy, however, will bring more flexibility in career and more movement between jobs (in church terms for "career" and "job", read "ministry"). Such organisational structures will mean that the middle manager as an occupation will be an endangered species, whilst the project worker, favoured for expertise rather than seniority will be preferred. Such organisational changes may be ones well suited for transference to education.

Yet this does not seem a description of what is occurring within education. Indeed, the degree of standardisation and inflexibility in education seems to be increasing, raising the possibility that education systems are being created, and educators conditioned in ways which make them singularly ill-equipped to help their students deal with these challenges. Part of this is because economic globalisation does not produce just greater demands for flexibility: paradoxically, it also increases demands for standardisation and predictability, and many organisations are being driven down this road rather than the road to flexibility. Educational organisations, and particularly universities, as they are increasingly required to compete in global marketplaces, find themselves pushed towards standardised rather than flexible destinations. It is therefore important to point out that the "knowledge economy" and the "knowledge society" are not universal phenomena.

Educators in particular are likely to experience tensions in their work. Their attempts to satisfy the greater demands of both clients and governments for an improved service will be hindered by the need to reduce expenditure and increase efficiencies. The need to respond to nation-state attempts to strengthen its legitimacy as the sole provider of citizenship will likely be in conflict with the increased claims by sub-national groups, and supra-national organisations, which may produce demands for more "nested" forms of citizenship. The pressure to use private sector concepts and practices, primarily based around questions of efficiency, economy, and profit, will likely conflict with public sector values and practices, based more around care and equity. Governments will continue to want to control and direct their thought and activity, yet will also wish them to be flexible and creative in developing students for a competitive knowledge economy. Educators are likely to experience a similar tension in terms of trust, as governments see the need to allow an enhanced autonomy and creativity, yet feel unwilling or unable to abandon policies which result in low-trust cultures of targets, performativity and compliance.

Such tensions are likely to be perceived as being generated by movement, on the one hand, towards decentralisation, flexibility, and empowerment, and on the other, to centralisation and control. There are likely to be then paradoxical perceptions of increases in both the fragmentation and the control of work.

Consumerism

The expansion of business into the areas of the personal and the cultural has the effect of turning cultural "goods" into articles or activities for consumption – they may be "commodified". Ultimately, the dominance of this agenda leads to an emphasis on economic functionality rather than the pursuit of things in their own right, and, in so doing, undermines the intrinsic value of other pursuits. One result is the encouragement of increased consumerism as an aid to expanding growth. This is most effectively done if people can be persuaded to see themselves, first and foremost, as consumers. As they do so, however, they will come to value the personal over the shared, the private over the public. This outcome has important implications for the Church.

Vincent Miller, commenting on the danger of liturgy becoming a production, refers to "consumer religion."[55] Consumer religion is linked to consumer culture which brings news which is both good and bad. The good news is that "consumer culture is experienced by most as a liberation," a liberation from closed culture, small communities and local authoritarian control. Critics sometimes complain that that such freedom from constraint invites moral relativism and anarchy. Moral relativism holds the position that moral or ethical propositions do not reflect objective and/or universal moral truths, but instead make claims relative to social, cultural, historical or personal circumstances. Moral relativists hold that no universal standard exists by which to assess an ethical proposition's truth. Relativistic positions often see moral values as applicable only within certain cultural boundaries (cultural relativism) or in the context of individual preferences (individualist ethical subjectivism). The most authoritative response to moral relativism from the Catholic perspective can be found in *Veritatis Splendor*, an encyclical by Pope John Paul II.[56]

A common phenomenon now is "church shopping" or "parish hopping." People intuitively accept that personal enrichment and fulfilment of desire are the highest goods. As a result, they choose the church that best satisfies their preferences without bothering to consult their community, the Bible or the Holy Spirit to gauge the legitimacy of those desires. After all, in consumerism a desire is never illegitimate, it is only unmet. Approaching Christianity as a brand (rather than a worldview) explains why the majority of people who identify themselves as Christians live no differently than others. According to George Barna: "Churchgoers didn't seem to have any real understanding of the Bible's distinctive message; many practising Christians believed that the Bible teaches that 'God helps those who help themselves. A morally relativistic American culture was shaping Christians more than Christians were shaping the culture.'[57]

Consumerism," he said, "represents an alternative source of meaning to the Christian gospel."[58]

Marketing strategies and secular business values are pervasive in today's ministry. Churches are in competition with other providers of identity and meaning for survival. Churches will have multiple services, now including Saturday as the Lord's Day, so people can choose a time that fits their busy schedule. One parent in an English parish, wishing her child to be prepared for first communion, found difficulty with the parish's proposed schedule of preparation and observed to the parish priest: "Your programme does not fit my life style."

Meanwhile a second result is the growth of "greedy" organisations which attempt to extract the maximum amount of physical and emotional labour and commitment out of individuals in an effort to reduce the costs of production and increase employees' work. This in part explains why many educators (and clergy, and indeed volunteers) now feel increasingly stressed by the quantity of work they are asked to undertake and the amount of themselves they are asked to commit to the good of the organisation. They can become disheartened by the view of their ministry/service simply as a job which becomes a burden and not a joy. Furthermore this ministry is seen to belong by right to the unfortunate individual and there is no hope of a process of succession – it is a job for life. The bad news is that in a consumer's paradise, as Miller observes, "where each person is free to pursue his or her own religious synthesis, whether ingenious and inspired, or banal and conforming… all of these are imprisoned in the private realm of individual insight, while globalising capitalism goes about its business unopposed."[59]

Consumerism produces commodification – "a social process in which the habits, practices and attitudes learned from buying and consuming products carry over into relationships with all other persons, places and things in our culture."[60] Consumerism and commodification lead to a culture based on market "value". All things, including people, have their price and are available for purchase. Estrangement and alienation may result but these are considered a small price to pay for the widespread availability of consumer goods. Value changes from being an intrinsic quality and becomes an arbitrary, extrinsic price and "goods and products to which 'value' is attached are themselves transformed into imaginary acts – a style, window dressing, props of an imaginary life."[61]

Commodification is the insatiable, driving desire to own stuff and a dogged determination to replicate the immediate past – a desire we call "retro chic" or nostalgia. This has a great deal to do with liturgy, as Miller says:

> Neo-traditionalist forms of Catholicism that repudiate the Second Vatican Council seem almost perfect illustrations of commodified nostalgia. Rejecting the Council's attempts to engage modernity critically, they dwell in the Catholicism of the recent past, revering its practices, beliefs, décor, and costume. Such nostalgic retrievals inevitably idealise the past by abstracting it from the particularities that created it and sunder it from any organic relation to the present…Inevitably, such "traditionalist" retrievals are not only innovative but also deeply contemporary. Fundamentalism is a thoroughly modern phenomenon. Traditionalism is deeply marked by the contemporary in that it easily conforms to the logic of nostalgia…Like souvenirs brought home from distant lands, the religion of the past is excised from its cultural political context and used to decorate the everyday life of our own time.[62]

Some have tried to argue that this neo-traditionalist retrieval of the recent past – sometimes noticed even among seminary students – is not retrograde conservatism but a new evangelical witness, a freshly embodied critique of our consumerist culture and values. This argument might have plausibility if we focus only on *what* is being retrieved without ever asking *how* it is being retrieved. The rush to reassert old-time religion falls victim to the very values it claims to criticise, values derived from a "shop till you drop" consumerism. Mitchell concludes:

Catholic nostalgia for the pre-conciliar is simply another symptom of late-capitalist, consumer culture in overdrive; it is a stretch indeed to call it evangelical witness, faith, or service. It is rooted, philosophically, in modernity's autonomous self which believes in its inalienable right to pick and choose what it prefers to believe about the past while pretending to inhabit the present. That is why nostalgia is not only elitist but abstract; it is a desire for goods *masking* as desire for God. We want stuff from the past – but only certain kinds of stuff.[63]

CHAPTER 4
Opportunities

Deconstruction

Two particular aspects of post-modernism which provide an insight into the dialogue of faith and culture are deconstruction and post-colonialism. Jacques Derrida coined the term *Deconstruction* in the 1960s. It is a word denoting a process of examining the *ways* that meaning is constructed by Western writers, texts, and readers and understood by readers – the texts and languages of Western philosophy (in particular) appear to shift and complicate in meaning when read in light of the assumptions and absences they reveal within themselves. Derrida's particular methods of textual criticism involved discovering, recognising and understanding the underlying – unspoken and implicit – assumptions, ideas and frameworks that form the basis for thought and belief.

According to Derrida, deconstruction is not an analysis nor a critique, a method, an act, or an operation.[64] Further, deconstruction is not, properly speaking, a synonym for "destruction". Rather, according to Barbara Johnson, it is a specific kind of analytical "reading":

> Deconstruction is in fact much closer to the original meaning of the word "analysis" itself, which etymologically means "to undo" – a virtual synonym for "to de-construct"... If anything

is destroyed in a deconstructive reading, it is not the text, but the claim to unequivocal domination of one mode of signifying over another. A deconstructive reading is a reading which analyses the specificity of a text's critical difference from itself.[65]

Some detractors claim deconstruction amounts to little more than nihilism:

> Post-modernists and post-structuralists deny the very grounds on which Western cultures have based their "truths": absolute knowledge and meaning, a "decentralisation" of authorship, the accumulation of positive knowledge, historical progress and the ideals of humanism and the Enlightenment. Jacques Derrida, whose deconstruction is perhaps most commonly labelled nihilistic, did not himself make the nihilistic move that others have claimed. Derridean deconstructionists argue that this approach rather frees texts, individuals or organisations from a restrictive truth, and that deconstruction opens up the possibility of other ways of being.... Deconstruction can thus be seen not as a denial of truth, but as a denial of our ability to know truth (it makes an epistemological claim compared to nihilism's ontological claim).[66]

The term "relativism" often comes up in debates over post-modernism. Critics of the perspective of deconstruction often identify its advocates with the label "relativism." Deconstruction is often termed a "relativist perspective" because of the ways it locates the meaning of a text in its appropriation and reading, implying that there is no "true" reading of a text and no text apart from its reading.

These perspectives do not strictly count as relativist in the philosophical sense because they express agnosticism on the nature of reality and make epistemological rather than ontological claims. Nevertheless, the term is useful to differentiate them from realists who believe that the purpose of philosophy, science or literary critique is to locate externally true meanings. This kind of "soft" relativism finds support in sociology, for example in the empirical studies of the social construction of meaning such as those of Berger and Luckmann. Further cultural relativism only implies that differing cultural contexts have to be taken into account when making judgments about what is good or bad relative to that culture. It does not limit one's ability to disagree with a cultural norm. A senior adviser to President Bush said, in the summer of 2002:

> [You people] in what we call the reality-based community . . . believe that solutions emerge from your judicious study of discernible reality. That's not the way the world really works anymore. We're an empire now, and when we act, we create our own reality.[67]

In April 2005, in his homily during Mass prior to the conclave which would elect him as Pope, then Joseph Cardinal Ratzinger talked about the world "moving towards a *dictatorship of relativism*":

> How many winds of doctrine we have known in recent decades, how many ideological currents, how many ways of thinking... Having a clear faith, based on the Creed of the Church, is often labelled today as a fundamentalism. Whereas, relativism, which is letting oneself be tossed and "swept along by every wind of teaching", looks like the only attitude acceptable to today's standards. We are moving towards a dictatorship of relativism which does not recognise anything as certain and which has as its highest goal one's own ego and one's own desires. However, we have a different goal: the Son of God, true man. He is the measure of true humanism. Being an "Adult" means having a faith which does not follow the waves of today's fashions or the latest novelties. A faith which is deeply rooted in friendship with Christ is adult and mature. It is this friendship which opens us up to all that is good and gives us the knowledge to judge true from false, and deceit from truth.[68]

Proponents of deconstruction deny this. It is not the abandonment of all meaning, but attempts to demonstrate that Western thought has not satisfied its quest for a "transcendental signifier" that will give meaning to all other signs. According to Derrida:

> Deconstruction is always deeply concerned with the "other" of language. I never cease to be surprised by critics who see my work as a declaration that there is nothing beyond language, that we are imprisoned in language; it is, in fact, saying the opposite. The critique of logocentrisim is above all else the search for the "other" and the "other of language"... I totally refuse the label of nihilism which has been ascribed to me and my American colleagues. Deconstruction is not an enclosure in nothingness, but an openness towards the other.[69]

One typical form of deconstructive reading is the critique of binary oppositions. A central deconstructive argument holds that, in all the classic dualities of Western thought, one term is privileged or "central" over the other. Examples might include:

- speech over writing
- presence over absence
- identity over difference
- fullness over emptiness
- meaning over meaninglessness
- mastery over submission
- life over death.

For instance, the structure of hierarchy, which Derrida sees as implicit in the kinds of binary oppositions which have traditionally informed, organised and ranked western thinking and have led us to value a concept such as order more highly than it opposite chaos, makes it imperative for Derrida to re-examine other such binary couplets. What the privileging of one term over and above the other (good/

evil, light/dark, reason/emotion, male/female, master/slave, model/copy, original/reproduction, literature/criticism, high culture/popular culture) reveals is that the preference for one term always works at the expense or exclusion of the subordinated term. Deconstruction is the means to expose, reverse and dismantle binary oppositions with their hierarchies of value. Each term differs from and defers to the other term (*'différance'*).

Liturgy

Sarah Irwin considers the application of deconstruction to the liturgy. She says that where traditions can be made into idols and dissenting voices silenced, deconstruction may be the opening of the door, an opening of the hand. Irwin offers an extensive reflection on the value of deconstruction in uncovering and enjoying the deeper experience of Christian faith in the liturgy:

> Deconstruction itself is "inherently" nothing at all; neither radical or conservative; the dichotomy between the two is undone. But as we deconstruct words, entire texts are loosed as well. What to do in the face of this deferral, this endless looking behind and beneath? It is easy to imagine a situation in which we slip from this recognition of instability to throwing up our hands in moral relativism and, later, nihilism. The text is based in a context, tied to a context, which is in turn tied other contexts and so on....We pay attention to context and thus to an incessant movement of recontextualiston. This multiple referencing disrupts every logic of opposition and dialectic. It delimits what it limits...context is not finite; there is an indefinite opening of every context... truth is not relativised and made impotent; truth is made bigger.[70]

Truth in this scheme requires archaeology. The *de* of *de*construction is not the demolition of what is constructing itself but rather what remains to be thought beyond the constructivist and destructionist scheme. That which remains to be thought is always buried under layers of context. We are left to do the hard work of excavation.

Irwin continues by considering the importance of community. Liturgy is a phenomenon of communities. It is an act undertaken by the community through which the church is constituted. There is no Christian individual identity prior to the Christian identity of the community. At the same time there is no Christian community without those particular individuals who through accident or intention or upbringing find themselves part of it. It is through liturgy that the church understands itself as the body of Christ. The project of liturgy is to place its participants in the presence of God, to appropriate for themselves that reality.

Our particular experience of liturgy is based on a prior context. Irwin refers to Joyce Zimmerman's perception of the aim of liturgy: "It is not so much perfect ritual as it is *prayer* that leads to appropriation of the Jesus-event in our lives. If a liturgy is performed flawlessly and according to liturgical law but does not make a difference in the lives of the people, then the liturgy ultimately has no authority, since it has no life."[71] There is something more complex than personal journey. By its fruits we know our faith. It is not just a matter of cause and effect – liturgy is formative. Our core identity established in baptism is nourished in early childhood by exposure to and experience of liturgy, of the dying and rising of Christ – the Paschal Mystery.

The community surrounds and supports and sends out the baptised person. Our bodies are energy in worship; worship is always an embodied experience. Liturgy is always experienced through the senses. People learn who they are and who they are becoming by what they say and do themselves and through the roles assigned to them in the community. Liturgy is text and performance. The experience of the assembled body happens in the context of the "cloud of witnesses" past and present that have made the assembly's presence at that event possible. The key to liturgy is repetition.

Derrida's philosophy of language – if indeed it is one – can be useful, says Irwin, for thinking about liturgy in two linked ways, one descriptive and the other analytical. The goal is not to deconstruct the liturgical text; the text, enacted, deconstructs itself. Liturgy gives us the language for how we encounter God. Liturgy is a process of translation. Liturgy provides us with a horizon of understanding – a horizon unimaginably far away but always present, however blocked our sight-lines may be at times. Bernard Lonergan's horizon is: "a boundary establishing a world of meaning within which that person lives. The horizon of the church is the web of shared meaning which constitutes the church as a collective subject. It is a corporate horizon and it is this horizon which is mediated in liturgical practice."[72]

Irwin suggests that the trouble with liturgy is that it works. The rule of prayer is the rule of belief. We do not pray our words casually, accidentally or only with our mouths. There are "only words"; but they are the only words that we have. As far as liturgy can form us in the realm of God, it deforms as well; a foot that is bound from birth, again and again, year after year, will not be straightened by sheer force of will.

Liturgy works with power: the power of words and also the power of institutions both clerical and secular. The critical task of the liberation liturgist is "to examine how liturgy reproduces the sinful power dynamics of the world. There is a question of justice, not of preference. When we choose only in the name of 'tradition' or 'history', we risk abandoning true *leitourgia*, the work of the people, in favour of nostalgic reassurance of past worldview."[73]

At the same time as liturgy binds us to a particular worldview, it frees us to step out of that worldview. Each utterance has the potential to destabilise all the oppressions enacted by the whole. Liturgy, however hierarchical or exclusive it may be, destabilises our assumptions about the world and about God. Participation in liturgy binds us but it also frees us, giving us a new imaginative faculty, giving us a liturgical sensibility that helps us to exist in the world in a different way. Liturgy is always a focus on others. There is always a tension in liturgy, indeed for liturgy to be "authentic and relevant" these tensions must be in evidence, as Don Saliers urges: "between the 'already' and the 'not yet', between the material form and the spiritual substance, the mediation of the divine and the critique of cultural idolatries, and between particular cultural means of communication and the humanely common."[74]

Radical, going to the root, getting under our cultural oppressions and evils, liturgy has a power we do not know apart from the shadows of it evident in our own transformation. But shadows, still: even our own metamorphoses are not visible to us. "The church is full of bad liturgy, oppressive and violent. Of this, too, there is no question. But there is no impotent liturgy, never a neutral one. Ambiguous, yes – there is both healing and hurting – but neutral, no."[75] What deconstruction can teach is to pay attention to the "space between" of *différance:* the space between the words we use and the reality we seek. Our words can only point to what we might mean. Our whole bodies are required to speak our liturgical prayers.

Discernment

All discourse, Irwin believes, all semiotics, conceal as much as they reveal. The task here is to excavate memories of the suppressed, the "incorrect" and the places where the experiences of the marginalised are whitewashed by the master story. Liturgy liberates, but its power is abused and it betrays itself when some are given voice at others' expense. The deconstructive move is a putting-into-perspective, but it is not a quietist move. It is to say, "Look! This that appeared so hegemonic, so water-tight, is neither of those things. See how it quarrels even against itself!" To make that statement, however, is not to erase the hegemonic or oppressive ways that text has been used. Deconstruction is an observation that comes from the underside. It is an upending process of exposure. It is not to erase the memory of struggle or to say that all forgettings are the same.

Deconstruction can help us to understand the way liturgy is formative. It is through the matrix of these symbols and experiences – enactments bodily as well as verbal – that liturgy makes us to be a particular kind of people in the world. Ritual is leaky, too. Just when we describe liturgy as something that happens to us, that we undergo, liturgy is shown to open itself. This is the space of *différance;* liturgy binds us and forms us both for good and for ill, helping us to appropriate the Realm of God at the same time as it binds our thinking to understand that Realm in particular ways, ways that both liberate and confine us.

What deconstruction helps us to do is to talk about how liturgy works both ways, how it is an unstable practice: just when we think we have an understanding, it slips out from under us. At the same time as deconstruction happens to the liturgy, we ourselves are deconstructed in liturgical practice, in our opening to God in word and sacrament. The economies of exchange in the world are undone by our participation in sacrament, a literally counter-cultural endeavor that will not be reduced to use-value, however spiritualised a one.

For liturgy to be fully transformative, for us to allow for the new thing that God is doing in us and with us, we have to allow it to grow and to change, and to mature. We are called to root out the places where liturgical practice is complicit in oppression and open the places where it heals. "Rather than continuing to bemoan the church's loss of privilege with 'the end of Christendom', we can be more critical and alive about our liturgical practice. This space of *différance* and resistance opened by liturgy cannot be summoned at will in a committee meeting. There is no shortcut or correct answer marked 'A' or 'B' or 'C'. This space of self-critique, of beauty and plenitude is only opened by the hard work of listening and discernment and prayer. Tradition is an important source of this discernment, as are the wider circles of community: local, regional, national church body, and world-wide community. But rote adherence to these does not enact justice."[76]

Any discernment is the work of the Holy Spirit. "As liturgy itself works only over time, through repetition and through patience, being faithful to the growth and maturation of the liturgy itself works only through that same patience and faithfulness. The maturation of our liturgy is not a question of fashion or social relevance. The goal is not to construct something more palatable for the kids or answering 'the woman question.' Justice is not about bowing to social convention or even about upending it. If we want for our liturgy to make of us people of justice, we have to be people who practice just liturgy."[77]

This interpretive move is a movement of hope, at the same time as it is a critical observation. What deconstruction can help us to do is to have faith that, where our understandings deconstruct each other, God's vision is expansive enough to hold them all together. Irwin advocates a deconstructive option for the marginalised. We need to reflect on our experience and how our inclusion frequently happens on the back of someone else's exclusion. The only way we are all included, all taken in, is by God; this will not be articulated in speech, or writing.

There is a risk in liturgy; as it goes in Tillich's understanding of sign and symbol, a sign points to what it represents and a symbol participates in it. The insights of deconstruction call us to humility; we are asked to tread a bit more lightly, and reminded not to confuse our signs for symbols. In the way that deconstruction works, we are helped to understand that liturgy works, too, that we can trust it to do so. We are called to trust in liturgy's promises of liberation and to examine how our liturgical practices work against this liberation. Deconstruction calls us to look at what narratives and what symbolisms stand in the way of others, and to think critically about who gets left out, and to allow ourselves to be opened by what comes in. As Irwin concludes: "The task of the historian is always to examine what has not been written; so too for the liturgist, and perhaps so much more. Each presence is made possible in the absence of another. Let us never forget our being formed by those absences, or, more importantly, our responsibilities to the absent."[78]

Post-colonialism

Post-colonialism or post-colonial theory refers to a set of theories in philosophy, theology, film and literature that grapple with the legacy of colonial rule. As a critical approach it deals with literature produced in countries that were once, or are now, colonies of other countries. It may also deal with literature written in or by citizens of colonising countries that takes colonies or their peoples as its subject matter. Post-colonial theory became part of the critical toolbox in the 1970s, and many practitioners take Edward Said's book *Orientalism*[79] to be the theory's founding work. Said is best known for describing and critiquing "Orientalism", which he perceived as a constellation of false assumptions underlying Western attitudes toward the East. In *Orientalism*, Said described the "subtle and persistent Eurocentric prejudice against Arabo-Islamic peoples and their culture."[80] He argued that a long tradition of false and romanticised images of Asia and the

Middle East in Western culture had served as an implicit justification for Europe and America's colonial and imperial ambitions. Just as fiercely, he denounced the practice of Arab elites who internalised the American and British orientalists' ideas of Arabic culture.

In 1980, Said criticised what he regarded as poor understanding of the Arab culture in the West:

> So far as the United States seems to be concerned, it is only a slight overstatement to say that Moslems and Arabs are essentially seen as either oil suppliers or potential terrorists. Very little of the detail, the human density, the passion of Arab-Moslem life has entered the awareness of even those people whose profession it is to report the Arab world. What we have instead is a series of crude, essentialised caricatures of the Islamic world presented in such a way as to make that world vulnerable to military aggression.[81]

Post-colonialism deals with many issues for societies that have undergone colonialism: the dilemmas of developing a national identity in the wake of colonial rule, the ways in which writers from colonised countries attempt to articulate and even celebrate their cultural identities and reclaim them from the colonisers, the ways knowledge of colonised people have served the interests of colonisers, and how knowledge of subordinate people is produced and used, and the ways in which the literature of the colonial powers is used to justify colonialism through the perpetuation of images of the colonised as inferior. The creation of binary oppositions structure the way we view others. In the case of colonialism, distinctions were made between the oriental and the westerner (one being emotional, the other rational). This opposition was used to justify a *destiny to rule* on behalf of the coloniser, or what was called the "white man's burden".

As Larbi Sadiki understood and noted, because borders have been drawn up by European powers that did not take into account people, old tribal boundaries and history, division of, for example, Kurds, the Middle East's present-day "identity problem" can be traced back to imperialism and colonialism. Indeed, "in places like Iraq and Jordan, leaders of the new state were brought in from the outside, tailored to suit colonial interests and commitments." Likewise, most states in the Persian Gulf were handed over to those who could protect and safeguard imperial interests in the post-withdrawal phase. Thus in the Middle East, there have been difficulties in defining national identity – at least partly because state boundaries have been defined by colonial boundaries, except "with notable exceptions like Egypt, Iran, Iraq, and Syria, most [countries]...had to [re-]invent, their historical roots" after colonialism. Therefore, "like its colonial predecessor, post-colonial identity owes its existence to force."[82]

Conquest

Amanda Pelletier offers a post-colonial reflection on the introduction of the gospel and the church to South America from which we may draw lessons for today.[83] She says, of Iberian Catholicism and Andean Inca, "ritual worlds they shared but a world of ritual they did not." There is a need to explore the possibility of shared meanings at a time in our history when the global and local cannot help but meet, to explore the implications of cultural encounter where religious meanings never meet.

Massive baptismal campaigns with the minimal if not non-existent catechesis made all the Andeans members of the church. But with regard to communion, Lima mandated post-baptismal catechesis. Now their souls were saved their minds had to be cleared of demonically inspired religious beliefs. The remedy was systematic catechetical indoctrination modelled on the Roman catechism. But instruction waned and few were permitted to receive communion. Prejudice against the Andeans' worthiness and aptness prevailed. Candidates were orally tested on the catechism – and had to answer questions about the Trinity, the Real Presence, the Incarnation, sin, grace and Redemption. Memorising came easily but doubt persisted about their understanding. However Andeans were not encouraged to receive communion a second or third time owing to doubts about their ability to live up to moral requisites that would make them worthy. The deaths of thousands in the reductions and the fact that many succumbed to drunkenness and asocial behaviour consolidated the view that Andeans would never be worthy of communion. Mass was mandatory but communion was only for the worthy.

José de Acosta defended staunchly the right of the Indians to receive the Eucharist more than once in a lifetime.[84] He noted that those who were properly prepared longed to receive communion again and again. Acosta challenged the destruction of their shrines, temples and the theft of their religious artefacts. Echoing Augustine, he reminded the missionaries that that first idols must be removed from their hearts and then from their altars. Without the support of religious symbols the door of their hearts is closed, locked and barred from the gospel.

Pelletier suggests that most Latin-Americanists agree with this reading of the colonial situation:

> The splendour and solemnity of the renaissance Mass did more to inculturate Catholicism among the Andeans than the indoctrination of the catechism. Since Andean religious tradition possessed a rich heritage of rituals, myths and beliefs, the Inca were naturally disposed to Catholic sacramentality. In view of the systematic destruction, desecration and denigration of their religious culture, Catholic signs, symbols and rituals provided a haven for their alienated religious imagination. As Inca shrines and temples were eradicated before their very eyes, Inca labourers and artisans were put to work building splendidly adorned catholic churches. In the very spot where *Inti Raymi*, the sun god, was honoured, the Catholic Son of God was worshipped with all possible pomp and solemnity. At these fabulous liturgies, music was of special importance. Schools for Inca choirs and cantors were formed. Native musical instruments were incorporated into the liturgy... mirroring a flourishing cult of the real presence in Spain. New World Corpus Christi processions developed into magnificent spectacles. In Cuzco, particularly, Corpus Christi was a feast whose splendour and solemnity surpassed all others. This fabulous display of faith and imagination included all manner of active, conscious participation: processions, dances, bonfires,

torches and religious drama honoured the Eucharistic Lord...
Andean melodies were adapted...the Andeans...dressed in
ceremonial finery reserved for ancestral cult...dances once
performed for the former sun god now honoured the new
God, Jesus Christ. Clearly the language that both the Old and
the New World shared was that of sign, symbol and ritual.
Sacrament and liturgy evangelised into a domain of Andean
soul what the catechism could not do.[85]

With what result? asks Pelletier. Were the indigenous cultures
thoroughly Christianised by a cultural adaptability of Catholicism?
Were the Andeans, according to post-modern ethno-history, chronically
resistant and only conditionally cooperative to missionaries? Or was
it just a case of syncretism where the meaning of the superficial
catechesis was missed and the Andeans remained pagans at heart.
Or were two cultural worlds united by a convergence of two similar
ritual worlds? In the case of the Andeans their religion was destroyed
before the onslaught of Christianisation so there was never a case of
inculturation. At best though there was never a dialogue between two
equals; a conversation of sorts emerged; it became the language that
continued a distant conversation between official catholicity and native
religiosity. For some Hispanics the Eucharist still remains a sacrament
celebrated but not shared.

Pelletier asks how can pastoral practice in our day facilitate communion
at the Eucharistic table. She offers three principles for our catechesis
today. Firstly, catechesis should be for communion, for *koinonia*.
The rate and intensity of globalisation generates more diverse local
churches. Boundaries are more permeable. In the past dialogue was
never possible between Iberian and native cultures. But now an over-
emphasis on diversity and an exaggerated focus on ethnicity accentuate
differences that easily compete. Both conquest and competition share
the same goal: the acquisition of power *over* and not communion *with*.

Secondly, catechesis should favour imagination over indoctrination.
Trust should be placed in the power of the symbolic in ritual gestures,
materials and space to convey meanings that indoctrination alone cannot
bear. Catechesis based on written or memorised texts tethers meaning

to concepts. The "rite" kind of catechesis engages the imagination to creatively assimilate the known with the new, and moves from the visible to the invisible.

Thirdly it is good to be acquainted with the history of the "other"; a good test of the sincerity of our discourse is to discover a friend with an accent or a different shade of skin. We need to favour a diversity that does not divide. The signs, symbols and rituals say what our words and works are often too weak to express. We must trust that the Body is one and we, though many and though diverse, are all significant parts.[86]

Michael Jagessar and Stephen Burns avow that a post-colonial perspective on Christian education and worship, liturgical studies, hymnody etc., will clearly want to build on the notion and practice of inculturation. However a post-colonial reading will want to include more than that.[87] Significantly it will be critical of and question the very notion of inculturation as in this example from 1996:

> The Pope, for his part, insists that true inculturation is the product of an ongoing "dialogue" between local cultures and the concrete, historical manifestation of Christ. In his exhortation *Catechesi tradendae*, the Pope writes: "the Gospel message cannot be purely and simply isolated from the culture in which it was first inserted, nor, without serious loss, from the cultures in which it has already been expressed down the centuries.... It has always been transmitted by means of an apostolic dialogue which inevitably becomes part of a certain dialogue of cultures" (CT. 53). In accord with this view, Cardinal Joseph Ratzinger, the Prefect of CDF, has recommended that the term "inculturation" be dropped altogether and replaced, alas, by an even more awkward neologism: "inter-culturality."[88]

However John Paul II had addressed the issue in several encyclicals and public appearances. The term inculturation was used again in his encyclical *Redemptoris Missio* (52) in 1990: "The process of the Church's insertion into peoples' cultures is a lengthy one. It is not a matter of purely external adaptation, for inculturation 'means the intimate transformation of authentic cultural values through their integration in Christianity and the insertion of Christianity in the various human cultures."[89]

The term was further explored in a number of documents, for example, here, at a Symposium on Faith and Cultures in Ethiopia in 1996:

> New terminology in missiology takes time to be accepted and to enter fully into the vocabulary and consciousness of the Church. In *Catechesi Tradendae* 53 we saw that *acculturation* was equated with *inculturation*. It is now acknowledged that *acculturation* is an anthropological term meaning the encounter between cultures; *inculturation* is a theological term which has been defined in *Redemptoris Missio* 52 as the on-going dialogue between faith and culture. But "faith itself is culture" unless it has "not been fully accepted, not thoroughly thought out, not faithfully lived."[90]

Culture

Jagessar and Burns question how the term *inculturation* is employed and whether it is another form of hegemonic control, empire building and colonisation. They say that imperialising texts assume many forms and can become the pen of the colonised who either collaborate with the dominant forces or yearn for the same power. Jagessar and Burns remind us that conversations on the influence of post-colonial studies in the areas of biblical studies, hermeneutics and, more recently, theology are ongoing.[91] For an example we see in Walther Brueggeman that:

> It is not the work of the Church (or of the preacher) to construct a full alternative world. That would be to act preemptively and imperialistically as all those old construals and impositions. Rather the task is to *fund* – to provide the pieces, materials and resources out of which a new world can be imagined. Our responsibility then is not a grand scheme or a coherent system, but the voicing of a lot of little pieces out of which people can put life together in *fresh configurations*.[92]

Such discussions have barely entered the realm of liturgy whose discussions on inculturation take their cue from Vatican 2's liturgy document *Sacrosanctum Concilium* and its concern with "legitimate variations and adaptations" of the Roman Rite "to different groups, regions and peoples, especially in mission countries."[93] The agenda of inculturation in this context will not be concerned with notions of empire, colonialism and the vested political interests and the relationship of these to the Catholic Church especially if they are conveyed in the symbols, language, imageries of the church and embedded in the liturgical texts. It is not surprising that the church "does not wish to impose a rigid uniformity in matters which do not involve the faith or the good practice of the whole community."[94]

Anscar Chupungco goes so far as to say of inculturation that "liturgical pluralism is an imperative, rather than a concession of Vatican II."[95] On the relationship between inculturation and the appropriation of the cultural practices of marginalised groups into the practices of a dominant group, Myke Johnson writes (in the context of the cultural appropriation of Native American symbols and ceremonies) that: "Cultural appropriation is a form of racism. Cultural appropriation is a weapon in the process of colonisation. Cultural appropriation is when a dominating [group] or colonising people take over the cultural and religious ceremonies and articles of a people experiencing a domination or colonisation."[96]

Jagessar and Burns subscribe to the complex and dialogical nature of cultures in relationship to and encounter with each other. How can we ensure that cultural and ideological assumptions do not dominate in the process of acculturation or translation? For example, Brazilian efforts to inculturate the celebration of the Eucharist, to introduce elements of Afro-Brazilian expressive culture into the Catholic liturgy, received much critique from the academic, secular Black movement and the practitioners of Afro-Brazilian religions who argued that this process perpetuated images encumbered by the history of white supremacy. The official caution with the so-called "Zaire Mass" shows how the development of what should have been achieved as a result of the vision of *Sacrosanctum Concilium* has in fact stalled.

"Post-colonial" is a term borrowed from literary studies as it offers some exciting possibilities of God-talk and religious discourse. It is not about the demise of colonialism as "post" since it embodies both "after" or "beyond". It is not about historical chronologies but more about a critical stance, oppositional tactic or subversive reading strategy. There is a historical sense in which the realities of today are seen in the light of the cultural, political and economic facts of colonialism. Post-colonialism as a critical, discursive practice has through its analysis of texts and societies (reading the texts from such post-colonial concerns as identity, hybridity and diaspora) given voice to the oppressed and offered viable critical alternatives to colonial domination. It further interrogates the political and ideological stance of the interpreter in for example biblical scholarship, leaving aside the virtuous aspects of Enlightenment and modernity and focusing on the vicious aspects of modernity – how colonialism and its legacy affected the promotion of the bible and the development of its interpretation.

In the struggle for liberation the insights of post-colonial biblical and theological scholars provide a framework for the critical scrutiny of liturgical discourse – to identify imperial and colonial references and influences and to interrogate the centre from which these discourses are happening. Do liturgical texts symbols and imageries perpetuate bondage and notions of empire? How do they represent minorities and signify their inclusion? A missionary, preaching on the Sunday lectionary readings in Nicaragua in 1987 at a time when the *Contras* (the rebel group opposing the Sandinista government) were raiding villages and stealing cattle and burning crops, found the text on David and Goliath was self-evident and when catechists in villages were being captured and killed, the text on Jeremiah in the well needed little explanation.

Jagessar and Burns suggest that racism is perpetuated when the colour black is used in negative and white in positive ways. These associations arise from European interpretations of the bible's use of light and darkness imagery. Blackness and darkness are quite distinct. "Representations are never exact or value free. Constructed images are not harmless likenesses. They convey messages that influence the ways that the Orient and its natives are perceived. They need to be interrogated for their ideological content."[97] A re-reading of the parable of the talents provokes the question why the richer and more powerful servants are rewarded and the least punished. The relevant point for us is the demanding nature and urgent need for new and liberating language and metaphors. "To critically confront and engage our beliefs, values, prejudices and assumptions in order to make sense or discern how they evolved and have become a natural part of one's life is very demanding. And the reality is for the dominant to enter the space of the subjugated and [to] learn how to exist in that space is an enormous and costly challenge."[98]

Image

Gail Ramshaw[99] has given some thought to the language of light in the liturgy with the dual aims of "keeping it metaphoric" and "making it inclusive." The season of Advent/Christmastide uses light and darkness imagery. One more sensitive approach might be to replace light with radiance or brightness, to replace darkness by shadows. Elsewhere in her work Ramshaw tackles other images central to Christian liturgy. Less problematical for her is the use of the image of "Body of Christ" which she suggests is more inclusive than "family of God". But there are problems of a post-colonial view of the Body of Christ on the cross related to the treatment of slaves. In a religiously plural context how will our "Body of Christ" discourse be inclusive? The image of "Kingdom of God" has implications as gendered language where "reign" might be a better choice.

The image of "Egypt" raises questions in the context of the Paschal Mystery and the celebration of the Triduum. In that context, Egypt is associated with the "perennial powers of evil and death", a shorthand to "denote the reality of evil."[100] Edward Said's *Orientalism* is useful as it shows how Orientalism is "a western style for dominating, restructuring, and having authority over the Orient."[101] Jagessar and Burns continue: "Hence, the Orient is conceptualised and represented in terms of difference, backwardness, strangeness, feminine penetrability, and uncivilised. The overarching agenda of Orientalism, as Said contends, is a self-justification of Western hegemony over the 'Egypts' of this world. Therefore textual representations, including liturgical texts as constructed images, need to be interrogated to denude them of their ideological content. 'Egypt' requires 'careful catechesis.'"[102]

Theological and liturgical texts are guilty of inscribing on bodies that are impaired "meanings that signify ignorance, evil, sin, moral deficiency, and lack of faith and consequently evoke a mixture of condemnation, pity and contempt."[103] The language of blindness is problematic not only because it may be related to the contrast between light and dark in relation to skin-pigmentation but because it may be offensive to the visually impaired. The use of the image applied to a part of the body must never become applied to the entire person to suggest stupidity, fault or an example of punishment (cf. John 9). Liturgical symbols, such as clothing and vestments, may bear witness to a colonial origin or a court of nobility, or even the desire to impose oppressively patterns of worship from the past.

Liturgical gestures can also be ambiguous. Janet Walton says that we do need to acknowledge God's authority but God does not require bowing our heads and closing our eyes. Bowing our heads is a non-reciprocal action. Closing the eyes is dangerous in an unjust society. Kneeling poses problems too – especially in feminist consciousness and perspective. "Feminist liturgies intend to provide occasions to practice gestures of resistance and expressions of shared power." [104]

A number of questions about self-representation are raised by these observations. Who decides on symbols and representations? Is the centre of authority the dominant culture or the marginalised voice? "Can the subaltern speak?" as Spivak asks in her seminal essay. Spivak contends that representation is a form of speech act implying a speaker and a listener. She observes that when the subaltern (the colonised or marginalised person) engages in self-representation, often outside "the lines laid down by official institutional structures of representation," such representations are usually not recognised by the listener.[105] Spivak observes that self-representation is a nearly impossible task and we should not underestimate the task of challenging status quo representations and their ideological agenda in reinforcing systems of inequality and subordination. In an inculturated church in Bangkok, there is an image of the risen Christ in the form of a golden image of Buddha, though of course neither reclining nor sitting. The parish priest, on being asked what response this had evoked, replied that "some Buddhists thought he had stolen their heritage while some Catholics thought he had sold out to the Buddhists."

Why this is important? An exploration of post-colonial perspectives on matters of education and worship has this value. In recent times we have seen the development and demise of liturgical inculturation which illustrates the potential threat to those whose cultural inheritance is not Euro-centred. Worship which legitimises classism, racism, casteism and sexism dehumanises and alienates. True worship is that which liberates and calls people to wholeness. It is not just that inclusivity is important but that all concerned experience a deepening sense of belonging to church, being Church, being a faithful people of God in the world, able to "grow up in every way" into Christ (Ephesians 4:15). Participating in the movement from inclusivity to the spirituality of belonging to one another is an image of the Christian way of life itself.

CHAPTER 5
Developments

Rise of the network

The information revolution and the new technologies enable small and dispersed actors to connect, coordinate and act jointly as never before. They favour and strengthen "network" forms of organisation. This trend raises questions not only about the importance of the network form by itself, but also relative to other forms of societal organisation like the churches. David Ronfeldt[106] in his essay on *Tribes* speaks of four stages of societal development:

- the kinship-based tribe, as denoted by the structure of extended families, clans, and other lineage systems;

- the hierarchical institution, as exemplified by the army, the church, and ultimately the bureaucratic state;

- the competitive-exchange market, as symbolised by merchants and traders responding to forces of supply and demand;

- and the collaborative network, as found today in the web-like ties among some NGOs devoted to social advocacy.

Ronfeldt suggests that each new development subsumes the old and, while changing it, also strengthens it. Each new development builds on all the previous stages. Kinship remains the core, defining dynamic. Tribe-like patterns, which once dominated the organisation of societies, remain an essential basis of identity and solidarity as societies become more complex and add state, market, and other structures. The term "institution" as used here refers to bounded organisations that are based essentially on hierarchy, and have leaders, management structures and administrative bureaucracies. Ronfeldt suggests that some of the worst ethnic conflicts today involve peoples who have lost their central institutions and reverted to ferocious neo-tribal behaviours (e.g. in the Balkans and the Middle East), or who fight to retain their traditional clan systems and resist the imposition of outside state and market structures (e.g., in Afghanistan). Some dictatorships that seem to rest on a strong state are really grounded on a particular predominant clan (e.g. in Iraq before 2004).

Ronfeldt observes that the term "network" is subject to loose and varied interpretations. Here, it is used to refer to organisational networks, mainly the "all-channel" design where all members are connected to and can communicate with each other. If we apply connection and communication as key factors in the understanding of the complexity of a church, which reveals elements of different forms of society, we might then engage in more effective education enterprises. The Catholic Church, as a traditional institution like the army and the monarchy, has hierarchy as an essential principle. This principle enables a society to address problems of power, authority and administration by having a centre for decision, control and coordination that is absent in the classic tribe. Ronfeldt suggests that the hierarchical form "excels at activities like dispensing titles and privileges, enforcing law and order, ensuring successions, imposing particular religious ideas, and running imperial enterprises."[107]

Partly borrowing from the tribal culture, this form thrives on ritual, ceremony, honour and duty. Yet, this form involves a new rationality. The development of authoritative institutions to govern a society involves, among other things, administrative specialisation and differentiation, professionalisation of office cadres, replacement of inscriptive by achievement criteria and the development of sanctioned instruments of coercion that spell an end to the egalitarianism of the tribal form. The information revolution erodes and makes life difficult for traditional hierarchies for they cannot process complex exchanges and information flows well.

In a hierarchical system, there should normally be only one of each specific institution – e.g. a society should not have more than one army or finance ministry. The market system involves new principles for relating specific institutions to each other – multiple competing actors may be the norm – there can be many banks and trading companies. Pluriformity of institutions, especially educational, was not originally to be found in the church. However with the handing over of former church ministries to lay leadership – colleges, schools, hospitals, care homes – there develops a pluriformity of provision for church members not subject to church control.

A society's ability to combine these distinctive forms of governance, many of whose principles contradict each other, renders an evolution to a higher level of complexity. The advent of the market system, the accompanying redistribution and pluralisation of power and the feedback of market principles into the realm of the state/church are all important for the development of political democracy. However the Church is not a democracy. Whatever pretence may be made of consultation and involvement in decision-making, Ronfeldt believes that the market system has mostly failed to penetrate the church structures and power remains in the hands of a few.

The key principle of the information-age network is heterarchic (or, to offer another term, "panarchic") collaboration among members who may be dispersed among multiple, often small organisations, or parts of organisations. Network designs have existed throughout history, but multi-organisational designs are now able to gain strength and mature because the new communications technologies let small, scattered, autonomous groups consult, coordinate, and act jointly across greater distances and across more issue areas than ever before.

Meanwhile, the network as a deliberate form of organisation was long viewed, especially by economists, as inefficient and inferior. Compared to hierarchies, networks (especially ones that operate like peer groups) involve high transaction costs, require dense communications, need high levels of mutual trust and reciprocity, are vulnerable to free-riders, and make for slow, complicated decision-making processes as all members try to have their say. Religious congregations, reformed and renewed after Vatican 2, might be said to have shown similar propensities.

New schools of thinking about networks began to cohere. The thinking looks beyond informal social networks to find that formal organisational networks are gaining strength as a distinct design – distinct in particular from the hierarchies and markets that organisational economists and economic sociologists normally emphasise. Why then does the information revolution, in both its technological and non-technological aspects, favour the rise of organisational networks?

In the first place, this revolution makes life difficult for traditional institutions. It erodes hierarchies, diffuses power, ignores boundaries, and generally compels closed systems to open up. This hurts large, centralised, aging, bureaucratic institutions. This does not mean that the institutional form is in demise; hierarchical institutions of all types – including especially the state – remain essential to the organisation of society. The capable, responsive ones will adapt their structures and processes to the information age. Many will evolve internally from strictly hierarchical toward new, flexible models that mix hierarchies and networks.

However, actors in the realm of what we may call civil society are likely to be the main beneficiaries. The trend is increasingly significant in this realm, where issue-oriented multi-organisational networks of NGOs – or, as some are called, non-profit organisations (NPOs), private voluntary organisations (PVOs), and grassroots organisations (GROs) – continue to multiply among activists and interest groups who identify with civil society.

The network form seems particularly well suited to strengthening civil-society actors whose purpose is to address social issues. Social and moral issues are seen much more to be the concern of the individual and network and less weight is given to hierarchies in this regard. At its best, this form may thus result in vast collaborative networks of NGOs geared to addressing and helping resolve social equity and accountability issues that traditional tribal, state, and market actors have tended to ignore or are now unsuited to addressing well. The network form offers its best advantages where the members, as often occurs in civil society, aim to preserve their autonomy and to avoid hierarchical controls, yet have agendas that are interdependent and benefit from consultation and coordination.

Organisational theorist Peter Drucker in particular sees that "the autonomous community organisation" is gaining strength as a "new centre of meaningful citizenship" in the United States.[108] And he foresees that, the post-capitalist polity needs a "third sector" in addition to the two generally recognised ones, the "private sector" of business and the "public sector" of government. It needs an autonomous social sector. Perhaps one might suggest that elements of this "third sector" exist already in church institutions.

Ronfeldt's TIMN framework (Tribes, Institutions, Markets and Networks) recognises a dynamic in which the rise of a new form (and its realm) reduces the scope of an existing form (and realm), yet strengthens the latter's power within that reduced scope.[109] He emphasises that this is a framework. It does not purport to be a theory, because, among other things, it does not specify explicitly what factors "cause" or otherwise explain the TIMN progression. Ronfeldt explains that each form is associated with high ideals as well as new capabilities. The forms are ethically neutral – as neutral as technologies – in the sense that they have both bright and dark sides, and can be used for good or ill. This latest technology revolution is enabling a heretofore weak form of organisation—the multi-organisational network—to come into its own.

Ronfeldt claims for the TIMN framework that:

> First, it makes a specific claim that the network is the next major form of organisation to mature, and in so doing, it is oriented more toward the future than the past.
>
> Second, the TIMN framework treats the evolution of "complexity" as an explicitly additive, cumulative, or combinatorial process in which a society is able to develop

various, specific sub-systems (realms) that operate according to different forms of organisation and their attendant operational principles.

Third, despite the fact that each form is different, the framework maintains that all systemic transitions – from the first to the fourth types of societies – are subject to general dynamics.

As this new form of information network continues to grow it will undoubtedly affect the church and its way of operating. The church will need both to preserve and to adapt its various structures in order to provide a continuing service to the world. There will be both continuity and discontinuity.

Ronfeldt is particularly in interested in the transition stage. We could apply his findings to a Church dealing with change. During the rise of a new form, subversion precedes addition. The network would bring to life a new set of values and norms which will need to spread for the form is to take root. But the values and norms, actors and issues favoured by one form tend to contradict those favoured by another.

Each form "brings to life" a new set of values and norms which must spread if the form is to take root. But the values and norms, actors and issues favoured by one form tend to contradict those favoured by another, e.g. the conflict between Latin and the vernacular. Practices are done before they are confirmed. Addition spells the creation and consolidation of a new realm: as a new form grows in legitimacy and utility, subversion and disturbance give way to adjustment, acceptance, and accommodation – to addition.

Combination has system-changing effects – systemic changes are set in motion – the new form's realm begins to separate from the older.

Each form's maturation, as Ronfeldt explains, increases social stratification. Early T-type societies had a single crucial rank: kinfolk. Then, +I dynamics resulted in a division into two strata: the rulers and the ruled. Next, +M dynamics created a middle class and the tripartite system so familiar today: upper, middle, and lower classes. Projection of this progression suggests that +N dynamics will generate new "haves" and "have-nots" with the defining referent this time being access to information, rather than to blood, power, or capital – and indeed this is already happening.

Each form has – but cannot realise - its ideal type. Yet, in practice, none operates according to its ideal, at least not for long. One reason for this is the presence of the other forms, and the unavoidability of having to function in relation to them. Incomplete adaptation may be best. While it is important to get a new form "right" and balance it vis-à-vis other forms, the balance principle does not mean that complete adaptedness to an environment is necessarily good for a society's potential for further evolution. This feature is apparent in the implementation of Vatican 2.

As Elman Service notes about ancient states, empires, and civilizations, the "potential for further advance decreases in proportion to adaptive success and maturity." [110] Is this a feature of the post-Vatican 2 era?

The framework also says that upward evolutionary transitions will lead to a transformation, but not a demise, of that realm – its demise would violate the principle that calls for a balanced combination.

Some activities currently associated with the public or private sectors are already being redesigned into multi-organisational networks – notably in the areas of health, education, and welfare – and these seem likely candidates to migrate into the new realm.

> States and their bureaucracies will be able to fight fission not only by resorting to force, but also by building education and communication systems to absorb and integrate varied ethnic groups. Chiefdoms still lacked such capacities, but they were a step in that direction.[111]

The distinction Ronfeldt is trying to make harks back to the distinction that Max Weber made long ago between two "types of solitary social relationships": communal relationships, and associative relationships. The former were "based on a subjective feeling of the parties, whether effectual or traditional, that they belong together." His examples included families and brotherhoods – exemplars of the tribal form in the TIMN framework. In contrast, the associative form mostly depended on "a rational agreement by mutual consent." Associative relationships included free-market exchange relationships, but also consisted largely of "voluntary associations" based on the members' "self-interest," meaning "the promotion of specific ulterior interests," and/or "motivated by an adherence to a set of absolutist values," such as serving a "cause."[112]

Institutional memory

Institutional memory is a collective of facts, concepts, experiences and know-how held by a group of people. As it transcends the individual, it requires the ongoing transmission of these memories between members of this group. Elements of institutional memory may be found in corporations, professional groups, government bodies, religious groups, academic collaborations and by extension in entire cultures. Institutional memory may be encouraged to preserve a group's ideology or way of work. Conversely, institutional memory may be ingrained to the point that it becomes hard to challenge if something is found to contradict that which was previously thought to have been correct.

The social conflict that precedes war or political violence, for example in the Balkans or the Middle-East, is replete with abnormal conduct and rhetoric. References to fears and grievances – real or imagined – proliferate. It is during these times, in particular, that other narratives function as community safeguards against organised aggression, xenophobia, vigilantes.

Jay Taber suggests that: "through participation in narrative events, they claim, those who feel as if they are alone, that they become connected to their community".[113] The stories we tell help to model the type of society we want to live in, who we are, and where we came from. It is this role of storytelling, the use of history, the preservation of memory that enables us to recognise patterns of conduct and rhetoric our communities have witnessed previously, in order for us to comprehend new threats and dangers. Replenished, renewed and repeated, these stories build a cohesive narrative of our collective understanding – our *institutional memory*.

Memories, however, do not reside in books or aging minds alone; indeed, they require the regular nourishment of ceremonies and conferences and public gatherings where they are spoken and heard and embellished with the perspective of time and maturation and contextual change. And by making the linkages between the past and the present, our stories – with luck – allow us to create the narrative of a future that embraces both. Without a widespread tribal support system or reliable public or private institutions (let alone markets) for the regular exercise of our new narratives incorporating our vital stories, values and norms, it is the network form we must now rely on as "curator" of these tales. Organisations within a civil-society network, more precisely, the individuals who retain these collective memories, are then crucial to keeping them alive. The communication of our stories will then determine who we will become. It is in this constructing of networks through face-to-face interaction, in pursuit of comprehending the forces against us, that we can discover our strengths and deepest values, and, with luck, develop enduring loci of memory and understanding to guide, comfort and console those yet to come

Looking at the post-colonial conflicts between nations and states, Taber quotes Jamake Highwater's assertion that, "Never has the interpretation of cultures been so worldwide, or disintegration so universal." Cautioning against the false isolation of individualism, Highwater proposes that "Freedom is not the right to **express** yourself, but the far more fundamental right to **be** yourself...The abiding principle of tribalism is the vision of both nature and a society which provides a place for absolutely everything and everyone."[114]

Addressing the UN in 1977, the *Six Nations* (Iroquois) spoke of native peoples being among the world's surviving proprietors of that kind of consciousness. "The great hope," as Epes Brown states, "is that a true and open dialogue may be established through which...each [society] may ultimately regain and reaffirm the sacred dimensions of their own respective traditions."[115]

As Highwater concludes, it is from primal peoples that there comes a new culture that replaces the exhausted one. "That is the ultimate irony of our era," he notes. "Those who have been most utterly defeated have become most influential. Another irony...is that the most linear and material minds are not aware that history has relentlessly moved past them, putting their values in a new perspective which they cannot yet see."[116]

Institutional memory is retained through telling the story, liturgical celebration, meeting, working together, hospitality, formally through education. Institutional memory is lost through individualism, consumer choice, living only in the present. Poor record keeping leads to poorly informed decision-making and loss of institutional memory. The network society has not yet solved the challenge of memory loss. Transient contents, technological obsolescence, what will remain of today's digital memory? Important efforts are made to overcome the decay but technological, institutional challenges are huge.

Sole use of e-mail usually means a dramatic loss institutional memory. Knowledge management is key and is lost in e-mail systems. Most knowledge is held within people and is not transferred if e-mail systems are the main collaborative tool. The legal profession offers this reflection on institutional memory:

> Loss of institutional memory when acquired lawyers never join or promptly leave. A large company that swallowed a succession of smaller companies during the past 10 years ended up keeping about half of the lawyers it acquired. One might assume that the 50% loss of institutional knowledge would hamstring those who remained. Not true. Clearing out veterans, to the contrary, could be cathartic. "*We don't have to do what we always did, and just because some initiative didn't work five years ago, perhaps it's different now.*" Analogously, this urban myth makes me wonder about the risks of moving litigation that is well underway from one law firm to another. My hunch is that competent lawyers can come up to speed quite quickly if the files of the transferring firm have been kept orderly.[117]

Joy and hope

The Pastoral Constitution *Gaudium et spes* (1965) is perhaps the first response of the church to the problems and opportunities of the incipient post-modern age. It shows an openness and inclusiveness to the wider world and it is not defensive:

> The split between the faith which many profess and their daily lives deserves to be counted among the more serious errors of our age. Long since, the prophets of the Old Testament fought vehemently against this scandal and even more so did Jesus Christ himself in the New Testament threaten it with grave punishments (GS 43).

The end of all theologising is the making of disciples. The theological manuals which came in to the post-Tridentine church dealt mainly with Christian misconduct rather than conduct. The obligations of the Natural Law were increasingly supplemented if not altogether overshadowed by the provisions of Canon Law. The approach of the manuals was act-centred, legalistic, minimalist and casuistic. There were no attempts to connect these many laws describing what is sinful and the degrees of sinfulness with the primary biblical injunction to love God with your whole being and your neighbour as yourself. Charles Curran says: "This theology tended to indoctrinate rather than inspire. Moral theology, supposedly the most practical of theological disciplines, was interested primarily in categorising personal sins for confessional practice. Personal moral development and social justice issues were not even discussed."[118]

Vatican 2 insisted that spirituality and morality cannot be separated. Curran explores the moral theology of Enda McDonagh who, he says, strives for a more integrated theology. McDonagh brings together morality and liturgy. Liturgy and Christian life have Trinitarian, covenantal and community aspects. Too often, Curran says, the emphasis on sacraments and liturgy has been too personal and has failed to recognise the important relationship to the community and the broader society.

> The liturgical and sacramental symbol and reality of communion confront the sacramental community with the problem of consumption and consumerism in our world. The rich consume the poor, the powerful consume the powerless, we consume our environment. Jesus was consumed by the political and religious leaders of his time – *consummatum est*. In contrast the communion of the sacraments in general and of the Eucharist in particular as a sharing in the bread of eternal life and the cup of salvation brings about a sharing in the love and the life of the triune God. The symbol and the reality of the communion celebrated in the sacraments radically confront the consumption so prevalent in our society.[119]

The tension between liturgy and ethics will only be overcome by a restoration of their close relationship. The element of "sacrament" is the symbolic place of the ongoing transition between scripture and ethics, from the letter to the body. The liturgy is the powerful pedagogy where we learn to consent to the presence of the absence of God who obliges us to give him a body in the world, thereby giving the sacraments their plenitude in the liturgy of the neighbour and giving the ritual memory of Jesus Christ its plenitude in our existential memory.

The memory of the exodus or of the arrest and trial of Jesus is most often told and retold from the viewpoint of the victor. Issues that do not conform or are contradictory are marginalised or left out entirely. The voice of the voiceless is often not heard in liturgical and sacramental ritual. Because of this, liturgical texts can be read with hermeneutical ease, and the lack of an ethical dimension is one reason why a hermeneutics of suspicion finds a dwelling place even in liturgy. Post-modern thought has raised for the western world at large profound questions of contemporary ethics and justice.

McDonagh proposes moving on from Vatican 2. *Gaudium et spes* certainly calls for a more theological approach, but this emphasis exists especially in the first part of the document dealing with more methodological and generic understandings such as the person, human actions, the human community and the role of the church in the modern world. The second part deals with five more specific issues of marriage, culture, socio-economic life, political life and the fostering of peace in the community of nations. The second part is much less theological. The Aristotelian and Thomistic notion of justice is still influential. McDonagh reminds us that liberation theology takes a biblical approach as distinct from a philosophical approach – it sees justice as characteristic of God and his dealings with the covenant people of Israel. The primary criterion of biblical justice is the treatment of the poor and needy, the disabled and the marginalised, the sick and the stranger.

Vatican 2 conceived of Catholic theology as a universal theology for the whole church throughout the world. Since Vatican 2 there has been a move towards particularity. McDonagh warns that the danger of the claim to universality is that this claim is really a particular theology at work, thus involving in its own way a theological imperialism. There remains however a need for the universal.

The re-entry of particularity, that is subjectivity, into a more commonly held objective onto-epistemology raises the issue of relativity. The issue of relativity has been deepened by the individualising and therefore privatising of subjectivity. The post-modern reaffirmation of subjectivity has only intensified this debate, but today the outsider has truly become the insider, and the objectivist who was the insider has become the outsider.

Gaudium et spes shows a characteristically modernist, positivist approach to all problems and an insufficient awareness of the tragic dimension of human existence. The belief in progress is too optimistic and the document fails to recognise the eschatological aspects and apocalyptic aspects of life. There is a failure too to recognise the presence of sin in the church and the world and the fact that the fullness of the reign of God will come only at the end of time. The church is a sign of the reign of God which will only come in the fullness of time. We are a pilgrim church always in need of reform.

Curran notes too the emphasis on authority and centralisation and the lack of creative leadership, the denial of any true leadership roles to women in the church and a failure to engage with issues of war, poverty, the gap between rich and poor and indeed with those who have left the church. "Cowardice and power-seeking have prevented the church from recognising a mediating-reconciling role proclaimed by Jesus Christ", he says. The Church lives in midst of the paschal mystery and this is only intermittently recognised in the documents of Vatican 2. The pilgrim community of the church should be generous in the boundaries and the welcoming of the gifts of all the faithful, not just the "party faithful," but of the partly faithful which in reality involves all of us.

The post-Vatican 2 church needs less emphasis on person than on community. The person is only a person-in-community and in dialectic with a community-of-persons. One becomes a person only in and through community. When community forms a person, so the person forms and changes the various communities of family, school, neighbourhood, city, nation, world.

Life is gift and call – the source of which is another person or group of persons. In transcending self to reach out to the other a certain disintegration of the subject occurs followed by reintegration of the subject in relationship to others and other communities. The other constitutes not only a gift but a threat. These two, gift and threat, call a person to conversion, true liberation and proper relationships.

Vatican 2 theology emanates from the centre. But the oppressed, poor and marginalised are not at the centre. The old world no longer provides the new world with the inspiration and theological analysis that they need. In reading the signs of the times *Gaudium et Spes* gave insufficient attention to the tragic aspects present even in Europe. We can be a people of hope only if we recognise the grief and anguish of the world and our complicity in it. The church is not the reign of God but its herald and servant.

However we need to recognise that not all post-modern thought is anti-theistic. Which god do they reject? Only the God of Christianity, the God who has to justify the injustices of the mighty of this world, who has to make the poor accept their wretched lot on earth, who must keep the oppressed in their social and political state of degradation. There is a Christian involvement in the appearance of modern atheism:

Atheism springs from various causes, among which must be included a critical reaction against religions and in some places against the Christian religion in particular. Believers can thus have more than a little to do with the rise of atheism [*partem non parvam habere possunt credentes*] (GS 19).

PART 2: FORMATION

CHAPTER 6
Inculturation

The Church and Inculturation

The Apostolic Exhortation on Catechesis *Catechesi Tradendae* (1979) said that the message of the gospels is embedded in cultures (CT 53). Inculturation is never a one way street. The Exhortation explains the new words *acculturation* or *inculturation* (here used without distinction) which express very well an aspect of the great mystery of the Incarnation. Catechesis, as well as of evangelisation in general, is the means to "bring the power of the Gospel into the very heart of culture and cultures." Catechesis will seek to know these cultures and their essential components; it will learn their most significant expressions; it will respect their particular values and riches. In this manner it will be able to offer these cultures the knowledge of the hidden mystery and help them to bring forth from their own living tradition original expressions of Christian life, celebration and thought (CT 53).

Catechesi Tradendae reminds us that the Gospel message was inculturated from the beginning; it cannot be purely and simply isolated from the culture in which it was first inserted (the biblical world or, more concretely, the cultural milieu in which Jesus of Nazareth lived) nor, without serious loss, can the Gospel message be separated from the cultures in which it has already been expressed down the centuries. It does not spring spontaneously from any cultural soil. Indeed and most importantly, it has always been transmitted by means of an apostolic dialogue which inevitably becomes part of a certain "dialogue of cultures." *Catechesi Tradendae* urges the thought that the power of the Gospel everywhere transforms and regenerates. When that power enters into a culture, it is no surprise that it rectifies many of its elements. There would be no catechesis if it were the Gospel that had to change when it came into contact with the cultures.

On the other hand, as part of this dialogue of cultures, the Exhortation tells us that it is important to receive, with wise discernment, certain elements, religious or otherwise, that form part of the cultural heritage of a human group and use them to help its members to understand better the whole of the Christian mystery. "Genuine catechists know that catechesis 'takes flesh' in the various cultures and milieux: one has only to think of the peoples with their great differences, of modern youth, of the great variety of circumstances in which people find themselves today. But they refuse to accept an impoverishment of catechesis through a renunciation or obscuring of its message…or by concessions in matters of faith or morals. True catechesis enriches these cultures by helping them to go beyond the defective or even inhuman features in them, and by communicating to their legitimate values the fullness of Christ" (CT 53).

The Instruction on Inculturation and the Roman Liturgy *Varietates legitimae* (VL) helpfully summarises previous texts on inculturation which it defines as "the incarnation of the Gospel in autonomous cultures and at the same time the introduction of these cultures into the life of the Church…an intimate transformation of the authentic cultural values by their integration into Christianity and the implantation of Christianity into different human cultures."[120] The Instruction reminds us of the change of vocabulary from adaptation to inculturation. Adaptation, taken from missionary terminology, could lead one to think of modifications of a somewhat transitory and external nature.

The term inculturation is a better expression to designate a double movement: "By inculturation, the Church makes the Gospel incarnate in different cultures and at the same time introduces peoples, together with their cultures, into her own community."[121] On the one hand the penetration of the Gospel into a given socio-cultural milieu "gives inner

fruitfulness to the spiritual qualities and gifts proper to each people…
strengthens these qualities, perfects them and restores them in Christ"
(GS 58). On the other hand, the Church assimilates these values, when
they are compatible with the Gospel, "to deepen understanding of
Christ's message and give it more effective expression in the liturgy
and in the many different aspects of the life of the community of
believers"(GS 58). This double movement in the work of inculturation
thus expresses one of the component elements of the mystery of the
incarnation (CT 53).

The Instruction (VL) refers to inculturation having its place in worship
as in other areas of the life of the Church. It constitutes one of
the aspects of the inculturation of the Gospel which calls for true
integration in the life of faith of each people of the permanent values
of a culture rather than their transient expressions. Inculturation is not
an accidental process or a by-product. It must "be in full solidarity with
a much greater action, a unified pastoral strategy which takes account
of the human situation. As in all forms of the work of evangelisation,
this patient and complex undertaking calls for methodical research and
ongoing discernment. The inculturation of the Christian life and of
liturgical celebrations must be the fruit of a progressive maturity in the
faith of the people" (VL 5).[122]

The church's critique of contemporary culture

At the same time as there is a positive move towards inculturation,
as Nathan Mitchell points out, several post-Vatican 2 documents
exhibit unease with the bewildering variety of modern cultures. This
is particularly true when the documents attempt to deal with inculturation *not* as it affects evangelisation in *missionary* contexts, but as it
impacts on gospel, worship and church life in familiar Western cultures
(especially those of Europe and the Americas).[123]

The ambivalence is evident, for example, in the Working Document
(Instrumentum Laboris) prepared for the meeting of the special Synod
for Europe in October 1999. On the one hand, the *Instrumentum* speaks
of a church that "announces, celebrates and serves the gospel of

hope" to a continent besieged by discouragement, doubt and social fragmentation, and it calls for "a renewed Christian proclamation which will help individuals and nations to combine freedom and truth, while providing spiritual and ethical foundations for the economic and political unification of the continent." Similarly, it envisions a renewed, "caring, mission-minded [church] community" that is enlivened by "an atmosphere of warm relationships, communication, service, shared responsibility and participation . . . attention to various forms of poverty; a culture of mutual concern; . . . an appreciation for the variety of charisms, vocations and responsibilities; [and] friendly collaboration [resulting in] . . . a revitalisation of participatory structures."[124]

On the other hand, despite the *Instrumentum's* rhetoric of "hope, caring, concern, compassion, warmth, shared responsibility, participation and collaboration", its assessment of contemporary continental society was rather negative, even antagonistic. "Pluralism has taken the place of Marxism in cultural dominance," the *Instrumentum* complained, "a pluralism which is undifferentiated and tending toward skepticism and nihilism. . . . In the context of the present increasing pluralism in Europe, the synod . . . intends to proclaim that Christ is the one and only saviour of all humanity and, consequently, to assert the absolute uniqueness of Christianity in relation to other-religions."[125]

The political evil of Marxism, these words suggest, has been supplanted by the equally pernicious social evil of "pluralism." Although the precise nature of this new malignancy is not defined, it seems closely connected to what a later *Congregation* for the Doctrine of the *Faith* document, *Dominus Jesus*, calls "relativistic theories which seek to justify religious pluralism, not only de facto but also de iure . . . presuppositions of both a philosophical and theological nature, which hinder the understanding and acceptance of the revealed truth . . . relativistic attitudes toward truth itself . . . subjectivism . . . eclecticism – all of which threaten to erode or degrade 'the character of absolute truth and salvific universality' possessed by 'the mystery of Jesus Christ and the Church.'"[126]

Despite the critique of *Dominus Jesus* of religious pluralism and "relativism," the Pontifical Council for Culture had issued – just a year earlier – a very different document which appreciatively examined the breadth of what is meant by "culture" today, urging sensitivity toward the distinctive cultural heritage of diverse peoples.[127] This document also spoke with great respect about the need to collaborate with persons of other religious traditions (e.g., Islam) "on the level of culture in [a] real reciprocity" that will "foster fruitful relationships".[128] In short, the Pontifical Council for Culture affirmed the pluralism and diversity of native cultures as fertile sources for the growth of faith, worship traditions, and "popular religion."

Taken together, these documents reveal a decided ambivalence toward modern cultures within the church's magisterium. The Synod for Europe's *Instrumentum* and the CDF's declaration *Dominus Jesus* both voice anxieties about cultural pluralism that are far less evident in documents like *Catechesi tradendae*, *Redemptoris missio*, and "Toward a Pastoral Approach to Culture." *Dominus Jesus* and the synodal *Instrumentum* seem to equate cultural pluralism with "eclectic relativism," the pervasive, unholy successor to Marxism's fatally flawed ideology. In such statements, the magisterium seems as uncomfortable with the early twenty-first century's "post-modern" pluralism as it was with the early twentieth century's "modernism."[129] And while *Dominus Jesus* does not explicitly discuss (or condemn) "post-modernism," its presence is perhaps implied in that document's reference to the "relativistic mentality, which is becoming ever more common" and hence requires that the magisterium "reassert the definitive and complete character of the revelation of Jesus Christ."

Despite their ambivalence, these documents do help to contextualise specifically *liturgical* "instructions" such as *Varietates legitimae* or the *Congregation* for *Divine Worship* and the Discipline of the Sacraments(CDWD)'s recent "translation manifesto," *Liturgiam authenticam.*[130] After all, despite nearly a quarter-century of retrenchment and "backpedalling," the fundamental structure of liturgical reform that emerged during the dozen years following the Council's conclusion remains intact. "Cautions" and "corrections" of alleged liturgical "excesses" and "abuses" have abounded during this period; yet in spite of everything Vatican 2's call for worship that invites the people's "full, conscious, and active participation" has continued to be heard and vigorously acted upon. All the documents discussed above – both the ones that deal with "evangelisation and culture" and those that deal directly with liturgical matters – have less to do with the church's worship than with the magisterium's ambivalent critique of contemporary Western culture (perceived sometimes as a perverse "successor" to Marxism and sometimes as a reality so natural and essential "that human nature can only be revealed through culture"[131]). In sum, the Catholic Church today seems caught in a kind of love-hate relation with both the plurality of cultures and the process of "inculturation" – and that is what drives recent pronouncements about worship, about the "substantial unity of the Roman Rite," and about (lay) ministries, rubrics, and vernacular translations.

Transition from "modern" to "post-modern"

A couple of years before the Council opened in 1962, Jesuit William F. Lynch's book *Christ and Apollo* drew attention to what the author called "the univocal mind," the tendency "to reduce everything, every difference and particularity . . . to the unity of a sameness which destroys or eliminates the variety and detail of existence."[132] A residue of this reductivism seems to cling to documents such as *Dominus Jesus* and *Liturgiam authenticam,* which tend to reduce complex phenomena (e.g. cultures and languages) to the status of labels or slogans (e.g. "relativistic theories which seek to justify religious pluralism"). What post-conciliar decrees sometimes forget is that SC appeared on the scene precisely at a time when Western cultures generally were shifting away from an increasingly discredited "modernity" to an astonishingly diverse and pluralistic "post-modernity." Unless that shift is understood, we cannot grasp either the nature of SC as a "reformist document" or the vigour of post-Conciliar reactions to it.

To speak of a shift from modernity to post-modernity is not, of course, to say that "modernity" itself was an invention of twentieth century cultures. On the contrary, the early modern era was already underway in the sixteenth century, and *mirabilis dictum* one of its early proponents was the Catholic Church, whose post-Tridentine programme of reform embraced both cutting-edge technology (printing) and humanist principles of literary criticism to produce a new liturgical library between 1568 and 1614. Three hundred years later, Western modernity had reached its zenith, especially in the fields of technology, social theory, literature and the arts. Ironically, by this point, the Catholic Church (which had resolutely snubbed theories of popular democracy throughout most of the nineteenth century) had embraced much of labour's social and political agenda in Pope Leo Xiao's great encyclical *Rerum novarum* (1891), with its dramatic defence of private property and workers' rights to a just wage – even as it deplored modernism's impact on biblical criticism and the history of doctrine.

At the very point at which the church had begun, perhaps grudgingly, to embrace limited aspects of modernity, artists and writers were fast becoming its fiercest critics. Far from exalting reason or lauding the captains of science and industry, early twentieth-century poets like T. S. Eliot had already begun to imagine modern culture as a toxic waste-land, "stony rubbish . . . / A heap of broken images, where the sun beats, / And the dead tree gives no shelter, the cricket no relief, / And the dry stone no sound of water."[133]

Two decades later, Auschwitz and Hiroshima revealed that, whatever its achievements, modernity had collapsed into genocide and nuclear devastation. What gradually emerged in the aftermath – during what we used to call "the post-war era" – was "post-modernism." Mitchell sums up as follows: "If modernity had united reason and science in a myth of limitless human progress, post-modernity is sceptical of *any* "totalising" myth or institution, whether secular or religious. If the modern world relied on *reason, purpose, design* and *hierarchy,* the post-modern world prizes *intuition, play, chance,* and *anarchy.* If the modern world stressed our need for *presence, centering, boundaries,* and *depth,* the post-modern world highlights *absence, dispersal, fluidity, the play of surfaces.* If the modern world demanded power and authority at the *centre,* the post-modern world favors a dispersal of power to the *margins, away* from the centre."[134]

That last word is plural precisely because the post-modern universe is, in fact, a dizzying mixture of cultures, identities, races, gender roles, technologies, economies, media, and cyberspaces. We live, quite simply, in a world of *interconnected differences,* differences daily altered and amplified at the speed of light. Ours is not a world united under a comprehensive "sacred canopy." There is no single system of meaning, faith, and values to which most humans officially adhere. We are all "minorities" of one sort or another, and are likely to remain so. Past mega-cultures (exemplified, for instance, by medieval "Christendom") have fragmented into thousands of micro-cultures, based often upon fluid, heterogeneous, interpersonal intimacies within small groups rather than upon stable, homogeneous, macro-structures supported by church and state.

As *Sacrosanctum Concilium* recognised forty years ago, our cultural context today is a post-modern one. For liturgy, this brings both good news and bad. The good news is that the post-modern sensibility welcomes a world of "interconnected differences," the dreamlike collage that unites diverse cultures, races, sounds and images into a kind of pluralistic Pentecostal community wherein each person – Galilean, Parthian, Mede, Cappadocian, Egyptian, Palestinian Jew and Arab, Asian, Anglo and Hispanic (cf. Acts 2) – hears of God's mighty deeds without having to sacrifice the richly diverse customs prized by each culture. The bad news is we post-moderns sometimes prefer surface to depth, play to purposeful action, consumption to contemplation, and "sound bites" to sound thought or careful analysis. As Fredric Jameson writes, post-modern cultures tend to dislocate people, splintering them into small linguistic communities, each one speaking "a curious private language of its own, each profession developing its private code or dialect . . . each individual coming to be a kind of linguistic island, separated from everyone else." [135] In short, post-modernism's good news is the pluralism of Pentecost; its bad news is the chaos of Babel!

Liturgy and life

Nathan Mitchell writes also on the relationship of the public worship of the church and the liturgy of the world, the liturgy and life, modern and post-modern.[136] He reminds us that the liturgy of the church exists for the sake of the liturgy of life, not vice versa. (In the thirteenth century, Thomas Aquinas expressed much the same thesis in even more lapidary fashion: *Sacramenta sunt propter homines,* "sacraments exist for the sake of people.") Sacramental worship is not an infomercial, says Mitchell, that advertises "Catholic identity," "Catholic character," or the church's politically correct response to cultural crisis. Nor is it palliative care designed to comfort Catholics besieged by the cruel "culture of disbelief"; liturgy is not hospice. Nor, finally, is it a species of countercultural resistance - a way to retard or reverse the storm of "secularism" spawned by the bankrupt philosophies of the twentieth century.

> Ritual, rather, is reading (a way to "read" the world), rehearsal (practice), and performance (repeatable deed); its words and acts are tablature – a musical score to be played, not a sermon to be endured or a syllabus to be taught. In the liturgy of Christians, ritual rehearses not beliefs, disciplines, or dogmas, but life itself. Much of human activity is devoted to hoarding, holding, and having – that is, to consumption, competition, and accumulation. But of course it does not have to be that way; life can also be seen as ritual enactment, ritual performance.[137]

Mitchell refers the reader to Herbert Fingarette who once proposed that human community itself is best understood as "holy rite":

> "The image of Holy Rite as a metaphor of human existence brings foremost to our attention the dimension of the holy in [human] existence. . . . Rite brings out forcefully not only the harmony and beauty of social forms, the inherent and ultimate dignity of human intercourse; it brings out also the moral perfection implicit in achieving one's ends by dealing with others as beings of equal dignity, as free co-participants in li [the Chinese word for rite or ritual] . . . [T]o act by ceremony [i.e., ritually] is to be completely open to the other; for ceremony is public, shared, transparent; to act otherwise is to be secret, obscure and devious, or merely tyrannically coercive. It is in this beautiful and dignified, shared and open participation with others who are ultimately like oneself that [we humans] realize [ourselves]. . . . Human life in its entirety [is] finally one vast, spontaneous and holy Rite: the community of [men and women].[138]

In 1997 Kevin Seasoltz wrote on the possibilities involved in the restoration of the arts in the transmission of catholic culture.[139] Rembert Weakland had already asserted that a formed and informed catholic identity is not found in the USA at the present time, even though a quest for catholic identity seems to permeate many institutions of the Catholic Church. Seasoltz urges that we retrieve, restore and support the role of the arts in the transmission of catholic culture.

> We have not created a catholic culture for our day and thus are at a loss on how to transmit our faith to the next generation. We have not given form to our belief…we have often focused on the transmission of precise verbal formulas that encapsulate the essentials of our teaching, or we have tried to find some kind of action that we could claim as our own, that would at the same time satisfy the nervous local bishop and give him the impression that all is well.[140]

Although formulaic assertions of beliefs, memorised by catholic adherents, are important, they are intellectual formulae which need to be incarnated in a common catholic culture, a meaning-system which pulls together and makes sense of the great variety of human experiences. A catholic culture is a way of looking at the whole of life – at life and death, at good and evil, at past, present and future, at human relationships and relationships with God. There are at present many cultural expressions among catholic people, but those expressions are generally undistinguishable from the culture of many others in our country.[141]

The inculturation of liturgical texts

One of the more contentious issues since Vatican 2 has been the revision and inculturation of liturgical texts followed more recently by a re-revision and a return to a more hieratic language. Chris Walsh explains the challenges of the revision of liturgical texts.[142] As early as 1980 ICEL began work on a revision of the original texts issued between 1968 and 1974. One of the earliest of the second generation was the Rite of Christian Initiation of Adults published in 1985.

In the case of translation, Walsh tells us, a differential criterion was agreed upon, partly on grounds of pastoral sensitivity and partly out of a better appreciation of the nature of ritual language, according to which congregational texts which were known by heart should not be altered except for reasons of inclusivity or serious doctrinal inadequacy, whereas texts which congregations heard regularly but did not themselves proclaim could be more readily revised for greater fidelity, for scriptural allusion, for rhythm or proclaimability, while those texts which they heard only infrequently should not simply be revised but newly translated from scratch to achieve a more elevated style of liturgical English.

The adoption of the vernacular was intended to achieve active and conscious participation of all the faithful; it was to become the "voice of the church". It should be a voice "accessible to the greatest number, easily understood by the uneducated and children, but which should be noble, worthy and not common."[143] However the spare and very basic English has proved unequal to the demands of a ritual language that should be formal without being elitist, accessible without being colloquial, sonorous and rhythmic, nourishing and memorable, rich in allusion and imagery, challenging and suggestive enough to bear regular repetition. However there are those who demand not only a functional or dynamic equivalence but in every instance a formal correspondence as well. A simply literal translation is clearly not the order of the day. The Vatican's own instruction required translators to employ dynamic equivalence and to take account of the demands of oral proclamation.[144]

Critics of new translations are unsympathetic to the fact that the available and working vocabulary of the English language is vastly greater than that of Latin or French or Italian. To require a fixed one-for-one equivalence would limit the ability of the translation to communicate the original and restrict the vocabulary of liturgical English to the same scope as the Latin. Given that the vocabulary of the New Testament in Greek is some 5,000 words, the corpus of Latin vocabulary is about 40,000 words and that English has some

700,000 words (250,000 in current use), there is an inherent difficulty in translating the scriptures and the liturgical texts. One word, occurring regularly in different passages of the original text, makes for the listener a connection in sense and meaning with diverse contexts. An English version may use several different words for the one Greek, depending on the context. In this case the verbal and mental connection is lost to the disadvantage of the listener.

Walsh discusses the growth of new texts organically from forms already in existence. He observes that liturgy is an oral medium; all our texts are printed but in the liturgical books are printed in sense lines. This practice is not followed in the lectionary, causing confusion and disorder among under-prepared readers. He contends that literary and formal English is in fact universally accessible and cites the speeches of Martin Luther King and Winston Churchill, of Patrick Pearse and Nelson Mandela, which are understood and admired wherever English is spoken. In commenting on the Eucharistic prayers, Walsh observes that:

> The resort to dynamic equivalence fails to capture the exact nuance, the literal sense intended by the original. This criterion of fidelity is appropriate to a biblical translation. Liturgical texts are not revealed and not inspired and not necessarily valid for all times and cultures. They are human responses in particular circumstances and conditions. It is strange that the Holy See explicitly allows dynamic equivalence in the translation of the scriptures but castigates ICEL for employing it in the translation of human liturgy.[145]

With regard to Scripture, allusion, of which there are a number in the Eucharistic prayers, is not the same thing as citation. Allusion is a far more subtle process, like that of symbolism, which makes connections by association, conjunction, hint, tangential reference, triggered memory. In addition at least six versions of scripture are authorised for liturgical use. In countries served by ICEL, quotations which are familiar and embedded in folk memory and culture are just as likely to be from other versions not authorised for liturgical use. It is not unknown for a priest, in proclaiming the gospel without an eye on the book, to revert to a translation better known since childhood. The Jerusalem bible used in the English and Welsh church is not as sonorous or congenial as for example the Revised Standard Version. The plethora of translations, using the facilities of the English language described above, can lead hearers to confusion about meaning and the consequent difficulty of making connections between different passages. Kevin Irwin has pointed out that the symbolic language of the liturgy "will often be less precise than the more technical language of dogmatic assertions."[146]

The Vatican has not been slow to supervise the work of Bishops' Conferences, slowing down or halting altogether "the process of adaptation and inculturation, and establishing hands-on control and micromanagement even of the vernacular liturgies, in defence of the 'substantial unity of the Roman rite' which they would see as imperilled if not already shattered."[147] We can see here a breakdown of two fundamental ecclesiological principles – collegiality and subsidiarity. Walsh continues: "Discernment of the needs of local churches and of the best pastoral strategies and resources to meet them must belong in the first place to the bishops and the Bishops' Conferences, and not to a civil service in Rome. A fortiori, judgments of appropriate language, literary style, cultural congruity, not to mention grammar and orthography, cannot be in the competence of a Vatican bureaucracy. We can happily recognise the necessary role of the Holy See in guaranteeing the orthodoxy of faith and unity in communion of the Catholic Church. It is the function of the Petrine ministry to confirm the faith of the brethren and preside over the churches in love – but surely not to dictate to us how we speak our own language."[148]

The intervention by the Holy See in matters of worship is not new. The earliest example among the English-speaking people was 1400 years ago, in a letter of Pope Gregory the Great to Augustine of Canterbury. It did not deal with language, as Anglo-Saxon was not yet a written tongue, but the principle is clear enough:

> You know, brother, the custom of the Roman church in which you were brought up; cherish it lovingly. But as far as I am

concerned, if you have discovered something more pleasing to almighty God – in the Roman, or the Gallican, or any other church – choose carefully, gathering the best customs from many different churches, and arrange them for use in the church of the English, which is still a newcomer to the faith. For we should love things not because of the places where they are found, but because of the goodness they contain. Choose, therefore, those elements that are reverent, devout, and orthodox, and gathering them all into a dish as it were, place it on the table of the English as their customary diet.[149]

Nathan Mitchell draws on the history of the Old Roman Canon for an understanding of literary inculturation.[150] The language of the Eucharistic Prayer I – the Old Roman Canon – contains few references to scripture and only twenty scriptural words. The language of the prayer is a perfect example of inculturation – of public prayer shaping itself to native customs, to the qualities and talents of particular people. Latin speaking Christians were not as fortunate as Greek speaking who had access to the Septuagint and the canonical gospels and letters. When the bible was finally translated into Latin, its style struck many as strange, eclectic and exotic. On the one hand the Latin bible drew on the strategies and resources of ordinary colloquial speech – and this made it accessible to people of all classes.

On the other hand, this same bible's language was full of odd neologisms, newly minted meanings for familiar words. Educated Romans found the Latin bible rather crude, bizarre, barbaric and embarrassing. Nevertheless it slowly gained in respectability so that, when the Roman Eucharistic liturgy finally shifted for good into Latin, a distinctive Latin Christian liturgical style levelled. This style imitated in many respects the formal, hieratic speech that characterised prayer in *pagan* Rome. It was language marked by formality, rigidity, juridical precision, solemnity and elegance, rhythm and balance and above all by a deliberate sacred quality. It differs dramatically from the simple everyday speech used at home among family and friends. It was not deeply rooted in the language of the Latin bible.

This hieratic style came to characterise much of the Roman Canon especially in its language of address and petition. We know from St Ambrose that at an earlier stage of its evolution the Roman Canon had used simpler speech. It petitioned God to accept our Eucharistic offering by saying:

"We offer you this holy bread and the cup of eternal life."

But over time this text was inflated, elevated and expanded to read:

"We offer to you, *God of glory and majesty*…the holy bread of *everlasting life* and the cup of *eternal salvation*."

The original language of "I" and "thou" suggests intimacy, interpersonal dialogue, ongoing conversation. Adding adulatory ascriptions suggests a very different kind of relationship – one in which the partners are *not* equal and can *never* be. This language emphasises God's uniqueness and otherness from all that is created. It ignores the fact and the scandal that in the incarnation God makes oneness with us the new definition. Pushed too far, hieratic language becomes quite artificial and is a radical departure from the way Jesus taught us to pray. For Jesus, God is not "Your Royal Highness" but "Abba", a word that connotes warmth, intimacy and familiarity. Mitchell concludes: "The models that shaped the Old Roman Canon were drawn not so much from the bible or Jewish liturgy but from the distinctive cultic and cultural heritage that characterised Roman life. If there is a problem with our English Eucharistic prayers today, the problem is unlikely to be resolved by an artificial effort to re-Latinise the translations."[151]

In the opinion of Mitchell, the anti-inculturationist attitude results from a fundamental misreading of *Sacrosanctum Concilium*. When SC 37 speaks of "respecting and fostering the qualities and talents of the various races and nations," it is actually laying down the proper hermeneutic for interpreting SC 30, 41, 48, and any other text that affirms the necessity of "full, active, conscious participation" by the people at Mass. SC 37-38 is not only the *magna charta* of inculturation (the legitimate use of native traditions and customs in the liturgy), it is the *magna charta of* participation.

CHAPTER 7
Evangelisation

Principles

The Apostolic Exhortation *Evangelii Nuntiandi*[152] (EN) opens with a mandate: "The task of evangelising all people constitutes the essential mission of the Church. It is a task and mission which the vast and profound changes of present-day society make all the more urgent" (EN 14). How does EN recognise the signs of the times and what does it offer to society undergoing vast and profound change? "For the Church, evangelising means bringing the Good News into all the strata of humanity, and through its influence transforming humanity from within and making it new: 'Now I am making the whole of creation new'" (EN 18). This has been the lifelong task of the church throughout its history, so there is no new charter for dealing with the changes of the present-day world. The interior change wrought by baptism is offered by the church in proclaiming her message to "both the personal and collective consciences of people, the activities in which they engage, and the lives and concrete milieu which are theirs" (EN 18).

The strata of humanity are not particular geographical areas or certain groups of people but for the church it is a question of "affecting and as it were upsetting, through the power of the Gospel, mankind's criteria of judgment, determining values, points of interest, lines of thought, sources of inspiration and models of life, which are in contrast with the Word of God and the plan of salvation" (EN 19). To evangelise is to proclaim liberation which cannot be limited to the simple and restricted dimension of economics, politics, social or cultural life; liberation must envisage the whole person, in all aspects, right up to and including openness to the absolute, even the divine Absolute; this perception of evangelisation is therefore attached to a view of the human person which it can never sacrifice to the needs of any strategy, practice or short-term efficiency (EN 33).

EN proclaims that the Gospel is the word of truth, a truth which liberates and which alone gives the peace of heart for which people are looking (EN 78). The world and history are filled with "seeds of the Word" so that it is a case of bringing the Gospel to where it already exists in the seeds that the Lord Himself has sown (EN 80). The gospel is not to be imposed on the consciences of hearers. But the truth of the Gospel and salvation in Jesus Christ is something to be proposed to their consciences, "with complete clarity and with a total respect for the free options which it presents". Far from being an attack on liberty, the proposition of the gospel is deemed to be "the choice of a way that even non-believers consider noble and uplifting." The church in France has been quick to latch onto the distinction between *imposition* and *proposition* and the proposition of the faith is a key interpretative tool for the task of evangelisation in that country.[153]

In a rhetoric typical of this Exhortation, the Pope asks: "Is it then a crime against others' freedom to proclaim with joy a Good News which one has come to know through the Lord's mercy? And why should only falsehood and error, debasement and pornography have the right to be put before people and often unfortunately imposed on them by the destructive propaganda of the mass media, by the tolerance of legislation, the timidity of the good and the impudence of the wicked?" (EN 80). The Exhortation goes on to examine two spheres of evangelisation, one called here "first proclamation", of those who have not heard the gospel and the other of those who are part of the Christian household but perhaps lack a firm grasp of their faith.

The first sphere (EN 55) of challenge is the one which can be called the "increase of unbelief in the modern world." The Synod of 1974 considered what it called the modern world, its many currents of thought, values and counter-values, latent aspirations or seeds of destruction, old convictions which disappear and new convictions which arise. In a typical response to the difficulties of the age the document views the world as "forever immersed in what a modern author [Henri de Lubac] has termed 'the drama of atheistic humanism.'" It is useful to remember that this was written in 1975, nearly fifteen years before the fall of the Berlin Wall. The next named enemy is secularism (not secularisation which is the just and legitimate effort to discover the inner laws of creation – culture and the sciences have a legitimate autonomy). True secularism is a concept of the world according to which it is self-explanatory, without any need for recourse to God, who thus becomes superfluous and an encumbrance. "This sort of secularism, in order to recognise the power of man, therefore ends up by doing without God and even by denying Him." Secularism is the source of an atheism which is no longer abstract and metaphysical but pragmatic, systematic and militant. The third enemy is the consumer society, the pursuit of pleasure set up as the supreme value, a desire for power and domination, and discrimination of every kind which are identified as the inhuman tendencies of "humanism." Yet the fathers of the Synod also identified the existence of real stepping-stones to Christianity, and of evangelical values at least in the form of a sense of emptiness or nostalgia. They conclude: "It would not be an exaggeration to say that there exists a powerful and tragic appeal to be evangelised."

The second sphere (EN 56) is that of "those who do not practice." Many of the baptised have not formally renounced their Baptism but are entirely indifferent to it and not living in accordance with it. This phenomenon of the non-practicing is recognised as a very ancient one in the history of Christianity. The reasons given for it are psychological as much as spiritual – a natural weakness and a profound inconsistency which they unfortunately bear deep within them. These reasons belong to human nature itself. But an additional challenge is the uprooting typical of our time. Furthermore Christians live in close proximity with non-believers and constantly experience the effects of unbelief. Consequently, the non-practicing Christians of today seek to explain and justify their position in the name of an interior religion, of personal independence or authenticity. So the result is either a refusal to accept the message or an inertia bordering on hostility of the one who has tried Christianity and found it wanting.

In discussing the roles of the faithful in evangelisation (EN 70) an interesting distinction is made between the clergy and the laity. The specific role of the clergy is to establish and develop the ecclesial community. The task of the laity, whose particular vocation places them in the midst of the world and in charge of the most varied temporal tasks, is to put to use every Christian and evangelical possibility latent but already present and active in the affairs of the world (in politics, society and economics, in the world of culture, of the sciences and the arts, of international life, of the mass media) and in more personal situations (such as human love, the family, the education of children and adolescents, professional work, suffering). The Synod fathers believed that the world paradoxically, despite innumerable signs of the denial of God, is nevertheless searching for Him in unexpected ways and painfully experiencing the need of Him. The world calls for and expects from evangelisers "simplicity of life, the spirit of prayer, charity towards all, especially towards the lowly and the poor, obedience and humility, detachment and self-sacrifice."

The sonorous language and the uplifting concepts of *Evangelii Nuntiandi* are the fruit of much dialogue and heart-searching. One interesting example of a moment in the process of the 1974 Synod of Bishops, convened by Pope Paul VI, which took up the theme "Evangelisation in the Modern World", is revealed in the following incident. Duraiswami Simon Amalorpavadass was a theologian who played a vital role in the renewal of life and mission of the Catholic Church in India, particularly after Vatican 2. He was fluent in French, English and Tamil. A Father Bevans, in a paper presented to celebrate 30 years of *Evangelii Nuntiandi*, writes that Amalorpavadass was one of the two special secretaries on the 1974 Synod. He proposed an interpretation that took into account many of the important movements in Asia and other parts of the Third World. His ideas, conceived in the spirit of Vatican 2, revolved around a greater role for the local church and the emergence of the theology of liberation. John Prior, a British missiologist, elaborates on his contribution:

> Amalorpavadass authored "a coherent, comprehensive, contextual theology of mission, drawing in both the bold new ventures of the majority and the questions of the cautionary minority," but his contributions, for all practical purposes, were ignored by the persons responsible for the official draft that was to come before the bishops in the Synod's final days. Amalorpavadass, when he realised this, had his own version duplicated and distributed among the bishops, who, when comparing it to the official draft, refused to approve it when it came to the final vote. It was four days before the closing of the Synod, and there was no time to write and then discuss another draft. It was then, as Cardinal Moreira Neves recalls, that Cardinal Karol Wojtyla suggested that "the Synod's recommendations be entrusted to the Pope so that he could transform them into the Synod's final document." The result, of course, was *Evangelii Nuntiandi*. [154]

Prior points out that Paul VI's document actually incorporated much of what was in Amalorpavadass' draft, and so it is a document that is much broader in scope than the document rejected by the bishops at the Synod. A mature development of Amalorpavadass' ideas can be found in the reflection[155] he wrote in 1997 in preparation for the Special Synod of Bishops from the Church in Asia, the final document of which reminded us in its opening paragraph that "Jesus Christ himself took flesh as an Asian" (*Ecclesia in Asia*).[156]

Liberation

Liberation is a key aim of evangelisation. A key figure in this quest for freedom has been Paulo Freire. Born in Brazil, he qualified as a lawyer but went into teaching. He became Director of the Department of Education and Culture of the Social Service in the State of Pernambuco. Working primarily among the illiterate poor (literacy was a requirement for voting in presidential elections), Freire began to develop a non-orthodox form of what later came to be considered liberation theology.

In 1961, he was appointed director of the Department of Cultural Extension of Recife University, and in 1962 he had the first opportunity for a significant application of his theories when 300 sugarcane workers were taught to read and write in just 45 days. In response to this experiment, the Brazilian government approved the creation of thousands of cultural circles across the country. In 1964, a military coup put an end to that effort. Freire was imprisoned as a traitor for 70 days. After a brief exile in Bolivia, Freire worked in Chile for five years for the Christian Democratic Agrarian Reform Movement and the Food and Agriculture Organization of the United Nations. In 1968 Freire published his most famous book, *Pedagogy of the Oppressed.* He worked in the USA and in Switzerland and in 1979 he was able to return to Brazil. In 1988, Freire was appointed Secretary of Education for São Paulo. He died in 1997.

In *Pedagogy of the Oppressed* Freire examines the struggle for justice and equity within the educational system and proposes a new pedagogy.[157] There are four main themes in the book. First he explores how oppression has been justified and how it is overcome through a mutual process between the "oppressor" and the "oppressed." Secondly he examines the "banking" approach to education – a metaphor used by Freire that suggests students are considered empty bank accounts that should remain open to deposits made by the teacher. He argues the banking approach stimulates oppressive attitudes and practices in society. Instead, Freire advocates a mutual approach to education. This attempt to use education as a means of consciously shaping the person and the society is called *conscientisation*, a term first coined by Freire in this book. Thirdly he devotes himself to dialogue. Freire argues that words involve a radical interaction between reflection and action and that true words are transformational. Dialogue requires mutual respect and cooperation to not only develop understanding, but also to change the world. "Authentic" education, according to Freire, will involve dialogue between the teacher and the student, mediated by the broader world context. He warns that the limits imposed upon both the coloniser and the colonised dehumanise everyone involved, thereby removing the ability for dialogue to occur, inevitably barring the possibility of transformation.

The last chapter proposes dialogue as an instrument to free the colonised, through the use of cooperation, unity, organisation and cultural synthesis (overcoming problems in society to liberate human beings). This is in contrast to anti-dialogics which use conquest, manipulation, cultural invasion and the concept of divide and rule. Freire explores the student-teacher dichotomy and the coloniser-colonised dichotomy. Critical pedagogy is a teaching approach which attempts to help students question and challenge domination and the beliefs and practices that dominate. It is a theory and practice of helping students achieve critical consciousness.

Freire maintains that the essence of education as freedom in practice is what he calls dialogicity. Man [sic] is not allowed to understand and transform the reality that encircles him when education is simply a method used to adapt him to this reality. The idea of Freire is that the individual learn to do just that – to understand and transform reality. This is what we have read in *Evangelii Nuntiandi*. In order to achieve this goal, it is necessary that dialogicity be established between teacher and student, since man does not create himself in silence, but through words, actions and reflection. The use of dialogue, therefore, is the key element in learning. The dialogue established between the two subjects helps to increase reciprocal kindness, something that is an act of bravery, not cowardice. This is the kind of thought that builds spaces and opportunities for liberation and the overturning of oppression through conscious action. Topics for learning can be found in the reality that surrounds the individual.

When we want to investigate a topic, we should first go to the place where the events take place in order to become familiar with the thinking of the oppressed and the second stage is to apply this thinking to systematic learning process by emphasising group interaction between the participants. The oppressor wants to maintain the status quo. He conquers the oppressed with an invariably unilateral dialogue. Some oppressors even use other ideological instruments to achieve their conquest – like that of "bread and circuses" – so that their conquest will be total. The oppressors also seek to prevent people from uniting through dialogue. In their implicit discourse they warn that it can be dangerous to the "social peace" to speak to the oppressed about the concepts of union and organisation, amongst others. One of their principal activities is to weaken the oppressed through alienation, with the idea that this will cause internal divisions, and that in this way things will remain stable. Compared to those who opposed them, the oppressors seem to be the only ones that can create the harmony necessary for life. But this is really an effort to divide. If any individual decides to begin a fight for liberation, he is stigmatised, included on the "black list", all in an effort to avoid the historically inevitable realisation of freedom. What is even more cruel is that when an oppressed individual attempts to liberate himself and fights to convince his fellows to do the same, he is negatively classified. For the oppressors, it seems impossible to listen to the unrest of the community. It is as if they see them as incapable of thought. This characteristic implies a single, inflexible view of reality.

Collaboration

Collaboration, according to Freire, is the form of community emancipation. This process does not happen through the presence of a messianic leader, but instead through the union created when a leader and the masses communicate and interact with each other to achieve their mutual goal of liberating themselves and discovering the world, instead of adapting to it. It happens when they offer each other mutual trust, so that a revolutionary praxis can be reached. Such a situation requires humility and constant dialogue on the part of all the participants.

In a later work, Freire explores more deeply the concept of dialogue and liberation.[158] He says: "It would be supremely naive to imagine that the élite would in any way promote or accept an education which stimulated the oppressed to discover the *raison d'être* of the social structure. The most that could be expected is that the élite might permit talk of such education, and occasional experiments which could be immediately suppressed should the status quo be threatened."[159] Work is not, for them, the action of men and women on the world, transforming and re-creating, but rather the price that must be paid for being human.

So it is that the more the masses are drowned in their culture of silence, with all the violence that this implies on the part of the oppressors, the more the masses tend to take refuge in churches which offer that sort of "ministry". They attempt the impossible: to renounce the world's mediation in their pilgrimage. By doing so, they hope to reach transcendence without passing by way of the mundane; they want meta-history without experiencing history; they want salvation without knowing liberation. Freire quotes Jurgen Moltmann here:

> From the beginning of modern times, hopes for something new from God have emigrated from the church and have been invested in revolution and rapid social change. It was most often reaction and conservatism that remained in the church. Thus the Christian church became "religious". That is, she cultivated and apotheosised tradition. Her authority was sanctioned by what had been in force always and everywhere from the earliest times.[160]

The history of Latin America shows that a new position begins to emerge when modernising elements replace the traditional structures of society. Development is acceptable, but it must not alter the state of dependence! Latin American societies, with the exception of Cuba since its revolution, and up to a point Chile, are "modernising" rather than "developing" in the real sense of the word. Their churches modernise too in certain respects, thereby becoming more efficient in their traditionalism. But the churches' pilgrimage toward modernisation never gets translated into historic involvement with the oppressed people in any real sense that leads toward that people's liberation. Freire concludes:

> Challenged by the increased efficiency of a society which is modernising its archaic structures, the modernising church improves its bureaucracy so that it can be more efficient in its social activities (its "do-goodism") and in its pastoral

activities. It replaces empirical means by technical processes. Its former "charity centres" directed by lay persons (in the Catholic Church by the Daughters of Mary) become known as "community centres", directed by social workers. And the men and women who were previously known by their own names are today numbers on a card index.[161]

That is why they defend structural reform over against the radical transformation of structures. But liberation becomes concrete only when society is changed, not when its structures are simply modernised. "The truth will set you free" (Jn 8:32).

The young people who are neither naive nor shrewd but are challenged by the drama of Latin America cannot accept the invitation of the modernising churches which support conservative and reformist positions; they reform so as to preserve the status quo. Hence the churches give the impression of "moving" while actually they are standing still. They create the illusion of marching on while really stabilising themselves. Ultimately they die because they refuse to die.

The modernising church speaks of "the poor" or of "the underprivileged" rather than "the oppressed". The young have all had to travel a hard route of experience from their idealistic visions toward a dialectical vision of reality. They have learned, not only as a result of their praxis with the people, but also from the courageous example of many young people. They now see that reality, a process and not a static fact, is full of contradictions, and that social conflicts are not metaphysical categories but rather historical expressions of the confrontation of these contradictions. Any attempt, therefore, to solve conflict without touching the contradictions which have generated it only stifles the conflict and at the same time strengthens the ruling class.

The prophetic position demands a critical analysis of the social structures in which the conflict takes place. This means that it demands of its followers a knowledge of socio-political science, since this science cannot be neutral; this demands an ideological choice. For to denounce the present reality and announce its radical transformation into another reality capable of giving birth to new men and women implies gaining through praxis a new knowledge of reality.

The prophetic church, says Freire, is no home for the oppressed, alienating them further by empty denunciations. On the contrary, it invites them to a new Exodus. Nor is the prophetic church one which chooses modernisation and thereby does no more than stagnate. Christ was no conservative. The prophetic church, like him, must move forward constantly, forever dying and forever being reborn. In order to be, it must always be in a state of *becoming*. The prophetic church must also accept an existence which is in dramatic tension between past and future, staying and going, speaking the word and keeping silence, being and not being. There is no prophecy without risk.

The theology of so-called development gives way to the theology of liberation, a prophetic, utopian theology, full of hope. Freire claims that this "is not an exotic attitude peculiar to 'underdevelopment', first because the original Christian position is itself prophetic, at whatever point in time and place. The concept of the Third World is ideological and political, not geographic. The so-called 'First World' has within it and against it its own 'Third World'. And the Third World has its First World, represented by the ideology of domination and the power of the ruling classes. The Third World is in the last analysis the world of silence, of oppression, of dependence, of exploitation, of the violence exercised by the ruling classes on the oppressed."[162] Education must be an instrument of transforming action at the service of permanent human liberation.

Religious education

Two authors have taken up Freire's line of thought and applied it to religious education *per se* and to religious education for the public sphere. Thomas Groome, in his seminal work *Christian Education: Sharing our Story and Vision*, develops the concept of praxis – which he defines as "a purposeful human activity that holds in dialectical unity both theory and practice, critical reflection and historical engagement." It aims for a way of being-in-communities that is active, reflective and creative. The word "shared" highlights that this reflective and purposeful activity is characterised by partnership, participation and dialogue, reflecting the social nature of the person. Groome says that "shared praxis" engages and nurtures the socialising role of the faith community. It sets up a dialectic between participants and their contexts, both social and ecclesial, and also between the Christian faith community and its own socio-cultural situation. It becomes possible to reflect critically through the medium of Christian faith.[163]

The process of shared praxis has several movements: engagement, expression, reflection, access, appropriation and decision – all to bring faith to life. While seemingly highly structured, the process allows for creating personal interest and fully engaging participants. Groome suggests that participants must bring three dimensions of themselves to bear self consciously on their place. Participants need to engage in (a) analytical and social remembering, an uncovering of the historical influences that shape their lives today; (b) there must be a cultural and social reasoning which questions and interprets the structures, values and meaning around which society organises itself; (c) finally and critically there must be creative and social imagining, which sees both the consequences and the responsibilities of actions and in addition questions what people can do to live together in more equitable and loving ways.

However if the life experience of the participants is not sufficiently thought through and critically reflected upon, the movement will result in a "thin" description, characterised more by anecdote than analysis. When thin descriptions are brought into conversation with Christian faith they inevitably lead to "thin" responses that are more appropriate to the private and personal dimensions of one's life. Groome points out that the religious educator needs to help participants to gain insight into their entire way of being a person-in-community; it is essential to develop people's consciousness of where and among whom they have been socialised. This consciousness can contribute to a deeper understanding of who they are, what they do and what they might become.

Dan O'Connell invites reflection on faith in action in the public forum and on what kind of education and formation might be needed for this to be effective.[164] O'Connell asserts that people need to be intentional about learning from the Christian faith and living a Christian way of life. Given the new context of a post-modern world, he suggests that this learning will require a capacity to enter into conversation with others who may or may not share something of the same tradition.

Christians will meet more and more people who do not share their basic world view and if they do, may not share the sources of such a belief. There are a number of responses to this emerging situation. If Christians are unable to engage in conversation with others who articulate definite values, they may be tempted to retreat from the discussion and retire to the private domain of their lives. They might be tempted to make generalised statements about the dignity of people and the reign of God but without the capacity to translate that into everyday life; others may stay silent because they are embarrassed about the hegemonic claims of the church over its history about truth and, given a new appreciation for the vale of tolerance an the belief that everyone has their own truth, think it best to keep their belief to themselves in case of causing offence. Religious education must become more mindful of the public dimension of Christian faith and educate deliberately to help participants find ways to bring their faith into that public sphere.

Bringing faith to life in a pluralistic and emerging multicultural society, says O'Connell, will require something new of religious education and theological education too. It will require forming people for a new context, one in which the ability to engage in sustained critical conversation with diverse others about the faith and life in the public sphere is of paramount importance – the public sphere where people add their voices and help to reach a consensus of compromise about what should be done in any given situation. These many different voices can leave us feeling that the public sphere has become downmarket, distracted by trivia and focus on what is entertaining, too fragmented, without enough rational debate about serious issues, contributing to a population that has become apathetic and disengaged from real politics. But there is a positive in the multiplicity of voices in the public sphere.

Christians need to be bilingual – we need to have the language of our own community – liturgy, scripture and traditions, but we also need to be able to talk with people outside our group from out own religious identity. For this translation is necessary. Religious education needs to help participants to become bilingual so they can make sense of Christian faith in dialogue with others who are agnostic, atheist, Muslim or Jew. There may also be a need for translation in order to speak to people within one's own community who are no longer practising their faith and have drifted way from the institutional church. Otherwise we will slip to the margins and become a sect.

The post-modern trend, the emergence of diversity and a new proximity to the other provide great opportunities and challenges to religious educators. Post-moderns place more emphasis on the local and the particular. It is in the local that we meet the other. We should not presume to meet the familiar in the other but someone who is genuinely strange and different. It should pull us out of our usual way of seeing the world and ourselves.

When we really see the face of the other in front of us, our knowledge shifts from knowing about them at a safe distance, a distance that serves to sustain the status quo, to one that really tries to see them in all their difference and dissimilarity. However this seeing is bi-directional. Rather than simply seeing them in their difference, we too allow ourselves to be seen, our assumptions to be questioned and our very selves to be shaken. This kind of relationship allows for the possibility of an ethical dimension to emerge.

We must be open to hearing the stories of others, questioned and persuaded ourselves, says O'Connell. It is essential to be open to conversion through the face of the other. The process is not about making quick, clean forays into the public sphere and returning unscathed with the goods, such as some new pile of legislation, funding or policy initiative. With this new post-modern sensibility, O'Connell notes the keen awareness of the importance of the role of community in shaping our identity. Today engagement needs to be characterised by conversation. It is through sustained, critical conversation that interpretations, even of Christian faith, can be tested and tried out in different public spheres.

The purpose of Christian religious education is to promote a lived and living Christian faith towards God's reign in the lives of participants and communities. Christian religious education involves shaping how people make sense of and relate to and engage in the world. It influences how and what people see around them and at the same time how they allow themselves to be seen by the world. The focus of Christian faith is that people are to effect in history the values of God's reign of justice, peace and freedom, wholeness and fullness of life for all.

CHAPTER 8
Lifelong Learning

The idea of lifelong education is hardly new and can be found as far back as Plato's republic. In recent times the idea was first fully articulated in 1929 by Basil Yeaxlee[165] who provided an intellectual basis for a comprehensive understanding of education as a continuing aspect of everyday life. In what R. D. Waller describes as a report without parallel, the Adult Education Committee of the British Ministry of Reconstruction had concluded in 1919:

> (A)dult education must not be regarded as a luxury for a few exceptional persons here and there, nor as a thing which concerns only a short span of early manhood, but that adult education is a permanent national necessity, an inseparable aspect of citizenship, and therefore should be both universal and lifelong.[166]

Lifelong education was taken up as a central organising idea by UNESCO in 1970. Perhaps the best known report arguing for the movement was prepared by Edgar Fauré and his associates (1972).[167] The commission laid stress above all on two fundamental ideas: lifelong education and the learning society. It called for a fresh look at the educational system until teaching becomes education and, more and more, learning. If learning involves all of one's life, in the sense of both time-span and diversity, and all of society, including its social and economic as well as its educational resources, then we must go even further than the necessary overhaul of "educational systems" until we reach the stage of a learning society.

More recently there has been a shift in much of the literature and policy discussions from lifelong education to lifelong learning. In Britain, this has been seized upon by New Labour thinkers like Tom Bentley (head of Demos and a former special advisor to David Blunkett). He describes "Labour's learning revolution" as follows:

> It requires a shift in our thinking about the fundamental organisational unit of education, from the school, an institution where learning is organised, defined and contained, to the learner, an intelligent agent with the potential to learn from any and all of her encounters with the world around her.[168]

The problem is that the sort of learning concerned is highly individualised and often oriented to employer or consumer interests. There has been little real interest in learning for democracy and community. Many adults now take part in organised learning throughout their lifespan; there has been a substantial increase in activities such as short residential courses, study tours, fitness centres, sports clubs, heritage centres, self-help therapy manuals, management gurus, electronic networks and self-instructional videos. The new adult learning is part of a much broader process. As individuals come to rely less on traditional institutions and the authority figures associated with them – church leaders, parents, aristocracy – to guide their behaviour, so they become more self-directed. At least in principle, they can select from a variety of possible role-models; traditional role-models certainly do not disappear (indeed, they are an important if little-understood resource for fundamentalist movements), but to select any role-model requires that individuals face up to an increasing range of biographical options. Changes in work organisation and management married to a focus on markets, consumption and lifestyle has certainly drawn policy makers to the rhetoric of lifelong learning. Government reports in

Britain, such as *The Learning Age* (DFEE 1998), demonstrate how far this movement has occurred.

Lifelong learning in the Church

In 1998-9, Michael Blades, Principal of Plater College, undertook an audit of providers of adult education and training within the Catholic Church in response to the Government report, *Learning for the Twenty-First Century* (1997) and the Green Paper, *The Learning Age* (1998), which set out the Government's commitment to the promotion of participation in lifelong learning.[169] The purpose of the audit was to identify lifelong learning needs, to identify best practice and to make proposals concerning the nature of a *Catholic Partnership for Lifelong Learning* with a view to furthering the Government's aims in the context of the Church community, supporting provision designed to address the needs of the Catholic community, disseminating best practice and developing provision to meet unaddressed needs.[170]

Part I of the report, *Vision and Lifelong Learning*, has thirteen paragraphs on the Government's agenda (1.1-1.13) and seven on the Church's agenda (1.14-1.20) with but one quote from a church document. Part II, *Adult Education in the Church*, provides information about formal church structures and refers also to training for the priesthood, voluntary activity and support for family life. Part III, *Responding to Change*, describes the challenge of changes in the church itself and in the society it serves. Part IV, *Conclusions and Proposals*, includes this key finding:

> The Church has always put the education of the poor at the heart of its mission. Many Catholic schools and colleges are in deprived areas and they are increasingly working in partnership to serve the needs of their local community. The audit discovered other evidence of a positive response to change within society and:
>
> - a thirst for learning;
>
> - a commitment to work for social justice;

- a desire to participate in the work of the church and the wider community;

- a desire for catholic education to engage with the wider world and the common good.[171]

The audit recommended new provision to fill significant gaps, the external accreditation of courses where appropriate, support for the disadvantaged communities and those with special needs and the appointment of a person to take forward the initiative of the Partnership. In the event the audit was limited to Catholic institutes of higher education; the full range of provision of adult education in individual dioceses and parishes was not included.

The report concludes that:

As a catholic community what we now do does not add up to a learning culture for everyone at the end of compulsory education (4.9). Bringing about the kind of change that would produce a revolution in attitudes towards adult training and formation within the Church would require the Bishops of England and Wales to consider setting out their vision and the framework by which they might wish the vision to be realised...a high level of participation in adult education within the Church would make a major contribution to the realisation of the vision of Vatican II – lay people playing their full part in the mission of the whole Christian people in the Church and in the wider world as sharers in the priestly, prophetic and kingly office of Christ (4.10).

Given "the decentralised structure of the Church" (4.7), "the principle of subsidiarity suggests...it would be necessary to get the right balance between the need for appropriate national coordination and accreditation and the imperative that local need should drive initiatives"(4.11).

One of the ongoing initiatives is the provision of the *Catholic Certificate in Religious Studies* (CCRS) in colleges and dioceses. The outcome of this course can be seen as, to borrow from the *Curriculum Directory*, "religiously literate people who have the knowledge, understanding... and capacity to think spiritually, ethically and theologically, and who are aware of the demands of religious commitment in everyday life".[172] Revised in 1991, this course provided for more than 10,000 students in the following ten years and many more since. Some students were teachers looking for an induction into the nature and life of the catholic school or teachers wanting a religious education qualification. Other participants were adults in the Christian community seeking sacramental preparation or a better understanding of their faith or support for their work in catechesis. The CCRS is the qualification for lay catholic prison ministry. The course is also delivered on the internet. No resolution was found to the debate about the desirability of the formal accreditation of the course outside the college structure.

Another initiative rising from the Audit was the establishment, in a partnership of church and state, of a suite of religious education accreditations, called Way of Faith, at levels 1, 2 and 3 on the National Framework of Accreditation. Courses provided under these arrangements attracted government funding for students, especially those studying religious education in the 16-19 age range.[173] Other students targeted by the accreditation were those adults wishing to gain a basic qualification in the study of their faith and those wishing to train for lay ministry in the church in the areas of teaching/catechesis, liturgy/worship and social concerns.

The general shift away from traditional classrooms into "learning centres" (in the secular world often situated in supermarkets and community projects) and more intensive use of distance and web-based learning has continued. The shift into individualised learning was also briefly accompanied by what is, effectively, an educational voucher scheme – the Individual Learning Account (ILA) of the 1990s. The government has not come to grips with lifelong learning and the tendency more recently has been to focus attention and funding on vocational and initial education.

The overall result is a paradox: "A shift in the responsibility for developing learning opportunities for adults from the state to individuals and employers is taking place at the very same time that there is a growing recognition of the need to move towards the notion of lifelong learning."[174] As we have seen, there is an increasing emphasis on individual, rather than collective, learning experience. Where *The 1919 Report* saw adult education resting "upon the twin principles of personal development and social service," the current concern with **the learning society** looks to personal change and economic development (and social control some would argue).[175] Lifelong learning is now a mechanism for exclusion and control. As well as facilitating development it has created new and powerful inequalities. There are issues around access to knowledge, and individualisation. In a knowledge-based economy, those who have the lowest levels of skill and the weakest capacity for constant updating are less and less likely to find paid employment.

Informal learning

Charles Leadbeater offers a broader view of education:

> We must move away from a view of education as a rite of passage involving the acquisition of enough knowledge and qualifications to acquire an adult station in life. The point of education should not be to inculcate a body of knowledge, but to develop capabilities: the basic ones of literacy and numeracy as well as the capability to act responsibly towards others, to take initiative and to work creatively and collaboratively. The most important capability, and the one which traditional education is worst at creating, is the ability and yearning to carry on learning. Too much schooling kills off a desire to learn...Schools and universities should become more like hubs of learning, within the community, capable of extending into the community...More learning needs to be done at home, in offices and kitchens, in the contexts where knowledge is deployed to solve problems and add value to people's lives.[176]

But for all the talk of lifelong learning and the learning society the focus remains on formal provision, qualifications and accountability. Generally, informal education is unorganised, unsystematic and even unintentional at times, yet accounts for the great bulk of any person's total lifetime learning – including that of a highly "schooled" person.[177] Formal education is linked with schools and training institutions, non-formal with community groups and other organisations; and informal covers what is left, e.g. interactions with friends, family and work colleagues. If it is deemed important that adults have opportunities to continue learning, the question arises about how best they learn and on the relationship between state and church as providers. For the most part adults' learning in faith is mostly informal.

There is an important point for policy in the distinction between formal and informal education. If schools and colleges have only a limited place in the learning that occurs in a society, questions must be asked about the focus on such institutions. Would funding be better deployed elsewhere? Does the current obsession with accreditation have any merit? Should researchers explore learning in everyday life in more depth?

A further issue is that many of those commentating on informal learning do not seem to make an adequate distinction between learning and education. The latter can be characterised as setting out to foster environments for learning that involve a commitment to certain values such as a respect for truth and for persons. Learning can be seen as a product or thing – a memory or understanding, or as a process – as a form of thinking. What is sometimes described as informal learning is, thus, better described as self-education, or self directed learning.

The use of the term "non-formal" invites dualism. We inevitably tend to contrast it with "formal" learning. This is learning that takes place in a situation where there is:

- A prescribed learning framework;
- An organised learning event or package;
- The presence of a designated teacher or trainer;

- The award of a qualification or credit;

- The external specification of outcomes.[178]

We may well want to question this characterisation of formal learning, but presumably non-formal learning could be seen as involving a non-prescribed learning framework, internal or non-specification of outcome, no designated teachers and so on.

Situated learning

People think in relationship with others. So it is that, particularly in a faith setting, we can talk of "situated learning." It can be seen as involving participation in communities of practice. Learning involves the whole person; it implies not only a relation to specific activities, but a relation to social communities – it implies becoming a full participant, a member, a real person. In this view, learning only partly – and often incidentally – implies becoming able to be involved in new activities, to perform new tasks and functions, to master new understandings. Activities, tasks, functions and understandings do not exist in isolation; they are part of broader systems of relations in which they have meaning. Novices enter at the edge – their participation is on the periphery. Gradually their engagement deepens and becomes more complex. They become full participants, and will often take on organising or facilitative roles. Knowledge is, thus, located in the community of practice. Furthermore, in this view, as Mark Tennant observes, "it makes no sense to talk of knowledge that is de-contextualised, abstract or general."[179]

Four propositions, Tennant continues, are common to the range of perspectives that come together under the banner of situated learning:

- High-level or expert knowledge and skill can be gained from everyday experiences at work, and in community or family.

- Domain-specific knowledge is necessary for the development of expertise (i.e. much of expertise relies on detailed local knowledge of a workplace, locality or industry).

• Learning is a social process.

• Knowledge is embedded in practice and transformed through goal-directed behaviour.[180]

From the above we can see how discussion on informal learning becomes linked with situated learning. There is a focus on communities of practice rather than dedicated learning environments; the interest is in implicit learning; and the concern with relationship and conversation can lead us in the direction of informal learning.

The key dimension, in many respects, is intention. Education is a conscious activity; learning isn't necessarily. People may not have a clear idea of the knowledge or skill they want to acquire but they are committed to a process. This focus on intention in education allows us to explore different ways of organising and articulating this. It is possible to separate those approaches that depend upon the planning and sequencing of learning (via something like a curriculum) and those that are essentially dialogical or conversational (and hence hold little prospect of pre-organising if we to stay true to their nature). The former can be seen as formal, and the latter as informal education.

Adult faith formation

There is some eagerness in policymakers, academics and practitioners to substitute learning for education (lifelong learning rather than lifelong education; adult learning rather than adult education). A focus on learning is important, but when it is at a cost of thinking about education (and the values it carries), then a grievous disservice is done to all involved. Learning is a process that is happening all the time; education involves intention and commitment. Education is a moral enterprise that needs to be judged as to whether it elevates and furthers well-being.

In a fresh consideration of adult faith formation, four key areas of exploration might offer food for thought:

Exploring tacit knowledge. It is often said that people do not know now what people used to know in years gone by or that young people do not seem to know anything about their faith these days. Informal learning is, perhaps, better approached as the revealing or unearthing of tacit knowledge. In the notions of "situated learning", reflection on action and skill acquisition, there are some possibilities. These fundamental processes require our attention.

Supporting self-education. The development of a range of accessible and usable opportunities for self-education is an obvious implication for policy and practice. Perhaps the most significant aspect here is the need to approach people, particularly adults, as both learners and educators. This means moving away from seeing learners as consumers of different packages and opportunities, into viewing them as creators and constructors of learning. This entails cultivating communities animated by dialogue, democracy and respect for truth – and seeing education and learning not as individual acts but as an aspect of living together.

Strengthening associational life. A follow-on from the above is the need to develop more democratic and elevating forms of group and organisational life. Not only do we need to attend to the significance of situated learning and distributed cognition, we also must look to building relationships and interactions that allow us to flourish and to grow, and to take responsibility for our lives and our part in the world.

Developing informal education. A further aspect is the need to focus attention on informal education and the place it has alongside formal education. Working with groups and associations, developing local forms of educating and learning, requires a special mix of dispositions, skills and knowledge.[181]

Moving from pedagogy to andragogy

There is little doubt that the most dominant form of instruction in Europe and America is pedagogy (the teaching of children), or what some people refer to as didactic, traditional or teacher-directed approaches. A competing idea in terms of instructing adult learners, and one that gathered momentum within the past three decades, has been dubbed andragogy (the teaching of adults).[182]

The pedagogical model of instruction was originally developed in the monastic schools of Europe in the Middle Ages. Young boys were received into the monasteries and taught by monks according to a system of instruction that required these children to be obedient, faithful and efficient servants of the church. From this origin developed the tradition of pedagogy which later spread to the secular schools of Europe and America and became and remains the dominant form of instruction.

In the pedagogical model, the teacher has full responsibility for making decisions about what will be learned, how it will be learned, when it will be learned and if the material has been learned. Pedagogy, or teacher-directed instruction as it is commonly known, places the student in a submissive role requiring obedience to the teacher's instructions. It is based on the assumption that learners need to know only what the teacher teaches them. The result is a teaching and learning situation that actively promotes dependency on the instructor.

Up until very recently, the pedagogical model has been applied equally to the teaching of children and adults, and in a sense, is a contradiction in terms. The reason is that as adults mature, they become increasingly independent and responsible for their own actions. They are often motivated to learn by a sincere desire to solve immediate problems in their lives. Additionally, they have an increasing need to be self-directing. In many ways the pedagogical model does not account for such developmental changes on the part of adults, and thus produces tension, resentment and resistance in individuals

The growth and development of andragogy as an alternative model of instruction has helped to remedy this situation and improve the teaching of adults. The first use of the term "andragogy" to catch the widespread attention of adult educators was in 1968, when Malcolm Knowles, then a professor of adult education at Boston University, introduced the term (then spelled "androgogy") through a journal article. In a 1970 book (a second edition was published in 1980) he defined the term as the art and science of helping adults learn.[183]

The andragogical model as conceived by Knowles is predicated on four basic assumptions about learners, all of which have some relationship to our notions about a learner's ability, need, and desire to take responsibility for learning:

- Their self-concept moves from dependency to independency or self-directedness.

- They accumulate a reservoir of experiences that can be used as a basis on which to build learning.

- Their readiness to learn becomes increasingly associated with the developmental tasks of social roles.

- Their time and curricular perspectives change from postponed to immediacy of application and from subject-centeredness to performance-centeredness.[184]

Knowles notes emerging evidence that people who take the initiative in educational activities seem to learn more and learn things better than what resulted from more passive individuals. He noted a second reason that self-directed learning appears "more in tune with our natural process of psychological development." An essential aspect of the maturation process is the development of an ability to take increasing responsibility for life. A third reason was the observation that the many evolving educational innovations (non-traditional programmes, Open University, weekend colleges, etc.) throughout the world require that learners assume a heavy responsibility and initiative in their own learning.

Knowles also suggested a more long-term reason in terms of individual and collective survival: ". . . it is tragic that we have not learned how to learn without being taught, and it is probably more important than all of the immediate reasons put together. Alvin Toffler calls this reason 'future shock.' The simple truth is that we are entering into a strange new world in which rapid change will be the only stable characteristic."[185] In summary Knowles makes the following assumptions about the design of learning:

- Adults need to know why they need to learn something ;
- Adults need to learn experientially;
- Adults approach learning as problem-solving;
- Adults learn best when the topic is of immediate value.

In practical terms, andragogy means that instruction for adults needs to focus more on the process and less on the content being taught. Strategies such as case studies, role playing, simulations and self-evaluation are most useful. Instructors adopt a role of facilitator or resource rather than lecturer or grader.

It is always important to remember that adult learners are volunteers. There is no compulsion involved when teaching adults and therefore motivation is not usually a problem. Adults tend to seek out learning opportunities. Often life changes, such as marriage, divorce, a job change or termination, retirement or a geographical change, serve as the motivation for the adult to seek new learning opportunities. They usually want to learn something that they can use to better their position or make a change for the better. They are not always interested in knowledge for its own sake. Learning is a means to an end, not an end in itself. These adults bring a wealth of information and experiences to the learning situation. They generally want to be treated as equals who are free to direct themselves in the education process.[186]

Critique of Andragogy

Some general issues have been raised with Knowles' approach to andragogy. First, his conception of andragogy is an attempt to build a comprehensive theory (or model) of adult learning that is anchored in the characteristics of adult learners. This approach may be contrasted with those that focus on an adult's life situation[187] or changes in consciousness.[188] Secondly, Knowles makes extensive use of a model of relationships derived from humanistic clinical psychology – and, in particular, the qualities of good facilitation argued for by Carl Rogers. Thirdly, Knowles adds in other elements which owe a great deal to scientific curriculum-making and behaviour modification (and are thus somewhat at odds with Rogers). These encourage the learner to identify needs, set objectives, enter into learning contracts and so on. In other words, he uses ideas from psychologists working in two quite different and opposing therapeutic traditions (the humanist and behavioural traditions). This points to an underlying deficit model of education. Throughout his writings there is a propensity to list characteristics of a phenomenon without interrogating the literature of the arena (e.g. as in the case of andragogy) or looking through the lens of a coherent conceptual system. Undoubtedly he had a number of important insights, but because they are not tempered by thorough analysis, they were a hostage to fortune – they could be taken up in an a-historical or a-theoretical way.[189]

Andragogy and pedagogy

As we compare Knowles' versions of pedagogy and andragogy, what we can see is a mirroring of the difference between what is known as the romantic and the classical curriculum (although this is confused by the introduction of behaviourist elements such as the learning contract). Perhaps even more significant is that for Knowles "education from above" is pedagogy, while "education of equals" is andragogy. As a result, the contrasts drawn are rather crude and do not reflect debates within the literature of curriculum and pedagogy. We need to be extremely cautious about claiming that there is anything distinctive about andragogy. In reference to romantic and classic notions of curriculum, what lies behind these formulations are competing conceptualisations of education itself. Crucially, these are not directly related to the age or social status of learners. There are various ways of categorising strands of educational thinking and practice – and they are somewhat more complex than Knowles' setting of pedagogy against andragogy.

In the twentieth century debates, four main strands can be identified; education can be seen primarily as:

- the transmission of knowledge (liberal education),

- product (the scientific curriculum),

- process (developmental/person-centred education), and

- praxis (education for radical social change).[190]

As Knowles developed his thinking, the child-adult dichotomy became less marked. He claimed that pedagogy was a content model and andragogy a process model. But the same criticisms apply concerning his introduction of behaviourist elements. Even if andragogy was an idea which gained popularity in a particular moment and says more about the ideology of the times than about learning process, J. R. Kidd, in his study of how adults learn, said the following, the last sentence of which may catch our attention:

> [W]hat we describe as adult learning is not a different kind or order from child learning. Indeed our main point is that man must be seen as a whole, in his lifelong development. Principles of learning will apply, in ways that we shall suggest, to all stages in life. The reason why we specify adults throughout is obvious. This is the field that has been neglected, not that of childhood.[191]

Vatican 2 and Education

The Vatican 2 Declaration on Education *Gravissimum educationis* (GE 1965) and the *General Directory for Catechesis* (GDC 1997) contribute, each in their own way, to the ongoing dialogue between faith and culture. Speaking of education in general, *Gravissimum educationis* begins optimistically with observation that "the circumstances of our time have made it easier and at once more urgent to educate young people and, what is more, to continue the education of adults" (GE Introduction). The reason given is that men [sic] are more are now aware of their own dignity and position; more and more they want to take an active part in social and especially in economic and political life. Enjoying more leisure, as they sometimes do, people find that the remarkable development of technology and scientific investigation and the new means of communication offer them an opportunity of attaining more easily their cultural and spiritual inheritance and of finding fulfilment one another in closer ties between groups and even between peoples.

The church on the other hand has a divine mandate to fulfil, that of proclaiming the mystery of salvation to all people and of restoring all things in Christ. The Church therefore must be concerned with the whole of life, even the secular part of it insofar as it has a bearing on our heavenly calling. Therefore she has a role in the progress and development of education.

The *Declaration* affirms that all people of every race, condition and age, since they enjoy the dignity of a human being, have an inalienable right to an education that is in keeping with their ultimate goal, their ability, their sex, and the culture and tradition of their country, and also in harmony with their fraternal association with other peoples in the fostering of true unity and peace on earth. The purpose of true education is the formation of the human person in the pursuit of his ultimate end and of the good of the societies of which (s)he is a member, and in whose obligations, as an adult, (s)he will share.[192]

Moving on to Christian education, we hear that baptism gives all Christians the right to a Christian education. The reason is that Christian education does not merely strive for the maturing of a human person, but that in the process the baptised:

- are gradually introduced the knowledge of the mystery of salvation,

- become ever more aware of the gift of Faith they have received,

- learn in addition how to worship God the Father in spirit and truth (cf. John 4:23) especially in liturgical action,

- learn be conformed in their personal lives according to the new man created in justice and holiness of truth (Eph. 4:22-24);

- develop into perfect manhood, to the mature measure of the fullness of Christ (cf. Eph. 4:13) and strive for the growth of the Mystical Body,

- aware of their calling…learn not only how to bear witness to the hope that is in them (cf. Peter 3:15) but also how to help in the Christian formation of the world that takes place when natural powers viewed in the full consideration of man redeemed by Christ contribute to the good of the whole society (GE 2).

The Council Fathers urged on pastors the most serious obligation to see to it that all the faithful, but especially the youth who are the hope of the Church, enjoy such a Christian education.[193] How is this to be achieved? The General Directory for Catechesis gives some more concrete directions.

The Directory has a particular focus on the *Ministry of the Word* which is at the service of the process of conversion. In the first place, the first proclamation of the Gospel is characterised by the call to faith; in the second place, catechesis is characterised by giving a foundation to conversion and providing Christian life with a basic structure; in the third place ongoing education in the faith, in which the place of the homily must be underlined, is characterised by being the necessary nourishment of which every baptised adult has need in order to live (GDC 57).[194]

With most significant insight, Directory proclaims that: "The model for all catechesis is the baptismal catechumenate when, by specific formation, an adult converted to belief is brought to explicit profession of baptismal faith during the Paschal Vigil" (GDC 59). This catechumenal formation of adults then should inspire the other forms of catechesis in both their objectives and in their dynamism.

In 1979, *Catechesi tradendae* had already referred to the "central problem of the catechesis of adults." It affirmed the adult form as the principal form of catechesis, because it is addressed to persons who have the greatest responsibilities and the capacity to live the Christian message in its fully developed form. The Christian community cannot carry out a permanent catechesis without the direct and skilled participation of adults, whether as *receivers* or as *promoters* of catechetical activity. The young are dependent on good adult catechesis, for the world, in which they are called to live and to give witness to the faith, is governed by adults. The faith of these adults too is not confined to the religious sphere or the household of faith but "should continually be enlightened, stimulated and renewed, so that it may pervade the temporal realities in their charge" (CT 43). Consequently, for catechesis to be effective, it must be permanent, and "it would be quite useless if it stopped short at the threshold of maturity, since catechesis, *admittedly under another form*, proves no less necessary for adults" [author's italics](CT 43). There is a little contradictory note here where the apologetic reference to the form of adult catechesis seems to undermine somewhat its previously stated priority – but then at the time of writing this form was perhaps a novelty for many, and it still is today a novelty to some.

Catechesis for initiation is to be *comprehensive* and *systematic*, and it cannot be reduced to the circumstantial or the occasional. As it is formation for the Christian life it comprises but surpasses mere instruction. Being essential and initiatory, it looks to what is "common" for the Christian, without entering into disputed questions nor transforming itself into a form of theological investigation. Being initiatory, it incorporates the recipients into the community, which lives, celebrates and bears witness to the faith. Its richness should serve to inspire other forms of catechesis (GDC 68).

The importance of the group receives great emphasis as an important function in the development processes of people. For children where the group fosters a rounded sociability, and for young people, groups are practically a vital necessity for personality formation. The same is true of adults where groups promote a sense of dialogue and sharing as well as a sense of Christian co-responsibility. Apart from its didactic aspect, the Christian group is called to be an experience of community and a form of participation in ecclesial life. It finds its goal and fullest manifestation in the more extended Eucharistic community. Jesus says: "Where two or three are gathered in my name, there am I in their midst (Mt 18:20)" (GDC 159).

The Directory speaks of "the need and right of every believer to receive a valid catechesis" in order to reach maturity of faith (GDC 167). It is thus a primary responsibility of the Church to respond to this need and right in a fitting and satisfactory manner. This requirement is explained as recognising that recipients of evangelisation are "*concrete* and historical persons," rooted in a given situation and always influenced by pedagogical, social, cultural, and religious conditioning. Finally in the whole process, those who are to be evangelised must be active subjects, conscious and co-responsible, and not merely a silent and passive recipients (GDC 167).

The adult who discovers, evaluates and activates what he has received by nature and grace, both in the Christian community and by living in human society, will be able to overcome the dangers of standardisation and of anonymity which are particularly dominant in some societies of today (and perhaps more generally in the post-modern world) and which lead to loss of identity and lack of appreciation for the resources and qualities of the individual (GDC 175).

An omnibus paragraph provides a comprehensive description of the post-modern world and is worth quoting in full as it is the backdrop against which all lifelong learning in faith is conducted:

> Many communities and individuals are called to live in a pluralistic and secularised world, in which forms of unbelief and religious indifference may be encountered together with vibrant expressions of religious and cultural pluralism. In many individuals the search for certainty and for values appears strong. Spurious forms of religion, however, are also evident as well as dubious adherence to the faith. In the face of such diversity, some Christians are confused or lost. They become incapable of knowing how to confront situations or to judge the messages which they receive. They may abandon regular practice of the faith and end by living as though there were no God – often resorting to surrogate or pseudo-religions. Their faith is exposed to trials. When threatened it risks being extinguished altogether, unless it is constantly nourished and sustained (GDC 193).

To combat these problems, formation especially of the catechist in the deepest human and Christian dimensions is of the utmost importance.

"Formation, above all else, must help him to mature as a person, a believer and as an apostle." This is what the catechist must know so as to be able to fulfil his responsibilities well. This dimension is permeated by the double commitment the catechist has to the message and to man. Maturity is marked by commitment both to the message and to the recipient in his/her social context (GDC 238).

Finally the locus of evangelisation is normally the parish. In the parish "adult catechesis must be given priority". In the parish "the proclamation of the gospel to those who are alienated or who live in religious indifference must be planned." To achieve this in the parish "it is necessary to have a nucleus of mature Christians" (GDC 258).

CHAPTER 9
Community

The search for community is as old as the human race. Angela Ashwin, writing on Spirituality and Corporate Worship[195] offers this insight from a more recently bygone age, quoting from Lambert Beauduin's *Liturgy the Life of the Church*, in which Beaduin identified "the abandonment of prayer" as one of the "sad consequences" of conditions in Catholic churches in 1914.[196] He observed that the "radiating warmth" that should come from "collective singing" and other forms of liturgical participation had been lost, and that people were cold, annoyed, in a hurry to get away, and no longer prayed. He went on to suggest that the very ambience of liturgy should inspire people in their own prayer life: "The soul formed in liturgical prayer will possess a facility of communion with Heaven, a pliancy and fervor, which will make its hours of prayer more spontaneous and more sweet."[197]

Romano Guardini, writing around the same time, lamented the separation of personal prayer and church worship. He believed that opportunities for growth were lost as personal spirituality and corporate worship need and nourish each other. He wrote: "It is hardly permissible to play off the spiritual life of the individual against the spiritual life of the liturgy…they are not mutually contradictory; they should both combine in active cooperation…They stand together in a vital and reciprocal relationship."[198]

The renewal of the church begun by Vatican 2 sought participation in the liturgy with purpose of achieving communion not only with Heaven but also amongst the participants. The Lord Jesus, "when He prayed to the Father, 'that all may be one . . . as we are one' (John 17:21-22) opened up vistas closed to human reason, for He implied a certain likeness between the union of the divine Persons, and the unity of God's sons in truth and charity" (GS 24). The church is the sign and instrument of communion with God and unity among all people (LG 1). The church is a "communion of life love and truth" (LG 9).

The Church, by the Spirit, is "unified in communion and in works of ministry" (LG 4). It is by God's power that the church is "a people brought into unity from the unity of the Father, the Son and the Holy Spirit" (LG 4). "All the faithful, scattered though they be throughout the world, are in communion with each other in the Holy Spirit" (LG 13). A cautionary note needs to be sounded that, not infrequently in Council documents, communion, while ideally it refers to the Trinity and to the Church, comes to be used more in making explicit the relationships within a hierarchical structure. Communion, as Paul McPartland says, is "juridically dominant rather than comunionally central."[199]

Further "the principal manifestation of the church" consists in the full active participation of God's people in the celebration of the Eucharist (SC42). Consequently the task of Christians in the world is "to reflect what God is like in the ways we live and work together", said a report on Collaborative Ministry, *The Sign We Give*.[200] The purpose of collaborative ministry is "to enable the church in mission. It must look outwards because God's life is for the whole world and all of creation."[201] Collaborative Ministry is not just a strategy but is "a spirituality in itself."

In his letter in January 2001, *Novo Millennio Ineunte*, Pope John Paul stressed that the Trinitarian mystery of unity in diversity is one that applies in every locality. The realisation of communion is closely linked to "the Christian community's ability to make room for all the gifts of the Spirit...for the unity of the church is not uniformity but an organic blending of legitimate diversities. It is the reality of many members joined in a single body, the one Body of Christ (cf. 1 Cor 12:12)"(NMI 46).[202] There could be no clearer statement of what is meant by collaborative ministry, and the Pope gives an equally clear indication that a serious commitment to it is required of us all:

> Therefore the Church of the third millennium will need to encourage all the baptised and confirmed to be aware of their active responsibility in the Church's life. Together with the ordained ministry, other ministries, whether formally instituted or simply recognised, can flourish for the good of the whole community, sustaining it in all its many needs: from catechesis to liturgy, from the education of the young to the widest array of charitable works (NMI 46).

Four dimensions

The four traditional dimensions of the pastoral activity of the Church, originating in the New Testament communities, are communication of and formation in faith *(kerygma)*; worship – symbols and rituals *(leitourgia)*; pastoral care and social commitment *(diakonia)* and identity and community *(koinonia)*.

Kerygma

Kerygma is derived from the Greek verb κηρύσσω (kērússō), *to proclaim or announce* and means *proclamation, announcement* of the faith. When Mark describes the beginning of Jesus' Galilean ministry, he writes: "Now after John was arrested, Jesus came to Galilee proclaiming the good news of God: 'The time is fulfilled, and the kingdom of God has come near; repent, and believe in the good news' " (Mark 1:14–15). Proclamation of the good news is the essential foundation for faith. Saint Paul says the same in his letter to the Romans: "And how are they to believe in one of whom they have never heard? And how are they to hear without someone to proclaim him?" (Romans 10:14).

Kerygma is the proclamation of the tradition and the words of the Lord. The question for today is how the Christian tradition of faith can be communicated and transmitted in a pluralistic context. *Kerygma* refers to the preaching of the Apostles as recorded in the New Testament.

Paul gives a summary of the *kerygma*, the Paschal Mystery: "For I handed on to you as of first importance what I in turn had received: that Christ died for our sins in accordance with the scriptures, and that he was buried, and that he was raised on the third day in accordance with the scriptures . . ." (1 Corinthians 15:3–4).

In addition to believers revisiting the *kerygma*, the New Testament indicates that the early converts receive teaching *(didache)*. This enables them to assimilate more deeply and integrate more fully the life-giving word they have received. The life of the early Jerusalem community is described in Acts 2:42-44: "They devoted themselves to the apostles' teaching *(didache)* and fellowship *(koinonia)*, to the breaking of bread *(klasis tou artou)* and the prayers *(proseuchai)*. . .And all who believed were together and had all things in common *(hapanta koina)*; and they sold their possessions and goods and distributed them to all, as any had need [*diakonia*]."

The teaching *(didache)* that develops the fuller sense of the basic proclamation also incorporates the moral implications of living by faith. This form of teaching is *paraklesis*, or exhortation. This is what Paul does in 1 Corinthians 1:10: "Now I appeal [*parakalo*] to you, brothers and sisters, by the name of our Lord Jesus Christ, that all of you be in agreement and that there be no divisions among you, but that you be united in the same mind and the same purpose."

Leitourgia

Liturgy is a Greek composite word meaning originally a public duty, a service to the state undertaken by a citizen (for example, in the 5th century BC, Athenian citizens paid up to build and equip a navy to resist the Persian invasion by sea). The public work of the church is to worship God together and to make provision for the poor; in Acts 2:42 there is described the complex activity of the teaching, the breaking of bread and the prayers. The question is how the content of what is celebrated in liturgy and sacraments can be explained and shared, given the kind of secularised society and the globalised world in which we live.

A very clear example of how coming to believe leads to worship and sacramental participation is found in the Acts 2. That momentous chapter begins with the coming of the Holy Spirit. The centre is Peter's speech at Pentecost, his proclamation of the *kerygma*. Luke describes the reaction and response of the listeners who come to believe Peter's proclamation of the good news: "Now when they heard this, they were cut to the heart and said to Peter and to the other apostles, 'Brothers, what should we do?'"(v. 37). Peter's response indicates the close and direct relationship between faith and sacramental/liturgical participation in the mysteries of faith: "Peter said to them, 'Repent, and be baptised every one of you in the name of Jesus Christ so that your sins may be forgiven; and you will receive the gift of the Holy Spirit' " (v. 38).

This formal participation in the sacraments leads to an entirely "worshipful" life marked by a contemplative, prayerful stance and a renewal of mind and heart. This is what Paul says to the Romans: "I appeal to you therefore, brothers and sisters, by the mercies of God, to present your bodies as a living sacrifice, holy and acceptable to God, which is your spiritual worship. Do not be conformed to this world, but be transformed by the renewing of your minds, so that you may discern what is the will of God – what is good and acceptable and perfect" (Romans 12:1–2). The New Testament tells us then that catechesis must focus on what we believe and what difference it makes.

Diakonia

Diakonia (ministry) is the consequence of hearing and believing in the good news. Jesus describes the very purpose of his coming among us as *diakonia*, service, that he defines not as doing favours but rather as the very gift of himself in self-sacrificing love. "For the Son of Man came not to be served but to serve, and to give his life a ransom for many" (Mark 10:45). In the remarkable depiction of the last judgment in Matthew 25, Jesus identifies the criterion of judgment as compassionate service, whether one has served one of the "least ones." For in serving them with compassion, those under judgment have served the Lord: "Truly I tell you, just as you did it to one of the least of these who are members of my family, you did it to me" (Matthew 25:40).

Acts 2:44 describes how "All who believed were together and had all things in common (*hapanta koina*); and they sold their possessions and goods and distributed them to all, as any had need." Indeed this ministry became more formalised as the community of believers grew, as we hear in Acts 6:1-4: "Now in these days when the disciples were increasing in number, the Hellenists murmured against the Hebrews because their widows were neglected in the daily distribution. And the twelve summoned the body of the disciples and said, 'It is not right that we should give up preaching the word of God to serve tables. Therefore, brethren, pick out from among you seven men of good repute, full of the Spirit and of wisdom, whom we may appoint to this duty. But we will devote ourselves to prayer and to the ministry of the word.'"

The underlying problems encountered in the conduct of the community meals and their development, to which the appointment of deacons was the solution here, is discussed by Gordon Lathrop where he concludes with this advice for today: "Make the meal clearly a meal. Continually reform the meal in the Trinitarian trajectory of the Crucified and Risen Christ toward the life of the world. In such a way Eucharistic practice, in all of its diversities, will remain continually in touch with its origin."[203]

The call to *diakonia* signals the practical consequence for living out the proclamation of the good news that has been believed and the holy mysteries in which believers have participated through the sacraments. *Diakonia* describes the mission of the followers of Jesus in the world. Through their service they give witness in the world to Jesus and, in that way, become salt and light for the world (see Matthew 5:13–16).

Koinonia

Koinonia is translated in various ways such as "fellowship," "community," "participation" or "communion." It is a central feature of the Christian life as presented in the Gospel of John and the First Letter of John.

Vatican 2 observes that God did not wish to save us individually, one by one, but decided to form us as a people "who might acknowledge him and serve him in holiness" (LG 9).

Koinonia describes a community of living witnesses to the faith, as in Acts 2:42 "They devoted themselves to...fellowship". The concept of *koinonia* contains as it were the *kerygma*, the *leiturgia* and the *diakonia*. Paul elaborates with a description of *koinonia* in action: "So if there is any encouragement in Christ, any incentive of love, any participation in the Spirit, any affection and sympathy, complete my joy by being of the same mind, having the same love, being in full accord and of one mind. Do nothing from selfishness or conceit, but in humility count others better than yourselves. Let each of you look not only to his own interests, but also to the interests of others. Have this mind among yourselves, which is yours in Christ Jesus" (Philippians 2:1-2). There follows a description of the ministry of Christ in his paschal mystery which is the rationale for the Christian way of life. Religion today is not infrequently seen to be an individual, personal and even private matter. For Christians this Paschal approach to religion reflects the fullness of our understanding and commitments to life in Christ which is both countercultural and communal.

Religious education

In the course of its development in the twentieth century religious education has become more and more separated from liturgy and catechesis. Where it existed within a catholic community such as a school the link was not severed; dwindling practice of the faith in worship has lead to its isolation.

One of the leading lights in the liturgical renewal of the twentieth century was Virgil Michel of St. John's Abbey, Collegeville, MN. Michel understood the problem of liturgical renewal to be fundamentally one of catechesis, which had become uprooted from its base in liturgy. His assessment was that the solution was not simply a matter of inserting the liturgy into religious education, but the recognition of the personal/relational knowing of religious truths that contextualise the Christian story in the life of the believer through liturgical participation. Michel states:

> We have given abundant religious instruction. But only too often such instruction has aimed chiefly at information of mind and not the living of faith. Just as Christ is the Way, the Truth and the Life, or King, Teacher and Priest – so all religion consists of morals, truths, and worship. To teach Catholic truths without relating these truths, both theoretically and practically, to actual worship, which is a living of these truths in real union with Christ, is a terrible neglect of the duty of religious instruction.[204]

Johannes Hofinger, a leader in the six International Catechetical Study Weeks (1959-1968), shared a common point of departure with the liturgical renewal movement in their assessment that the propositional theology of the church was the root cause of the perceived "lifelessness in the modern church."[205]

In the kerymgatic call for a return to the sources, the model of the early church at worship, which expressed itself in the proclamatory nature of the good news of salvation in Christ, pointed to a pastoral theology grounded in *kerygma*. The roots of kerygmatic movement were grounded in the liturgy and Hofinger taught that "the contemporary nature of the history of salvation is engagingly communicated in the liturgy."[206] In his view, the fullness of the liturgical cycle brings forth the unity of the Christian message and active participation in the liturgy points to "an essential element in religious pedagogy: the bringing into relief of the principles of experience and activity."[207]

In his classic, *The Art of Teaching Christian Doctrine*, Hofinger describes how the liturgy educates through the pedagogy of "doing" and the experiential dimension of ritual action. He says: "The abstract truths of our religion become visible in the liturgy. This is what we stress so much in modern catechetics, but the liturgy does more that just make the truths visible; religion is more than just 'knowing', it is a 'doing'. Therefore we have to learn by doing. Liturgy is an action, and the more we participate in this action of the family of Christ, the more our religion becomes active and pertinent."[208]

The kerygmatic approach and a renewed liturgical catechesis provided a good overture to Vatican 2. The Council set about restoring the communal dimension of liturgy (see especially its recognition of the community dimension of the history of salvation in *Lumen Gentium* 9). However where the reform was not received, we find a polarisation with origins in a bifurcation of the current religious sensibility, the separation of the quest for transcendence from the quest for community.

Transcendence without community

There appears to be a widespread yearning for the experience of transcendence; it is a feature of the human spirit, distinctive in that it often takes place outside traditional religious communities and is seen in the popularity of New Age movements, the attraction of Eastern religions, particularly from the 1970s onwards, all of which lack an adequate communal foundation. In this post-modern era those who are disenchanted with established religious denominations construct their own credo; it becomes a solitary quest for a religious experience or outlook tailored to the individual's own spiritual needs. A privatised search is also to be found within denominations. Many look to denominations not for communal commitment but for a product or commodity – religious experience. This attitude is reinforced by the consumerist ethos of our society where we are "booth-keepers in an emporium of transcendence."[209]

This privatised search can be found also in "traditionalist" parishes "where some seek a return to the 'smells and bells' from the past and relish the passivity of this worship experience."[210] Communality is purged in retro style, or at least muted. Such practice "is informed not by sound liturgical theology but by an uninformed liturgical romanticism. Advocates of a return to Tridentine are not those who have significant memories of the Latin Mass but those who project their private yearnings for the experience of the supernatural on a liturgical rite."[211] In such parishes it is not so much a retrieval of the liturgy of the past as a romanticised recreation which is little more than a superimposition of this individual longing for transcendence on a form of a past rite. "They want God but not God's people."[212]

What are the consequences of this privatised quest for transcendence? Is there still a role for religion as a motivation for moral behaviour? Are religious people more other-regarding? Richard Gaillardetz suggests that "It is not the religious motivation itself which [is] a decisive factor in…other-regarding behaviour, but the association of the quest for the transcendent with religious community."[213]

Larry Rasmussen, exploring the relationship between morality and religion, concludes: "Privatised religion apparently dampens concern for others, while commitment to a community sets in motion those dynamics that draw us into the webs of association that bind us together, sensitise us to needs beyond our own and call forth active response to and with others."[214] It is a central Christian conviction is that communal life is the essential context for authentic Christian living.

Community without transcendence.

Gaillardetz, viewing the many flourishing support groups, twelve-step programmes, charitable organisations and the like in our society, contends that they are examples of a longing for community but primarily for psychological, emotional and spiritual healing and support. Other kinds of community are comprised of autonomous individuals, each possessing certain gifts and abilities, who voluntarily join with other individual to form an association. They come together to share common interests, find support in others or to exercise acts of charity. But they often "sustained by a consumerist mentality – I belong while I derive benefit. Membership is strictly voluntary, and while withdrawal may have some cost, my personal identity is not essentially affected."[215] Other groups are designated communities by ethnicity or of life-style choice. Post-enlightenment liberalism has shaped our culture; it does not grant to community any significant formative or transformative power.

Gaillardetz suggests that we have come to identify this connectedness and sense of belonging with intimacy. He says that the contraction of our public life, manifested in the weakening of relationships with extended family, the demise of neighbourhoods as meaningful communities and negative associations often connected with the loci for public interaction (e.g. public transport, public parks – linked with crime) have lead us to stress only those few relationships capable of real intimacy and vulnerability.

The familial model is imposed on all communities. Religious congregations call themselves "families." The tacit assumption is that an experience of connectedness and solidarity is only available through experiences of warmth, informality and intimacy. This approach to community with its consumerist assumptions, its individualistic starting point and its stress on warmth and informality can be found in many catholic parishes. It is reflected in the liturgical life of those parishes. Ritual and symbolic dimensions are consistently downplayed and the experience is "lukewarm and limp...half-hearted... What is all too often not communicated is a sense of participation in the communion of the faithful."[216]

Trinity and Eucharist - foundations of the Christian community

In summary, Gaillardetz says that: "Transcendence without community degenerates into a base supernaturalism and unhealthy fascination with the otherworldly or ecstatic and emotion-based religious experience... Community without transcendence is prone to the consumerist, individualistic cult of intimacy which makes of the community that sphere of relations which exist solely for the fulfilment of my personal needs."[217]

Today's common cultural assumptions are challenged by the Christian tradition's Trinitarian and Eucharistic foundations of the Christian community. The doctrine of the Trinity is of a God whose very being, whose very essence is personal relationality. The early Christian community's experience was of the God of the Covenant who showed his commitment to his people in a radical way by fully embracing human history in the person of Jesus Christ and by the power of the Holy Spirit he drew all creation into divine communion.

The call to a Trinitarian life of communion dissolves any opposition between community and transcendence. For the life of communion is always at the same time communion with God and communion with one another. Paul describes this twofold communion in 1 Cor 10:16-17: "The cup of blessing which we bless, is it not a participation in the blood of Christ? The bread which we break, is it not a participation in the body of Christ?" and "Because there is one bread, we who are many are one body, for we all partake of the one bread." The Eucharistic celebration is the central sacramental expression of the Christian life of communion.

The notion of *koinonia* flows from the theology of the body of Christ as in 1 Corinthians 12:12: "For just as the body is one and has many members, and all the members of the body, though many, are one body, so it is with Christ." In this individualist and consumerist world we frequently act as though we come to services of public worship simply to receive rather than to generate, to be nourished rather than to nourish. Some produce, others consume. "The Church is not an aggregate of individual members – it is a participation in community which is formative and transformative. We discover our personal identities in the life of communion. What makes a person 'unique' is not 'individuality', but one's particular contribution to the common life of believers."[218] The liturgy celebrates the unity of communion with God and communion with one another.

Too often transcendence is understood as "other-worldly". The Tridentine mass took us into another world. Understood in this way transcendence will always be opposed to community. But ritual action, by ritualising ordinary human gestures and postures, highlights the transcendent dimension of our human existence. Ritual actions draw us into the life of the communion. The transcendent dimension of the liturgy is not found in some arbitrary set of actions and gestures but in the dignity with which all ritual actions are expressed. Liturgy is act of communication and celebration of a meal. These are at heart social actions. Sociality is not something we inject into the liturgy; it is in fact at the heart of the liturgy. Good liturgy highlights and develops what is embedded in the rituals. These rituals are not just social; they are communal.

The liturgy we celebrate shapes our identity as Christians. It is the narrative framework which makes our lives intelligible. That is why the Christian community can never be one group among many groups in our lives. It is not one social commitment among many. Rather my ecclesial identity as a member of this community of disciples provides the context, the horizon against which I assess my other life commitments.

The Paschal Mystery revealed and celebrated in the proclamation of God's word and in the action of the Eucharist proper "offers the very grammar of our salvation."[219] The transformation of the gifts is at the same time our transformation. The transformation effected in us in the Eucharist is not in the first instance a private one; it is a personal and therefore a communal transformation. As ancient tradition has it: we become what we receive.

The human search for transcendent mystery calls for full engagement with the great liturgical symbols of the tradition: gathering, processing, eating, drinking, touching, gesturing and singing. "Eucharistic liturgy has never exhausted the Church's resources in encountering the mystery of the transcendent."[220]

PART 3: LITURGY

CHAPTER 10
The Paschal Mystery

The Paschal Mystery of the suffering dying and rising of Jesus Christ is at the centre of Christian faith and therefore it may be approached from many directions. One direction was that of Dietrich Bonhoeffer, imprisoned in Berlin Tegel military prison for his Christian faith, who wrote in *Letters and Papers from Prison* in 1944:

> Socrates mastered the art of dying; Christ overcame death as "the last enemy" (1 Cor 15:26). There is a real difference between the two things; the one is within the scope of human possibilities, the other means resurrection. It is not from *ars moriendi*, the art of dying, but from the resurrection of Christ that a new and purifying wind can blow through our present world. ... If a few people really believed that and acted on it in their daily lives, a great deal would be changed. To live in the light of the Resurrection – that is what Easter means.[221]

Not only did his Christian faith sustain the heart and life of Bonhoeffer, but it enabled him to see possibilities for the future far beyond the bounds of his personal circumstances.

St Maximus of Turin, writing in the fifth century, sees possibilities far beyond the present moment; in one of his sermons, entitled *Christ is the Day*, he says:

> Christ's resurrection is life for the dead, pardon for sinners, glory for the saints. And so the holy prophet invites every creature to the celebration of Christ's resurrection; we should rejoice, he says, and be glad on this day which the Lord has made...

> "The light shines in the darkness, and the darkness has not overcome it." And so, my brethren, we ought all to rejoice on this holy day. No one should separate himself from the general rejoicing because he has sins on his conscience; no one should refuse to take part in the public worship because of the burden of his misdeeds. However great a sinner he may be, on this day he should not despair of pardon, for the privileges granted this day are great. If a thief was thought worthy of paradise, why should not a Christian be thought worthy of forgiveness?[222]

The writer of the Letter to the Hebrews, after describing the dying, rising and perfection of Jesus, has these words of hope and encouragement for the generations to come:

> Since, then, we have a great high priest who has passed through the heavens, Jesus, the Son of God, let us hold fast to our confession. For we do not have a high priest who is unable to sympathise with our weaknesses, but we have one who in every respect has been tested as we are, yet without sin. Let us therefore approach the throne of grace with boldness, so that we may receive mercy and find grace to help in time of need (Heb. 4:14-16).

A purifying wind, a light shining in the darkness, a throne of mercy and grace – how may we describe the Paschal Mystery in our post-modern day?

The Paschal Mystery is the centre of our faith. Through the liturgy, especially the Eucharist, the Paschal Mystery of the dying and rising of Christ and our dying and rising through, with and in him are made real and engage us now. We share in the Paschal Mystery of Christ through the action of the proclaimed word and our participation in the gifts of bread and wine becoming the body and blood of Christ that we share in communion. Maria Boulding asserts that: "All liturgy is paschal."[223] As the Vatican 2 decree on the liturgy affirms:

> Just as Christ was sent by the Father, so also He sent the apostles, filled with the Holy Spirit. This He did that, by preaching the gospel to every creature, they might proclaim that the Son of God, by His death and resurrection, had freed us from the power of Satan and from death, and brought us into the kingdom of His Father. His purpose also was that they might accomplish the work of salvation which they had proclaimed, by means of sacrifice and sacraments, around which the entire liturgical life revolves.

> Thus by baptism men are plunged into the paschal mystery of Christ: they die with Him, are buried with Him, and rise with Him; they receive the spirit of adoption as sons "in which we cry: Abba, Father" (Rom 8:15), and thus become true adorers whom the Father seeks.

> In like manner, as often as they eat the supper of the Lord they proclaim the death of the Lord until He comes. For that reason, on the very day of Pentecost, when the Church appeared before the world, "those who received the word" of Peter "were baptised." And "they continued steadfastly in the teaching of the apostles and in the communion of the breaking of bread and in prayers . . . praising God and being in favour with all the people" (Acts 2:41-47).

> From that time onwards the Church has never failed to come together to celebrate the paschal mystery: reading those things "which were in all the scriptures concerning him" (Luke 24:27), celebrating the Eucharist in which "the victory and triumph of his death are again made present", and at the same time giving

thanks "to God for his unspeakable gift" (2 Cor 9:15) in Christ Jesus, "in praise of his glory" (Eph. 1:12), through the power of the Holy Spirit (SC 6).

Paschal Mystery in history

What is this mystery? Since the fourth century the main liturgical functions and particularly the rites associated with Christian initiation culminating in the Eucharist have been described in Greek speaking churches as *mysteria*, in Syriac speaking churches as *raze* and in the Latin Church either as *mysteria* or *sacramenta*. The original meaning of these words faded in the course of time. *Sacrament* became reserved to the seven rites whose importance was discerned by the development of doctrinal reflection. The word *raz*, the translation of an Iranian term, appears in apocalyptic texts and had eschatological overtones. The Greek translation of scripture uses *mysterion* in the same sense.

St Paul used the word *mysterion* frequently, while the synoptic gospels have only one use (Mt 3:11; Mk 4:11; Lk8:10); there are several uses in the Book of Revelation. For St Paul, while the word mysterion is rooted in apocalyptic contexts, it refers to the Kingdom and the lordship of Jesus, manifested as the Christ (1 Cor 1:23; 2:1, 7; Rom 16:25-26). It is through the preaching of Christ and him crucified that the mystery is being revealed as it was the on the cross that the radical opposition of the mysterious and previously hidden wisdom of God to the supposed wisdom of the world was shown. In the letters to the Ephesians and the Colossians Paul shows the consequences of all this for the life of the early church communities while emphasising the eschatology which is being brought to fulfilment.

Tertullian rejected the transposition of *mysterium* into Latin, preferring the term *sacramentum*, rich in overtones in Roman usage (for example, *sacramentum* was the oath sworn between a Roman general and his soldiers expressing mutual obligations). The more allusive sense of mystery in Greek is noted in Ignatius of Antioch who refers to the observance of the Lord's day replacing the observance of the Sabbath because Sunday is the day on which "our life was raised up through him and his death", adding "it is through this mystery that we received the faith, and it is because of it that we persevere in order to be acknowledged as disciples of Jesus Christ, our only Master."[224]

The celebration of the new Passover, the memorial of the death and resurrection of Christ, was from an early date seen and proclaimed as the supreme mystery of the Christian faith. Justin makes reference to "the mystery of the lamb" in the Mosaic Passover as the "prefiguration of Christ."[225] Melito of Sardis uses the phrase "mystery of the Pasch."[226] Eusebius of Caesarea adopts "mystery" in speaking of "the memorial of the great sacrifice of Christ, according to the mysteries he has passed on to us," "for David already alluded [Ps 39:3-9 LXX] to the mystery of the new covenant of Christ that is today celebrated openly among all peoples."[227] A little later he is more explicit: " First our Saviour and Lord himself offered sacrifice and now all the priests of all nations who derive their priesthood from him do likewise, when ...they enact the mysteries of his body and blood under the symbols of bread and wine."[228]

From the middle of the fourth century, because of the different origins and the nuances each had in Latin use, *mysteria* (in the plural) was used for baptism and for Eucharist. In Latin *mysterium* was preferred when the emphasis was on the spiritual realties hidden beneath the letter of the Scriptures, while *sacramentum* was preferred for the actions by which Christians were initiated into those realities.[229] Only in the Scholastic period did *sacramentum* acquire the technical meaning it has kept down to our time.

Once we give "sacrament" its older and broader meaning, we see that in the church, the "universal sacrament of salvation", everything is sacramental, that is, everything is the vehicle of a meaning and an efficacy belonging to a different order from the realities of direct experience, and that is because the church of Christ is a sign and anticipation of the "mysteries of the kingdom."[230]

The idea of "mystery", perhaps too rich and imprecise, became replaced by the idea of "sign" linked particularly to the seven sacraments in the Middle Ages with an emphasis on the effect of the sacraments and therefore on their causality. The end result was a twofold theology of the Christian rites: a sacramental theology based on a "descent", that is the communication to humans of a salvation worked directly by God and a liturgical theology based on an "ascent", which would restore to the church's rites their value as the external and social manifestation of the virtue of religion.

Liturgy belongs to the order of "doing" (*ergon* – a work or action) rather than of "knowing" (*logos* – word, mind and reason). Liturgical actions reveal their meaning in their performance at a level of sensible reality, awakening the mind and heart to acceptance of realities of a different order. Instead of trying to explain divine realities by means of analogies from the created world, we describe the manifestation of the divine in the universe that is accessible to us, for "mystery" implies "revelation" (*apocalypsis*) which is made to those whose ears are already open to hear God speaking in the Scriptures.

In the Israelite mind, time is linear and consists of three main phases: time before creation, the duration of time between creation and the "Day of the Lord" and the last times that follow that Day. The time in between is historical time interspersed with divine manifestations (theophanies) and numerous covenants (Noah, Abraham, Moses). Christ broke this continuum because the kingdom is now "at hand" and "among you". The resurrection establishes Jesus as Christ and Lord, being now the fulfilment of all that went before and the revelation of all that is to follow. This new and final time of fullness and fulfilment is the time of the Church, the time of the Spirit who brings about a new creation, a time of "mystery" that will end in "revelation" (*apocalypsis*) of the unveiled presence (*parousia*) of the Lord.

Until then the Spirit is given as the "first fruits" (Rom 8:23) and a pledge (2 Cor 1:22) for the kingdom is present but not yet fully revealed. The Spirit is given through the death and resurrection of Jesus (John 7:39) as the first gift[231] and is manifest in his gifts. Every Christian liturgy has at its heart an "epiclesis" or fervent prayer that the Spirit may descend on the ecclesial assembly and make known there the mysteries of the kingdom. Meanwhile the Lord is at once present and absent, present and acting directly in the sacraments, absent for he is seated at the right hand of the Father. The time of the church is then both historical and eschatological. The Eucharistic celebration recalls the meal Jesus took with his disciples and foretells the eschatological fulfilment often presented in the form of a messianic banquet.

Whatever the origins of the paschal celebration, the Mosaic Passover was associated with the freeing of God's people at the Exodus and the making of the covenant on Sinai. The prophets concern for the Day of the Lord linked the Passover to creation as the beginning of God's plan of salvation and to the foreshadowing of its eschatological fulfilment and therefore a source of messianic hope. In the early church two themes emerge, one pairing *pascha* and *passio*, emphasising the fulfilment of the saving plan through the passion and resurrection of Christ, in which we participate in baptism and the Eucharist and the other pairing *pascha* and *transitus* emphasising what believers do in actualising what it prefigured in the Mosaic Passover and fulfilled in the passion and resurrection of Christ. However the tendency to celebrate all the mysteries of the life of Christ and the church lead to a diminution of the overriding importance of the Paschal Mystery as the one all-embracing mystery and the importance of its celebration, not once only a year at Easter but on Sundays throughout the year.

From the second century onwards the faithful's active participation in the Eucharistic prayer was expressed in the great *Amen* and from the seventh century also in the *Sanctus* acclamation. In the revised liturgy from the Second Vatican Council, a memorial acclamation was added. In response to the invitation: "Let us proclaim the mystery of faith", we proclaim our faith in the dying, rising and final coming of Christ. In the *anamnesis* or memorial which follows we remember not only past events of salvation but the action of Christ bringing God's promises to fulfilment. Our response draws us into the event taking place and we share in the paschal mystery of Christ. The opposite of *anamnesis* is *amnesia* – in the institution of the church we keep fresh the memory of Christ in a world where institutions are rapidly losing their corporate memory. As a rabbinic adage observes: "To remember is to give life – to forget is to let die." In liturgical memorial we do not repeat, re-enact or re-do anything from the past. The Roman missal offers us the terms "enact", "participate in" and "perpetuate." History becomes present in a graced event of salvation in the here and now, and a glimpse is given of what the future holds when the kingdom comes. "Active participation" in the liturgy is the right and vocation of the assembly – the liturgy is the privileged school of faith and the central means of salvation; it is first the action of God and then the action of the faithful in their response.[232] Irwin sums up this train of thought saying that the repeated ritual enactment of Christ's Paschal Mystery needs to take deep root in our lives.

> It can then become the way we measure success and failure, happiness and suffering, hopefulness and despair, triumph and humiliation….apparent failure in the world's eyes is the very thing that leads us to deeper conversion to Christ, …apparent despair is a dark night of the soul leading to a new appreciation of the brilliance of Christ's light; that what we experience as humiliation is really a purgation leading us to a fuller life in God's sight, even if that is not the way others see it or us.[233]

Paschal Mystery today

Since the Second Vatican Council the renewal of the Roman liturgy has once more put the Paschal Mystery, understood in its traditional fullness, at the heart of liturgical actions and celebrations. The liturgical mystery now more clearly calls to mind not only the manifestation of the incarnate Word from his first appearance on earth to his glorious return to heaven but the mystery of salvation in history from creation to consummation ritually through the temporal cycle. In addition the liturgy celebrates the moments and acts of the individual's participation in the mystery of salvation from baptism into divine life through to the entry into the kingdom. Throughout the year the mystery of the Pasch – the "passage of the Lord" by which he delivers his people and the "passage" of his people in union with Christ – is reflected.[234]

To this end the Liturgy of the Hours expresses and effects the sanctification of time in a threefold cycle. The annual cycle celebrates the mystery of salvation summed up in Christ. The weekly cycle, reflecting the phases of the moon, an ancient symbol of the mutability of earthly life, transposes the order of creation into the mystery of salvation where the great poem of the Hexaemeron (the six days of creation) is anchored to the cycle of redemption centred on the

Lord's Day – Sunday. The daily cycle derives its rhythm from light and darkness, bringing out the symbolic resonances of day and night. In this prayer the church bears witness to its paradoxical situation on the boundary between time and eternity. Odo Casel sums up mystery in this way:

> Christianity in its full and original meaning – the "Gospel of God" or "of Christ" – is …not a world-view with a religious background nor a religious or theological system of doctrine nor a moral code, but "mystery" in the Pauline sense, that is, a revelation of God to human beings through theandric acts that are full of power, as well as the passage of human beings to God that is made possible by this revelation and the gift of grace; it is the attainment of the eternal Father by the redeemed church through the sacrifice of total self-giving and through the glory that this produces.[235]

We participate in the mystery of salvation through a mystical and real participation in the life and death of Christ. Christ lives and dies in the very sacramental action that makes us sharers in him. But, as A. G. Martimort says: "Care must still be taken, however, that the symbolic expression of the mystery is not obscured by an arid ritual and by mediocre formularies, especially in the lyrical parts of the service."[236]

At the present time we can see that the restoration of the *Rite of Christian Initiation of Adults* gives us an opportunity to focus on two particular and distinct phases of the catechesis which unfolds the Paschal Mystery. The first phase is the journey of the community accompanying through Lent those who are preparing for initiation into the Body of Christ through baptism, confirmation and Eucharist. Maury Schepers reminds us, remembering the words of Conrad Pepler O.P. from her student days, that: "The Lenten pilgrimage begins with a strong emphasis on our moral fitness (or lack thereof). The initial focus is on the three ascetic practices (works of mercy, prayer and fasting) that were given even the primitive church's seal of approval (Mt 6). Then as the weeks go by there is a shift of attention, away from the insistence on self-denial to a quite different concern, namely, Jesus' own journey to Jerusalem, and eventually his suffering, death and vindication."[237] Through its recognition of the development of this phase, the community is able to enter more deeply into the mystery of the dying and rising of Christ.

The second phase encompasses the fifty days following Easter, culminating in the celebration of Pentecost. Here the catechist is the risen Christ himself. His teaching unfolds in the Johannine readings – the dialogue between Jesus and Nicodemus on new birth (Jn 3), the discourse on the bread of life (Jn 6) and the words spoken in the Upper Room, revealing the gifts of the spirit (Jn 14-17). These readings unfold the endowment of the two-fold gifts of Sacrament and Spirit.

Schepers goes on suggest two spiritual laws, the *law of the cross* and the *law of the resurrection*, derived respectively from Jesus' self-sacrifice on Calvary and from his deliverance from death. He believes that the fruitfulness of the Paschal Mystery is measured by our living in conformity with them. These laws are not the negative and then the positive side of the total celebration of the Paschal Mystery but both laws each have a positive and a negative side. The Law of the Cross prescribes the way in which evil is to be dealt with but precisely in order that a greater good may be harvested. It is God's plan that evil is to be overcome by not by the exercise of naked power but by suffering willingly and lovingly undergone to the effect that the evil is converted into a greater good. The foundation of this law is in the dangerous hope that God has dominion over evil. The exercise of naked power will not bring about peace; rather it will breed more violence. The combatants are deaf to any appeal to suspend hostilities; they dare not stop the violence for fear that "the silence will reveal an alternative and they will be proved to be in the wrong."[238] The only adequate response to evil is suffering lovingly undergone; it is the example Jesus gave that is in effect even down to our own time. The key is not in getting rid of evil but in becoming non-violent persons. It is not that evil will cease to exist but that it will be transformed through the presence of a community that is the Body of Christ, a community who find in the Cross their hope and who consecrate themselves to making the Law of the Cross their rule of life.

The Law of the Resurrection, while oriented towards progress in hope, demands a radical renunciation of an altogether different kind. After the resurrection Jesus does not speak to anyone to whom he appears about the past. (The apparent exception is on the road to Emmaus where the disciples think Jesus is unaware of the recent events in Jerusalem while he is only too aware, having been at the centre of the storm.) Schepers suggests a connection between the silence of Jesus and the baptism of the catechumens. The conversion of the catechumens is a turning away from the past. The symbol of their baptism is the font where entry into it is going down into the tomb and coming out from it is an emergence from the womb. The past is dead and buried in the rite. At Easter members of the community are invited to recall their baptism and to renew the promises of their initiation. The past is not to be remembered. Burying the past is therefore is integral to the Easter ritual. The challenge is to do this on a regular basis. Our success is partial; we are never without sin and our proclivity to deny it is significant. Our habitual sins come back to haunt us. Our sins are not to be denied but they are to be consigned to oblivion as Jesus is the victor over sin and death. He knows the past but chooses to disregard it. The challenge is to let go of something about which we spontaneously feel that we should do something. Our living faith is not the adherence to external law but the interior transformation of our hearts and our lives through the spirit which is poured into our hearts through the Paschal Mystery.[239]

Presence and gift

Nathan Mitchell explores, in an article entitled *Mystery and Manners,* the thoughts of two post-modern philosophers who express the Paschal Mystery in terms of presence and gift.[240] The French philosopher-theologian, Jean-Luc Marion, begins his 1983 essay *The Gift of Presence* with these words: "Easter innovates, and does so radically. Either Christ no longer has any importance on this day, or 'he brought all newness in bringing himself'…The innovation has a name – Christ – and a function – to render [us] new. As well as the things of life…Since the resurrection…we must relearn everything…We are thrown forward in a world too new for us." Louis-Marie Chauvet, following the Jewish philosopher Emmanuel Lévinas, speaks of the practice of what he calls "the liturgy of the neighbour." Both explore how, in the light of that subversive "innovation", Easter and the Eucharist are related to ethics, to the working out of Christian identity in the world.

Both are critical of western metaphysics; both see Easter as the starting point for interpreting sacramental "presence." Indeed Christianity is the starting point of the dissolution of metaphysics because the gospel seems to "shift the centre of philosophical interest from the natural world to human spirituality, from intellect to the practice of charity." Marion calls into question the metaphysical determination of God, maintaining that we must affirm the absolute freedom of God with regard or all determinations; we must return to God's own most properly theological name – charity/love.

For Chauvet, when metaphysics thinks "God" it thinks "cause" and when it thinks "cause" it thinks "effect"; this is a productionist scheme; it assumes the cause can be known through the effects. Post-moderns perceive phenomena not as produced from a "causal cloud of being" but only as "given." The true horizon of meaning therefore is not being but givenness. If phenomena are given, then there could be both and given and a giver.

Chauvet and Marion speak of a "pragmatic theology of absence." Such a theology does not assert the "non-presence" of God. It says rather that God is to be shielded from presence i.e. from confinement to or containment within causal categories. God is utterly beyond signification and therefore utterly beyond both "presence" and "absence." The name of God "does not name God as an essence; it designates what passes beyond every name. The name designates what one does not name and says that one does not name it."

Mitchell explores what he calls the case against metaphysics.[241] For our purposes we will refer here to points which have provoked thought and caused discussion in recent pastoral situations. First, metaphysics is impatient with progress. It privileges being over becoming; being completes becoming; process is inherently inferior because it is perpetually in motion, because it is looking toward something to complete it. Process destabilises because it is open-ended, boundless, limitless. This view echoes an understanding of the world as more dynamic than static, of the experience of becoming rather than of stability. Secondly metaphysics promises presence but ends by binding it to production and thereby reduces the sheer gratuity of gift to a circular cycle of cause, debt and obligation.

Thirdly metaphysics is not only reductive but is anthropomorphic and utilitarian. God is not an innovator but an operator; it erases being's radical otherness. Descartes *Cogito ergo sum* (I think therefore I am) is the ultimate example of being reduced to rationality. In a culture of technology being is reduced to representation, to the image. We have traded icon for idol and the real for mere voyeurism. In such a world being is equated with economic capital. Fourthly metaphysics neglects the relation of reciprocity and reversibility that characterises human subjects. The relation between lover and beloved is not the same as the relation between a shipbuilder and a ship. The truly human cannot be reduced to a productionist, technological model of causality. Because persons are not trophies, achievements, they are works in progress, unfolding without end.

Therefore to see the Eucharist as presence and gift is a new starting point from the Paschal Mystery that can neither be derived nor deduced from the metaphysics of presence and causality. Easter's innovation is counterintuitive because it compels us to talk "real presence" without relying on "empirical place." Presence and location are not to be equated. The resurrected body is only encountered by putting aside the logic which governs empirical experience and the conceptual organisation of all which is. It is a real presence without succumbing to a metaphysics of being and causality. In the Eucharist, the body of Christ is not given to us in the dead, discredited language of this world but in the innovative word of Easter. Christ's presence needs a body built for it and this is the work of the Holy Spirit who acts in Eucharist, in church and in the glorified humanity of the Lord who, by these very means, makes of himself a gift, gives himself as a present by that same Spirit. But how can it be built? If one cannot appeal to the usual suspects being and causality, if one cannot produce a presence through empiricism or the mechanics of signification, how can we receive Christ's Eucharistic body daily?

Easter transforms Christ's bodily presence from (now absent) empirical fact to divine gift. Thus what builds presence a body, what gives presence is Easter. More especially the unique act of blessing and disappearance we call the Ascension. Note the parallel between Ascension and Emmaus where Jesus disappears in the very act of blessing his bewildered disciples and vanishes just as the disciples' eyes are opened and recognition dawns. Emmaus is a dark story – we want everything to be as it was. We want the comfort of the empirical body. We thought in Jesus we had forever found it. The disciples on road to Emmaus are not merely confused and disappointed; they are resentful and angry because God destroyed the very One they had hoped and believed in. *And we are exactly like them.* As Rahner said in a homily for the feast of the Ascension, grief is the right response. He took it all with him and we want it back.

Chauvet says that the presence and the absence are not separate but form one ambivalent reality. Christ's presence may be inscribed on our bodies but it can never be circumscribed in a place. The "here" of the Eucharistic presence while not an empirical "here" always refers us back to the body, to its history and particularity, to its communion with others. Presence needs to have a body built for it because God is "not 'nowhere in particular'; God is somewhere." The glorious Lord's presence is not within an closed object, an edible loaf – that loaf is meant to be broken so that Christ's presence is not the bread as such in its unbroken state – rather it is indeed the bread but in its essence bread-as-food, bread-as-meal, bread-for-sharing. It is in the breaking of bread that the reality is manifested.

Blessing

Blessing is the theological act, a Trinitarian act, whose source is God's own life. Marion sees an essential bond between blessing and presence and between recognition and gift. Because presence depends on blessing, Christ discloses himself as gift – this gift can only be recognised when we bless God as Jesus did.[242] Easter is our confession, our recognition, that the glory of God is present and given to us in the crucified and risen body of Jesus, the body which in glory still bears its wounds. It is the spirit who makes it possible for God in Jesus to efface God's very self inside humanity; it is the spirit at work in the cross, resurrection, ascension and Pentecost who makes it possible for God to take on an eschatological body in humanity and so be present to us and gift to us forever.

This presence launched the mission of the church. Presence becomes a gift to us from the beyond of the Trinity. Christ's absence at the ascension results in the intensification of presence not its diminishment. The Ascension is the radicalisation of the gift of presence that makes possible the more insistent presence of the Eucharist. God's own life as persons in communion consists precisely in their constantly being given away to one another. So too is the economy of Easter, Ascension and Pentecost. Hence the Ascension marks less of a departure and separation or indeed an abandonment than the setting up of a gap/distance crossed by the blessings. Presence becomes possible because of distance. As Marion says, distance allows the disciples to become not servants but friends, not spectators but actors of the redemptive and revelatory action of Christ.

The goal of post-modern theology is not to deny or diminish Eucharistic real presence but to affirm it in terms other than those of metaphysical being and causality. Post-modern theologians seek "to build a body" for Christ's presence. Marion describes the process in these terms:

> [T]he ascension does not mark the disappearance of Christ in the expectation of a new (empirical) presence at the end of an all too long absence. It marks the Paschal conversion of all presence into gift: blessing, submission to the Spirit which makes us act in and as Christ, and mission...constitute the three dimensions of the gift of presence in distance. For if the Word became flesh, it is necessary, ever since the Ascension, that is, in us, "flesh become word – and the word fall" [a quote from the poet Octavio Paz]. Our flesh becomes word in order to bless the Trinitarian gift of the presence of the Word, and to accomplish our incorporation in Him.[243]

Mitchell sums up this paradox as follows: "We do really participate in the 'presence of the absence'. For what is present to us at the Eucharistic table is eaten, yet never consumed; present, yet never contained; broken, yet never destroyed; shared, yet never used up; distributed to all, while remaining inexhaustible, irreducible."[244]

St Andrew of Crete, whose ministry straddled the seventh and eighth centuries, sums up the Paschal Mystery and its ongoing paradox of presence and absence:

> Come then, let us run with him as he presses on to his passion. Let us imitate those who have gone out to meet him, not scattering olive branches or garments or palms in his path, but spreading ourselves before him as best we can, with humility of soul and upright purpose. So may we welcome the Word as he comes, so may God who cannot be contained within any bounds, be contained within us.
>
> So it is that we must spread under Christ's feet, not coats or lifeless branches or shoots of trees, matter which wastes away and delights the eye for only a few brief hours. But we have clothed ourselves with Christ's grace, or with the whole Christ —"for as many of you as were baptised into Christ have put on Christ" – so let us spread ourselves like coats under his feet.
>
> Today let us too give voice with the children to that sacred chant as we wave the spiritual branches of our soul: "Blessed is he who comes in the name of the Lord, the King of Israel."[245]

CHAPTER 11
Liturgy

All liturgy is Paschal

All liturgy is a union of word and act/sacrament/symbol. Liturgy is not something imposed, divinely or not, from outside or above. Liturgy is the people's work, it being the public duty of the people – the word *liturgy* itself originating in an ancient Greek secular context from the duty of the people to promote the welfare of every individual and of the state itself.

As the Vatican Council said: "The liturgy, 'through which the work of our redemption is accomplished,' most of all in the divine sacrifice of the Eucharist, is the outstanding means whereby the faithful may express in their lives, and manifest to others, the mystery of Christ and the real nature of the true Church." The liturgy is Paschal for in the liturgy: "in Jesus Christ, the Son of God made man, who died and rose from the dead, salvation is offered to all men, as a gift of God's grace and mercy" (SC 2).

Liturgy is first of all "the work of Christ the Lord in redeeming mankind and giving perfect glory to God." Christ achieved his work "principally by the paschal mystery of His blessed passion, resurrection from the dead, and the glorious ascension, whereby 'dying, he destroyed our death and, rising, he restored our life.'" The Paschal Mystery is the origin of the sacraments and above all "it was from the side of Christ as He slept the sleep of death upon the cross that there came forth the wondrous sacrament of the whole Church" (SC 5).

The Paschal Mystery is no mere past event for "by baptism men are plunged into the Paschal Mystery of Christ." Since the time of Christ "the Church has never failed to come together to celebrate the paschal mystery: reading...the scriptures...celebrating the Eucharist...and at the same time giving thanks to God...through the power of the Holy Spirit" (SC 6).

A significant and much used concept is that of presence, in particular the presence of Christ in the liturgy. Christ is always present to accomplish his work:

- in His Church, especially in her liturgical celebrations,
- in the sacrifice of the Mass,
    o   in the person of His minister,
    o   under the Eucharistic species,
- in the sacraments, so that when a man baptises it is really Christ Himself who baptises,
- in His word, since it is He Himself who speaks when the holy scriptures are read in the Church,
- when the Church prays and sings (SC 7).

The church is active before the liturgy is celebrated when it calls people to faith and to conversion. For "How then are they to call upon him in whom they have not yet believed? But how are they to believe him whom they have not heard? And how are they to hear if no one preaches? And how are men to preach unless they be sent?" (Rom. 10:14-15) (SC 9). The liturgy itself is the summit toward which the activity of the Church is directed; at the same time it is the font from which all her power flows. The faithful, filled with "the paschal sacraments," become "one in holiness" and are urged to hold fast in their lives to what they have grasped by their faith" (SC 10).

In whatever way the liturgy was to be "restored" (note this description of post-Vatican 2 liturgy) and promoted, the "full and active participation by all the people is the aim to be considered before all else; for it is the primary and indispensable source from which the faithful are to derive the true Christian spirit" (SC 14). In promoting the instruction and participation of the faithful, pastors need to "take into account their age and condition, their way of life, and standard of religious culture, with zeal and patience, and leading by example" (SC 19).

The liturgy is made up of immutable elements divinely instituted, and of elements subject to change. These latter "not only may but ought to be changed with the passage of time if they have suffered from the intrusion of anything out of harmony with the inner nature of the liturgy or have become unsuited to it" in the general restoration of the liturgy (SC 21). Texts and rites should express more clearly the holy things which they signify so that the people should be enabled to understand them with ease and to take part in them fully and actively.

Sacred scripture "is of the greatest importance in the celebration of the liturgy. For it is from scripture...that actions and signs derive their meaning...it is essential to promote that warm and living love for scripture to which the venerable tradition of both eastern and western rites gives testimony" (SC 24). In sum the Church "earnestly desires that Christ's faithful, when present at this mystery of faith, should not be there as strangers or silent spectators...they should take part in the sacred action conscious of what they are doing, with devotion and full collaboration" (SC 48).

The importance of Sacred Scripture cannot be underestimated.[246] "What was handed on by the Apostles includes everything which contributes toward the holiness of life and increase in faith of the peoples of God" (DV 8). Indeed "the Church has always venerated the divine Scriptures just as she venerates the body of the Lord, since, especially in the sacred liturgy, she unceasingly receives and offers to the faithful the bread of life from the table both of God's word and of Christ's body" (DV 21).

Karl Rahner observes how Origen perceived the word of God sacramentally and how the word mediates divine presence in the

Eucharist.[247] In word and Eucharist the incarnational character of Christian salvation as a whole is sacramentally present in them. Word and sacrament are so similar because they are constituted by the same divine presence. The symbolic nature of the word allows it to bring what it proclaims; the word effectively renders the grace of God present. The word does not merely carry communication about God, it is a communication of God's very self, or as Herbert Vorgrimler expressed it: "This communication is not 'news about', information', 'tidings,' – it is God's very self."[248]

Nathan Mitchell observes that the *aggiornamento* (updating, later to be called restoration) of the liturgy, launched by John XXIII and completed by Paul VI, "reclaimed as both 'work of the people' *(leitourgia,* action of an assembly) and 'work of God' *(opus Dei,* God doing for us what we cannot do for ourselves) was a radical event. The other three radical components of Vatican 2, according to Mitchell, are: "an ecclesiology that is populist and Christocentric rather than papal and curialist; a renewed episcopate, seen once more as an authoritative college including (but not competing with) the pope; and a renewed social order based on love rather than justice."[249]

Mitchell reminds us that the Liturgy Constitution (debated at Vatican 2's first session in 1962) attracted not a little opposition. He tells us that Cardinal Montini had worked constantly behind the scenes to contact the experts needed "to legitimate liturgical reform on historical grounds."[250] As Pope Paul VI, Montini wasted no time in establishing a working Consilium so the liturgical reforms could be implemented right away. Article IX of the text of the Pope's *motu proprio, Sacram Liturgiam* (1964), gave episcopal conferences the right to oversee their own liturgical translations. But a "doctored" text, published in *L'Osservatore Romano* (29 January 1964), called the conferences' right into question by omitting a crucial passage. As Peter Hebblethwaite writes: "Cisalpine indignation flared up" once this deception was discovered; the trickster was forced to back down, and the original text (affirming the role of episcopal conferences) was reinstated when *Sacram Liturgiam* appeared in the *Acta Apostolicae Sedis.*"[251] The importance of this story is that the obvious intent of *Sacram Liturgiam* was to let episcopal conferences decide matters of translation particular to their language groups.

The real significance of the Pauline liturgical reform was "the insight (so radical in its implications) that worship is simultaneously the 'work of God' (pure gift, to which we can only surrender in love and gratitude) and the 'work of the people' (where the liturgical assembly is the active *subject* of liturgical acts, not simply the *object* of ministrations by the clergy). Given this insight, one can, without fear, affirm *both* the inherently 'vernacular' nature of worship (its populism, cultural distinctiveness, and inclusive character) and its 'impossibility' (liturgy as a *divine* gift that can never be controlled by those who celebrate it)."[252]

Active participation

The Vatican Council had this aim in view: "to adapt more suitably to the needs of our own times those institutions which are subject to change" (SC 1). Active participation – *actuosa participatio* – does not mean so much active as actual participation – full, actual participation in what the rite itself participates in and makes the people of God present to, that is, the history of God's revelation of his plan of salvation for all and the culmination of that plan in the Paschal Mystery. *Active participation* is not a description of what we must be doing but a synonym for our life in the spirit, the means by which we are drawn into the life of the Trinity. We are drawn into the mutual relationship of the father and the son – in the spirit. This kind of participation requires much more than saying, doing and singing something. We need to see into and behind what is said, done and sung so that we understand its sacred meaning.

Keith Pecklars grapples with the future of liturgy at a time of exceptional confusion and uncertainty in the Christian Churches. Christian renewal, he says, must always be liturgical renewal. After a conference assembled in Rome in the summer of 2002, he tells in an essay how Cardinal Daneels, after evaluating the liturgical reforms of Vatican 2, tackles the problem of incomprehensibility in a world whose symbolic system has been lost. He calls for the recovery of liturgy's contemplative dimension, which is at once sensual and "inculturated" and expressive of the full liturgical assembly.[253]

The deposit of Christian experience over centuries is shaped to the exigencies of one particular moment – the present. The really crucial issue is, does liturgy bring the present under its sovereignty or is it the other way round? The issue is not for many the style of the performance of the rite. It is truth not style that is at issue and whether the liturgy should challenge and redeem an age or simply reflect back to it its spiritual concerns. What is done and the way it is done matters in its ability to convey truth.

In the same conference a Father Leonard claimed that: "As liturgists... we need to enter the modern media market place where, these days, we have unashamedly to compete with other groups for minds, hearts and values." Pecklars asks whether, here, the nature of the Liturgy has not been missed. For the Liturgy is not an advertisement for the faith, but a celebration and renewal of its most sacred mysteries for the baptised faithful. Initiation and formation are required before the Liturgy begins to be comprehensible. Certainly the Church must find evangelical tools which speak to the post-modern world. The Liturgy, he asserts, is the "daily exercise of our collective memory" through which we can recollect ourselves and concentrate on the "essential and vital" questions: "Who am I, where do I come from, where am I going?"

Peter Phan finds that the 1994 magisterial instruction on liturgical inculturation *Varietates Legitimae* fails to offer "an adequate strategy" for the inculturation of the liturgy, "especially in view of the challenges of postmodernism."[254] The work of the Filipino Benedictine, Anscar Chupungco, is held up as a healthy alternative. Inculturation is envisaged by such proponents as "only an intermediate step; one must move beyond it to...'liturgical creativity'." The future is put more firmly: "the result of liturgical inculturation can no longer be the Roman rite as it currently exists." Yet the author goes further than this, asserting that "a vibrant new way of being Church" is in fact what is required. The envisioned mode of being is that of "dialogue."

Post-modern liturgical reform is also focused on the experience of God's presence. The post-modern person is looking for something beyond modernity, some source of meaning and value that transcends the assumptions of modernity. Post-moderns are seeking worship that is more reflective and meaningful, yet throughout, a period of corporate worship

The culture of children

One early example of liturgical inculturation within the western hemisphere is the publication of the Children's Eucharistic Prayers in 1973 (DMC).[255]

Clare Johnson suggests that this paradigm "within" our world is able to help us to understand inculturation "outside", beyond our own world.[256] Here is a dialogue, indeed, a dynamic interaction between the Roman *editio typica* and the culture of children in the early 1970s. The Children's Eucharistic Prayers are compositions based on a model, for a particular defined group, in the vernacular. The authors wrote for a first world European context. DMC 5 says that prayers must be adapted to the local cultural contexts in which children worship. These prayers herald a clear departure from the dominant model which consisted mostly of translation rather than adaptation. "A faithful translation," she says, "therefore, cannot be judged on the basis of individual words: the total context of this specific act of communication must be kept in mind, as well as the literary form proper to the respective language."[257]

The CEPs are composed in the vernacular according to a model as "features proper to Latin (which never developed a special style of speaking with children)" and "the Latin preference for compound sentences, the somewhat ornate and repetitious style, and the so-called cursus" make the language of a direct translation too difficult for children to understand.[258] The authors had in mind too the importance of avoiding the danger of childish language.

Johnson notes that a "culture" of children is assumed by the authors of the CEPs which arose out of a western European cultural mindset. Children are described thus:

1. Children have a different mentality than adults.

2. Children need simple language and concepts.

3. Children need clearly defined structures and relationships.

4. Children respond to the attitude of adults.

5. Children have short attention spans.

6. Children need to be taught the ways and words of worship.

7. Children need repetition to fully learn the ways and words of worship.

8. Children need interaction to be fully engaged in worship.

9. Children respond well to musical expression to help engage them in worship.

10. Children are essentially self-focused.

Given the popularity among some adults of these prayers, for their ease of comprehension, one wonders if the liturgical needs of adults are not all that different in some respects from those of children. One wonders too if at Sunday celebration of Word and Eucharist the children should in fact listen to the word of God with the whole congregation and then retire to reflect on it at their own level while the community celebrate the Eucharist, rather than the other way round as is common practice. After all the children are still catechumens and this is what catechumens do.

Johnson adds some further questions for reflection on the role of children:

- Who is the child in the church? What is meant by full, conscious, and active participation in the church when some or all of the children are non-communicating?

- What is the underlying theology of childhood developed in these prayers?

- What is the relationship between God and the child assumed in these prayers?

- Can adults understand how children relate to God?

- How do children pray to God?

- Given the clearly first-world, western European authorship of the *editio typica* of the CEPs, how readily do such prayers and their assumed "culture " of children "translate" into the broader cultural contexts in which the children of the world worship?

- Do the CEPs enable or hinder children's participation in adult liturgy?

- The CEPs were designed primarily for use at weekday liturgies where mostly children are present, and it was assumed that children would participate in Sunday worship with their parents...but what if they do not attend Sunday liturgy?

Johnson concludes that, whatever the answers to these questions, we find here a model of liturgical inculturation in which the dynamic interaction between the Roman *editio typica* and the local "culture" results in the development of a new and arguably successful liturgical form which is concrete historical evidence that the process of liturgical inculturation can and does work.[259]

Inculturation

The term "inculturation" was coined by G. L. Barney, a Protestant missionary, in 1973 who stressed the need to keep the Christian message intact throughout the course of cultural exchange.[260]

According to Anscar Chupungco, liturgical inculturation may be defined as:

> the process of inserting the texts and rites of the liturgy into the framework of the local culture. As a result, the texts and rites assimilate the people's thought, language, value, ritual, symbolic and artistic pattern...Liturgical inculturation is basically the assimilation by the liturgy of local cultural patterns... The liturgy is inserted into the culture, history and tradition of the people among whom the church dwells...Inculturation is not creativity (though this is not ruled out), but the dynamic

translation of the typical editions into the cultures of the local churches.[261]

There are two poles involved in the process by which liturgical inculturation occurs, according to Chupungco – the typical editions of texts and the people's cultural pattern. He suggests that this process "should normally start from existing models, and in practice the models are the typical editions of the liturgical books published by the Vatican after the Council."[262] The cultural pattern of a people plays a principal role in the process of liturgical inculturation, as the dialogue partner of the typical edition of the liturgical text. Chupungco defines the cultural pattern of a people as:

> the typical mode of thinking, speaking and expressing oneself through rites, symbols and art forms. It affects society's values and ideology, social and family traditions, socio-economic life, and political system. Cultural pattern cuts across everything that constitutes the life of a society. It is a people's prescribed system of reflecting on, verbalising, and ritualizing the values, traditions and experiences of life.[263]

Chupungco states that the aim of liturgical inculturation is to "graft liturgical texts and rites onto the cultural pattern of the local church."[264] He notes that there are various methods by which this can be achieved, and highlights four in particular: dynamic equivalence, creative assimilation, organic progression and liturgical creativity. In describing the potential of the fourth method he notes that "liturgical creativity" covers a wide spectrum of meaning ranging from absolutely new forms of liturgy to a simple case of adaptation.

Jesus whom we worship was born into a specific culture of the world. In the mystery of his incarnation are the model and the mandate for the contextualisation of Christian worship. God can be and is encountered in the local cultures of our world. A given culture's values and patterns, insofar as they are consonant with the values of the Gospel, can be used to express the meaning and purpose of Christian worship. Contextualisation is a necessary task for the Church's mission in the world so that the Gospel can be ever more deeply rooted in diverse local cultures.

Dynamic equivalence

Dynamic equivalence consists in replacing an element of the Roman liturgy with something in the local culture that has an equal meaning or value. Dynamic equivalence goes beyond mere translation; it involves understanding the fundamental meanings both of elements of worship and of the local culture, and enabling the meanings and actions of worship to be "encoded" and re-expressed in the language of local culture. The linguistic, ritual and symbolic elements of the Roman liturgy are re-expressed following a particular pattern of thought, speech and ritual. The result is a liturgy whose language, rites and symbols admirably relate to the community of worship.

Eugene Nida, an American linguist, coined the phrase "dynamic equivalence." He took to heart the experience of missionary translators who were trying to put the Bible into the local languages of South-American and African tribes (most of which lacked even a system of writing at the time).[265] He gathered up a number of ideas about language that were current among linguists in his time and he applied them to the task of Bible translation. Nida himself coined this phrase in an effort to distinguish his method from unrestrained "paraphrase." In his later writings he distanced himself from the term "dynamic equivalence," preferring instead "functional equivalence."

It is important to notice that Nida was not primarily concerned with English translations. A missionary orientation is conspicuous in his writings on the subject. In addition to the purely linguistic constraints that he discusses, Nida also imposes some constraints which are non-linguistic in nature.

> Our communication is primarily sowing the seed, not transplanting churches. It is lighting a spark, not establishing an institution. This does not mean that the communication of the full revelation of God is unconcerned with the church; but

the indigenous church we are committed to, whether in central Africa or central Kansas, is not the church we have structured, but one raised up by the spirit of God...The development of an indigenous church will always be the living response of people to the life demands of the message. The source of the information...is never more than a catalyst.[266]

We can see that Nida was concerned with producing versions of the Bible which might be useful outside the context of an established church. Along the same lines Nida later wrote that translators who rightly discern the "needs of the audience" will see that: "*Non-Christians have priority over Christians. That is to say, the Scriptures must be intelligible to non-Christians, and if they are, they will also be intelligible to Christians. Not only is this principle important in making the translation of the Bible effective as an instrument of evangelism, but it is also necessary if the language of the church is to be kept from becoming an esoteric dialect.*"[267] Here Nida is making statements as a missiologist, not as a linguist; and he is using a particular philosophy of ministry as the basis for his philosophy of translation. The most fundamental presupposition of the method is the idea that the Bible precedes the Church.

The inspired authors of the New Testament favoured literal translation of the Old Testament, with Hebrew and Aramaic idioms carried straight over into Greek. There are too important conceptual differences which uncommon "biblical" phrases and words often serve to convey. Michael Marlowe gives a number of examples. One may suffice at present:

In 1 Peter 1:13 the expression "girding up the loins of your mind" has been rendered "prepare your minds for action" in the New International Version. Peter's use of the peculiar "girding up the loins of your mind" may at first sight seem clumsy and even a little weird to many people. It certainly is not idiomatic in English. But neither was it idiomatic in Greek. Peter deliberately uses this odd Hebraic expression as a way of bringing to his readers' minds the words spoken to Israel concerning the Passover: "And thus you shall eat it, with your loins girded, your shoes on your feet and your staff in your hand" (Exodus 12:11). But readers of the NIV (and most other modern versions as well) will miss [this] reference entirely. Instead of an accurately translated verbal allusion, they are given an "equivalent" expression.[268]

Opponents conclude that the dynamic equivalence method represents a departure from tradition and from the principles of translation used by the Biblical authors themselves and results in a simplification of the text in which important features of the Bible are erased. Such a method proceeds from false assumptions about the relationship of Scripture to the Church and to the reader.

Organic progression

Organic progression is "progressive because of the new shape it gives to liturgy. At the same time it is organic its result complies with the basic intention of the liturgical documents and, on a wider breadth, with the nature and tradition of the liturgy."[269] Chupungco's desire is to move beyond dynamic equivalence, even creative assimilation, and into organic progression where liturgical creativity can be released from the letter of the typical editions of the Roman books.

David William Antonio presents an Inculturation Model of the Catholic Marriage Ritual, showing how the rite might be adapted to the language, culture and traditions of a particular people, specifically, the Ilocanos of Northern Luzon in the Philippines.[270]

Vatican 2 called for the revision and adaptation of the rite of marriage, exhorting local churches to develop their own rites suited to their people's particular customs and traditions. Antonio shows that the work of preparing a rite of marriage for a particular region cannot be limited to merely translating the typical edition. There has to be a thorough examination of both the *editio typica* and the people's religious and cultural traditions, the socio-economic and political realities that confront them, attending to the positive values expressed therein. Only a dialogical process such as this will guarantee a liturgy that is faithful to the Christian tradition and meaningful to a given people.

In developing organic progression, he analyses the theology of marriage, the principles of liturgical celebration and its directives for the work of inculturation or preparation of regional texts. He discusses the liturgical and theological principles which must guide the development of an adapted rite. This is followed by an investigation of the customs, rites and beliefs of the Ilocano people surrounding marriage. Finally, he presents a liturgical ritual that is adapted to and suited for the Ilocanos. This continuous rite begins at the time of engagement and carries through to the wedding and is marked with catechesis and celebration in the various stages. The adapted ritual offers dynamic translations of formularies as well as new texts. His work on an Inculturation Model may serve as a model for people of other cultures who have to do similar liturgical preparation and will be important especially to churches whose membership includes people who experienced colonisation but never lost the riches of their own cultures in the blending of cultures and beliefs that followed.

Creative assimilation

Local churches might also consider the method of *creative assimilation*. This consists of adding pertinent components of local culture to the liturgical *ordo* in order to enrich its original core. The baptismal *ordo* of "washing with water and the Word", for example, was gradually elaborated by the assimilation of such cultural practices as the giving of white vestments and lighted candles to the neophytes of ancient mystery religions. Unlike dynamic equivalence, creative assimilation enriches the liturgical *ordo* – not by culturally re-expressing its elements, but by adding to it new elements from local culture. The fundamental values and meanings of both Christianity and of local cultures must be respected. An important criterion for dynamic equivalence and creative assimilation is that sound or accepted liturgical traditions are preserved in order to keep unity with the universal Church's tradition of worship, while progress inspired by pastoral needs is encouraged. On the side of culture, it is understood that not everything can be integrated with

Christian worship, but only those elements that are connatural to (that is, of the same nature as) the liturgical *ordo*. Elements borrowed from local culture should always undergo critique and purification which can be achieved through the use of biblical typology.

Jesus Christ came to transform all people and all cultures, and calls us not to conform to the world, but to be transformed with it (Romans 12:2). In the mystery of his passage from death to eternal life is the model for transformation, and thus for the counter-cultural nature of Christian worship. Some components of every culture in the world are sinful, dehumanising and contradictory to the values of the Gospel. From the perspective of the Gospel, they need critique and transformation. Christian faith and worship necessarily involves the challenging of all types of oppression and social injustice wherever they exist in earthly cultures. It also involves the transformation of cultural patterns which idolise the self or the local group at the expense of a wider humanity, or which give central place to the acquisition of wealth at the expense of the care of the earth and its poor. The tools of the counter-cultural in Christian worship may also include the deliberate maintenance or recovery of patterns of action which differ intentionally from prevailing cultural models. These patterns may arise from a recovered sense of Christian history or from the wisdom of other cultures.

Liturgical creativity is not a new notion in the history of the church as the church has always used its creative skill in "shaping new rites in order to transmit the message in ways that could be understood and appreciated by the worshipping community."[271] Chupungco concludes that "creativity, which has always been an inherent feature of the church's worship, is sometimes not a mere option but an imperative for a local church that wants its liturgy to be relevant and have impact on the life of the faithful."[272]

CHAPTER 12
Initiation

The General Directory for Catechesis (1997) proclaimed: "The model for all catechesis is the baptismal catechumenate when, by specific formation, an adult converted to belief is brought to explicit profession of baptismal faith during the Paschal Vigil" (GDC 59, referring to CT 65). Recent developments in the field of initiation have kept faith with long established tradition. The key ingredients of the process remain spiritual journey, community and ministry. Luke 24, the road to Emmaus, is a well-known paradigm for the journey of coming to faith. There are however other examples which may illustrate this pattern in greater breadth and depth.

The reading of the Law Nehemiah (8:1-8)

> All the people *gathered together* into the square before the Water Gate. They told the scribe Ezra to bring the book of the law of Moses, which the LORD had given to Israel. Accordingly, the priest *Ezra brought the law before the assembly*, both men and women and all who could hear with understanding. This was on the first day of the seventh month. *He read from it* facing the square before the Water Gate from early morning until midday, in the presence of the men and the women and those who could understand; and *the ears of all the people were attentive*

to the book of the law. The scribe Ezra stood on a wooden platform that had been made for the purpose…And Ezra opened the book in the sight of all the people, for he was standing above all the people; and when he opened it, all the people stood up. Then *Ezra blessed the* LORD, the great God, and *all the people answered, 'Amen, Amen', lifting up their hands.* Then *they bowed their heads and worshipped the* LORD *with their faces to the ground…the Levite, helped the people to understand the law,* while the people remained in their places. So *they read from the book, from the law of God, with interpretation. They gave the sense, so that the people understood the reading.*

This passage from Nehemiah gives an account of the day when Ezra and his fellow-ministers of the Word gathered the people together and began to teach them the contents of the "Book of the Law of Moses." This is the time after the return from exile when the people re-discover the Word of God. On their spiritual journey of rediscovery the people hear the word and in response to the blessing stand, lift up their hands and praise God. The gathered community draws inspiration and understanding from the ministry of the Levites who help them with an explanation of the meaning of the word they have heard. The italicised phrases point to links with the process of the Rite of Christian Initiation of Adults.

Jesus and Zacchaeus (Lk 19:1-10)

Jesus entered Jericho and was passing through it. A man was there named Zacchaeus; he was a chief tax-collector and was rich. *He was trying to see who Jesus was,* but on account of the crowd he could not, because he was short in stature. So he ran ahead and climbed a sycamore tree to see him, because he was going to pass that way. When *Jesus* came to the place, he *looked up and said to him, 'Zacchaeus, hurry and come down; for I must stay at your house today.'* So *he* hurried down and *was happy to welcome him.* All who saw it began to grumble and said, *'He has gone to be the guest of one who is a sinner.'* Zacchaeus stood there and *said to the Lord, 'Look, half of my possessions, Lord, I will give to the poor;* and if I have defrauded anyone of anything, I will pay back four times as much.' Then *Jesus said to him, 'Today salvation has come to this house*, because he too is a son of Abraham. For the Son of Man came to seek out and to save the lost.'

Zacchaeus was on his own spiritual journey – "he was trying to see" in more than one sense. There follows an encounter and dialogue between Jesus and the seeker. A community gathers. Zacchaeus joyfully testifies to his conversion and takes up his own ministry. This is no mere historic moment but an action valid for eternity – "today" is every day as it recalls the "today" of the Paschal Mystery and the salvation it brings. Again the italicised phrases point to moments of the spiritual journey celebrated in the RCIA.

Philip and the Ethiopian eunuch (Acts 8:26-35)

Then an angel of the Lord said to Philip, "Get up and go towards the south to the road that goes down from Jerusalem to Gaza." (This is a wilderness road.) So he got up and went. Now there was *an Ethiopian eunuch*, a court official of the Candace, queen of the Ethiopians, in charge of her entire treasury. He *had come to Jerusalem to worship* and was returning home; seated in his chariot, *he was reading the prophet Isaiah*. Then the Spirit said to Philip, 'Go over to this chariot and join it.' *So Philip ran up to it and heard him reading the prophet Isaiah. He asked, 'Do you understand what you are reading?'* He replied, *'How can I, unless someone guides me?'* And he invited Philip to get in and sit beside him. Now the passage of the scripture that he was reading was this: 'Like a sheep he was led to the slaughter, and like a lamb silent before its shearer, so he does not open his mouth. *In his humiliation justice was denied him. Who can describe his generation? For his life is taken away from the earth.'* The eunuch asked Philip, *'About whom, may I ask you, does the prophet say this, about himself or about someone else?'* Then *Philip* began to speak, and starting with this scripture, he *proclaimed to him the good news about Jesus*. As they were going along the road, *they came to some water; and the eunuch said, 'Look, here is water! What is to prevent me from being baptized?'*

> He commanded the chariot to stop, and both of them, *Philip and the eunuch, went down into the water, and Philip baptized him.* When they came up out of the water, the Spirit of the Lord snatched Philip away; *the eunuch* saw him no more, and *went on his way rejoicing.* But Philip found himself at Azotus, and as he was passing through the region, he proclaimed the good news to all the towns until he came to Caesarea.

Another journey and another enquirer are to be found here. The eunuch made the journey to Jerusalem to worship, but needed more than that. He needed an interpreter of the scriptures. Philip fulfilled this ministry as one of the community of early disciples. Joy again is the fruit of this ministry as it unfolds the meaning of the Paschal Mystery. The relationship between the word of God and its recipients is not simple and direct. It is conditioned by the hearer's relationship to Christ and to the community. The italicised phrases describe the coming to faith and the acceptance of the gift of the Spirit in baptism.

The Vatican Council's Constitution on the Sacred Liturgy (SC) called for the preparation of a new rite of adult baptism and a catechumenate of adults "divided into several stages" and "sanctified by sacred rites to be celebrated at successive intervals of time" (SC 64). In response to this request the Rite of Initiation was restored and published in 1972.[273] This move was partly in response to the needs of the mission to the nations but quickly became recognised as an appropriate and valuable response to burgeoning post-modern pressures on the Church of the West. Here we highlight some of the key points.

Rite of Christian Initiation of Adults

In the introduction we read: "The rite of initiation is suited to a spiritual journey of adults that varies according to

- the many forms of God's grace,
- the free cooperation of the individuals,
- the action of the church, and

- the circumstances of time and place" (RCIA 5).

This complexity and flexibility of the faith journey which give importance both to the work of God and to the individual circumstances permit a fruitful dialogue between the seeker and the word of God mediated through the community. The whole initiation must bear a markedly paschal character, since the initiation of Christians is the first sacramental sharing in Christ's dying and rising (RCIA 8).

The formation of the catechumens is not to be merely intellectual but a matter of living. Their deeper knowledge of God and Christ must be accompanied by an ongoing effort at the renewal of their lives, an effort that the church accompanies and supports by sanctifying action and prayer – blessings, exorcisms, scrutinies and so on. All this requires that the sacred ministers, aided by community authorities, catechists and sponsors acquire a direct knowledge of the catechumens so that they may accompany, encourage and guide them and be sure that they deserve admission to the sacraments.

The prime ministry is that of the people of God who "should understand and show by their concern that the initiation of adults is the responsibility of all the baptised" (RCIA 9). Members of the community have an apostolic vocation to give help to those who are searching for Christ and an obligation to spread the faith according to their abilities in the various circumstances of their lives and to help candidates and the catechumens throughout the process of their initiation. These principles are spelled out by the exhortation that in making known Christ's message by word and deed they should "show themselves ready to give the candidates evidence of the spirit of the Christian community and to welcome them into their homes, into personal conversation, and into community gatherings." All of these activities challenge the individualism and isolation of post-modern living.

Individual ministries merit attention. The ministry required from the sponsor who accompanies the candidate, and knows and assists the candidate, is to stand as witness to the candidate's moral character, faith and intention (RCIA 10).

Godparents have a ministry to show the candidates how to practise the Gospel in personal and social life, to sustain the candidates in moments of hesitancy and anxiety, to bear witness and to guide the candidates' progress in the baptismal life (RCIA 11). In a post-modern world guidance and encouragement along with personal example are perhaps of greater value than some current more or less scientific aids to happiness in life.

The ministry of the catechist is "for the progress of the catechumens and for the growth of the community." Catechists may perform the minor exorcisms and blessings contained in the ritual. In their ministry, "catechists should see that their instruction is filled with the spirit of the Gospel, adapted to the liturgical signs and the cycle of the church's year, suited to the needs of the catechumens, and as far as possible enriched by local traditions"(16). Catechists thus demonstrate the close links between catechesis and liturgy. The question of what are "local traditions" raises much discussion and reflection when put to groups of ministers and indeed to the whole community.

The ministries of the clergy (RCIA 12-15) are here expressed in conventional, institutional terms, except for a brief mention that priests in their exercise of the pastoral and personal care of catechumens should attend especially to those "who seem hesitant and discouraged."

Thus journey, community and ministry are woven together in a bond of connection and support.

The candidates themselves, in preparing to enter into the catechumenate, begin to "show evidence of the first stirrings of repentance, start the practice of calling upon God in prayer, develop a sense of the Church, and enjoy some experience of the company and spirit of Christians through contact with… the community" (RCIA 42).

During the extended period of the catechumenate, the combination of catechesis, prayer, worship and Christian living assists the catechumen in entering more deeply into the mystery of salvation. In their spiritual journey the catechumens manifest a progressive change of outlook and conduct as "already sharing through faith in the mystery of Christ's death and resurrection, they pass from the old to a new nature made perfect in Christ" (RCIA 75).

The instruction that the catechumens receive "enlightens faith, directs the heart toward God, fosters participation in the liturgy, inspires apostolic activity, and nurtures a life completely in accord with the spirit of Christ" (RCIA 78). This process is holistic and inclusive and combats the fragmentation typical of the post-modern world.

The period of post-baptismal catechesis or mystagogy is a time for the community and the neophytes together to grow in deepening their grasp of the paschal mystery and in making it part of their lives through meditation on the Gospel, sharing in the Eucharist, and doing the works of charity. As they begin to walk in newness of life, the catechumens are supported and inspired by the community of the faithful, including those in ministry, who "give them thoughtful and friendly help" (234).

Reform

Annibale Bugnini was Secretary of the Pontifical Preparatory Commission on the Liturgy, the body which drafted the document that would become *Sacrosanctum Concilium*, the Council's Constitution on the Sacred Liturgy. At the Council Bugnini was appointed as a *peritus* or expert theologian. In January 1964 Paul VI appointed him as Secretary of the Consilium for the Implementation of the Constitution on the Liturgy. He describes in detail the process of the reform of the liturgy prior to and after the Second Vatican Council as well as providing a lively commentary on the work of the Council itself. [274]

The early draft of SC produced a surprise name for the period of catechesis after initiation, that of "mystagogy" instead of "post-baptismal" catechesis. Bugnini relates that unsurprisingly there was lively discussion of the draft particularly over details rather than the structure and especially from Consilium fathers who were not from mission countries and had no experience of the catechumenate, who also had a fear of artificiality and archeologism. Bugnini summed up the discussion as follows:

Despite all this, the Fathers' fear of archeologism led them to challenge the terms "initiation" and "scrutinies", to regard as complicated the rite of entrance into the catechumenate, and to think of the presentations as artificial. Of the latter one Father said: "They already know the gospel and the creed!" The relator replied: "It is one thing to know them, another to receive them officially from the Church in a celebration in the presence of the community." Again: in the entrance into the catechumenate the celebrant asks the candidate's name. "What's the point of that? He already knows it!" said one Father. The relator answered: "True, but the statement of the name in the presence of the entire community enhances and personalises the act being performed."[275]

The term "initiation" was regarded by some as an "archeologism", "unintelligible" and "ambiguous". The study group insisted that the word be kept as it brings out well the spirit of the catechumenate as a gradual introduction to the mystery of God and the Church which was not simply intellectual but concerns one's manner of life. The adjective Christian removed any ambiguous reminiscence of ideas from pagan mystery cults. The group also wanted to ensure the unity of the three sacraments of initiation (Baptism, Confirmation and Eucharist) so as to have the catechumen experience a complete Christian initiation. The group recognised the difficulty that some might have over the Latin terms, especially the translation of *electio*, *scrutinia* and *mystagogia* and desired to retain for the time being these terms, now well known and consecrated by tradition, while searching for appropriate translations. Such translations have sadly not yet emerged in the English language over the course of time.

At the same time a revised rite for infant baptism was drawn up and sent out for consultation. The structures of the rites were significantly different for the rite of infant baptism. The rite for adults was not intended to be celebrated in its entirety on one occasion but over a lengthy period of time. However with the increasing use of the adult rite, the rite for adults begun to serve as a model for the initiation of children of catechetical age and even for infants, with the separation of the rite into parts celebrated over a suitable period of time.

By a process of inverse deduction from the observations made at the end of the period of consultation we can see how the revised rite responded to the needs and culture of today. Bugnini notes four points made by members of the Consilium. The beginning and the end of the process of initiation were seen to be periods devoid of suitable rites. It was suggested that the period prior to the entry into the catechumenate, a time of evangelisation, sympathetic welcome and hospitality, might be provided with some rites while the period of mystagogy was felt to be liturgically empty and the catechumenate in general to be thin on content. A second observation was that there were some rites not adapted to the (post-)modern mentality (scrutinies, presentations and exorcisms) or too involved (the rite of introduction into the catechumenate) or artificial (the rite of election) or not practicable (the dismissal of the catechumens after the Liturgy of the Word). A third observation was that the prayers sometimes used negative ideas to express conversion to God and the progressive purification of the catechumens. Finally it was thought that catechists should have a larger role, even in the liturgy, as they had in many cases to bear most the burden of the catechumenal instruction. These observations were taken into account by the study group. After clarification and revision the Ordo was published on January 6th 1972. However, these objections, while remaining today as not un-common objections to aspects of the implementation of the rite, have not proved insuperable but the use of the correct terms has even been deemed extremely fruitful.

Language

The problem of translation is not new. Pagans accused the Christians of sullying the purity of the Latin language with neologisms and new meanings. But St. Augustine replied (*Sermones* 299.6) concerning *salvator*:

> *Nec quaerant grammatici quam sit latinum, sed christiani quam verum.*
> *"Salus" enim latinum nomen est. "Salvare" et "salvator" non fuerunt*

Peter Humfrey

haec latina antequam veniret salvator. Quando ad latinos venit, et haec latina fecit.

Schoolteachers should not ask how Latin a word is, but the Christians should ask how true it is. *Salus* is a Latin word. The Latin words *salvare* and *salvator* did not exist before the Saviour came. When he came to the Latin world, he made these Latin words also.

Christian Latin was profoundly influenced by the language of the Bible which everyone heard in church, even the most humble who did not know how to read. The early translations of sacred scripture were very literal and in this way Hebrew and Greek exercised a certain influence, even in syntax. This example illustrates the mechanism and result of this biblical influence.

In their translation of the Hebrew text, the translators of the Greek Old Testament, the Septuagint, often chose one Greek word to render a certain Hebrew word without bothering about the *polysemy* (one word with two or more different meanings) of the original – that is to say, the ambiguity of an individual word or phrase that can be used (in different contexts) to express two or more different meanings. The Hebrew *masal*, "comparison", "proverb," "discourse," "word," is always translated by *parabole*, although the Greek word only possesses the sense of "comparison". In the Latin versions of the Bible, the translators borrowed the Greek word parabola in *all* the senses of the original Hebrew, even those of "word", and "expression". The use of *parabola* as "word" from the language of the Bible spread to the everyday language of Christians and when Christianity, after the peace of Constantine, spread to all of society, *parabola* became an everyday word. Even a verb *parabolare* appeared, which we meet for the first time in a text of the Merovingian era, the *Visio Baronti*, ch. 1: "ille nihil homini valuit parabolare sed digito gulam ei monstrabat," [he was able to say nothing to the man but with his finger pointed to his throat].[276] Italian *parlare*, and French *parler* show that in spoken Latin of late antiquity this verb had already replaced the classical Latin *loqui*, which left not a trace in the Romance languages. Given the current, sometimes lively discussion about the use of Latin, it is worth reflecting on the evolution of Latin during the medieval period and the consequences for the modern and post-modern eras, according to Dag Norberg:

> We have stated…that all the episcopal schools were responsible for providing the learned of the eleventh and twelfth centuries with the detailed linguistic preparation which allowed the brilliant flourishing of Latin literature in this period. But from the thirteenth century on the situation rapidly changed. In the universities, which replaced the episcopal schools in ever growing numbers, dialectic surpassed grammar, facts attracted the interest of students much more than elegant form, the classical *auctores* were abandoned in the pursuit of the study of theology, law, medicine, philosophy, and the sciences… From the fourteenth century on, the friends of literature undertook a relentless struggle against the technical Latin of education in the field of dialectic. In their enthusiasm for the beauty of classical literature, they rejected not only the language of scholasticism, but all that had been created since antiquity… For Latin, however, the success of the Renaissance was disastrous. Literary geniuses ceased to express themselves in a language in which imitation was the highest principle, and a rigorous normativism did not provide much freedom of expression. Scholars later followed their example, when they discovered the limits of usage of the school language. After the Renaissance, Latin ceased to develop and its history presents nothing of further interest from a linguistic point of view. It became what is often called a dead language… From the moment when Latin ceased to be understood by all the people – which varies from place to place – its usage was limited to an exclusive element of the population. Latin was no longer a mother tongue but a scholarly language whose secrets were inaccessible to the greater part of society.[277]

When it comes to translating Greek words into English, there is often a wide choice of synonyms. It is difficult not to confine the meaning of the Greek to one concept in English and exclude the possibility of seeing in a text an allusion to larger clusters of ideas. The word *logos* in Greek means to do with instances of speaking and is used as the antithesis of *ergon* – work. Its semantic field extends beyond "word" to notions such as "thought, speech, account, meaning, reason, proportion, principle, study, standard", or "logic". Logos is usually translated as "Word" in English Bibles. The term *Logos* also reflects the term *dabar Yahweh* ("Word of God") in the Hebrew Bible; *dabar* has two strands of meaning – speech and reason, and can mean word, statement, act, thing etc. *Dabar* comes from a root that has truly vast domains of application. The root, its many derivations and the many meanings of each derivation occur over 2,500 times in the Old Testament (first in Genesis 12:4) – the King James Bible uses more than 110 different English words and expressions to translate this one Hebrew word *dabar*. Besides its enormous significance in the phrase Word of God, the root is used to indicate the "order" of Melchizedek, the "inner sanctuary" of the Holy of Holies, the Ten "Commandments" and to supply two out of five books of Moses with their titles: the original title of Numbers is *And He spoke*. The original title of Deuteronomy is *The Words*.

Perhaps some of the resistance to using the original technical words in the Rite is linked to the fact that, although, in the 600,000 words of the written English language towards a third come from Latin and another third from French, 80% of English common speech uses words of Anglo-Saxon origin. Foreign words claim no high ground. A useful lesson may also be had from Nelson Mandela who learned Afrikaans in order to understand and communicate with the Afrikaners and his advice to politicians is: "Speak to people in a language they understand, it goes to their head; speak to people in a language they know, it will go to their heart." Even Saatchi in its advertising campaigns uses an extraordinarily high level of everyday language.

Implementation of the reform

The Sacred Congregation for Divine Worship in November 1970 had suggested an apostolic constitution on Christian initiation that would consider the rites of all three sacraments together. It was noted that "serious problems, caused by the dechristianisation of broad sectors of society and also by supposed requirements of a psychological and educational kind, have arisen today with regard to the appropriateness of infant baptism, the age of confirmation and the age for admitting children to the Eucharist."[278] This suggestion was not accepted so there is even today a variety of opinion and practice with regard to the Christian initiation of children and adolescents.

The Introduction (RCIA 30-35) ends with a section on adaptations by the Episcopal conference, the local bishop and the minister of the celebration. The liturgical constitution (SC 65) allows for a more radical adaptation that is linked to the cultures and social traditions of the various peoples. Many peoples have rites of passage to mark the most important moments in life. In particular each episcopal conference is "to carefully and prudently weigh what elements of a people's distinctive traditions and culture may suitably be admitted to divine worship…to retain distinctive elements of any existing local rituals as long as…they correspond to contemporary needs…and to prepare translations of the texts that genuinely reflect the characteristics of various languages and cultures." In the church also there are vestiges of this perception of sacraments as rites of passage. When first Holy Communion was celebrated around the age of 12 it was considered to be a rite of passage into young adult life. After 1910 when the age for first Holy Communion was reduced to the age of reason, generally interpreted as around 7/8 years old, the sacrament of confirmation, celebrated between the ages of 12 and 16, replaced it as a perceived rite of passage.

The Scrutinies are intermediate rites of exorcism and blessings which give spiritual aid to those who are endeavouring to advance toward a full Christian life; the scrutinies signify and mediate the action of the God who "searches (*scrutatur*) hearts" and penetrates and transforms them by his grace; and there is the presentation of the Creed and the Lord's Prayer. Objections to a perceived obscurity of these rites are answered by Dominic Serra who observed: "Concern for the liturgical tradition has more in common with horticulture than with taxidermy."[279]

A new example of adaptation is the provision made for special cases, for example, *Rite of Initiation for Children of Catechetical Age* (Chapter V). The situation of a child differs from that of an adult because a child is still under the authority of its parents who take part in the liturgical rites. In addition the instruction and rites must be adapted to the age of the candidates. This rite represents the first time in history that such an effort of adaptation has been made. The rite for the reception of baptised Christians into the Catholic Church has been reduced to a minimum. This generally takes place during Mass. The text also expressly says that any display of triumphalism and any publicity are to be avoided. Above all there should be some link with a parish community. Privatisation is overcome by community participation.

Mark Wedig offers some reflections on the success of this renewed Rite. He observes that one of the principal measures of the success of Christian evangelisation always has been the degree to which the worship of the church was adapted to the local culture.[280] The liturgical historian Josef Jungmann narrated the development of early medieval worship in Europe as a pastoral success story because the Roman rite was malleable to Franco-Germanic culture and piety. A people were evangelised by the way a Roman imperial Christian ordo was adapted and assimilated by Teutonic cultures.[281] The cultural adaptation of catholic worship remained a European phenomenon for over a thousand years. More recently and especially after Vatican 2, the synthesis of faith and culture has become a more complex worldwide phenomenon. Worship evangelises when it authentically embodies multiple and diverse ecclesial expressions. The genius of the revised Roman liturgy lies in its adaptability to manifold local cultures.[282]

Since Vatican 2 the RCIA has provided a foundational method for Christian evangelisation. The rituals embody the process for the formation for a local church. They reveal the programmatic schemata for the evangelisation of a local culture through liturgical means. The RCIA bridges church tradition and local culture. As far as the rituals embody the complexities of inculturation, they function as effective modes of evangelisation. So the failure to embody culture specific ritual processes indicates the RCIA's failure to evangelise. In the post-modern world Christian faithful witness is confronted by a greater cultural and social complexity than existed even a few decades ago. Religious claims are undermined by increasingly complicated and competitive social, economic, philosophical and religious factors. If the RCIA remains a source for continued evangelisation in the church, it bears an ever greater burden of adaptation, integration and even resistance to post-modern cultural factors.[283]

The RCIA serves as a primary means of evangelisation. Since Vatican 2 the church itself is conceived of essentially as missionary. Ecclesiology does not precede missiology; church and mission belong together.[284] Traditional purposes and objectives of mission are radically altered by a new consciousness of the relationship between the church and the world. The church is no longer pitted against the world but stands squarely in the midst of global struggles for justice, reconciliation and peace. Mission is viewed as God's involvement in the world and not as a hostile retreat from it. Mission is the work of the local church as the universal church finds its true existence in the particular churches (LG 26). Consequently Christianity's most basic missionary objective becomes the recovery of the cultural integrity of its particular ecclesial communities. Evangelisation then is seen no longer as church extension but as the ministry of the local church. Evangelisation is seen as the integration of the gospel within a particular cultural context. Evangelisation does not exist except as adapted and integrated by a local culture. There is a two way process here, the inculturation of Christianity and the Christianisation of culture. The gospel remains the good news while becoming a cultural phenomenon.

Inculturation

Liturgical inculturation is the dynamic relationship between a cultic tradition and a local culture. Worship without inculturation remains an abstraction and therefore an ineffective means of evangelisation. Vatican 2 underlined a primary purpose of the Roman reform directing that a *typical edition* necessitates cultural adaptation and integration in a local church (SC 37-40). Without a dynamic interaction with the local cultural context the revised texts and rites remain empty and lifeless forms and fail to evangelise the local church and society. Chupungco explains the double movement of inculturation from the standpoint of liturgy as: "the process of inserting the texts and rites of the liturgy into the framework of a local culture. As a result, the texts and rites assimilate the people's thought, language and value, ritual, symbolic and artistic pattern."[285] Chupungco delineates four methods by which the liturgy is grafted to cultural patterns: dynamic equivalence, creative assimilation, organic progression and liturgical creativity.[286]

From the point of view of culture, liturgical inculturation can be identified as "the cultural components which interact, dialogue and combine with the Christian *ordo*. Cultural components consist of values, patterns and institutions that form part of the system of the rites of passage of a society."[287] These components cannot be supplanted without destroying the very fabric of the local society. The shape of baptism, Eucharist, reconciliation, marriage, healing and funerals was dependent on uncompromising cultural factors. Aidan Kavanagh argues that the most creative innovation that resulted from Vatican 2 concerned baptism. With the development of the RCIA there is a fundamental shift from the conventional norm centring on infant baptism to a more traditional norm centring on adults.[288] The change reflects a dramatic movement in the church's ecclesiological self-understanding. The retrieval of adult initiation parallels the recovery of local church identity. The RCIA promotes and forms the intentional membership that engenders the particular ecclesia. The RCIA is not a specious resurrection of an ancient *ordo* but the creative integration of baptism and post-modern, post-Enlightenment culture. Furthermore the RCIA represents a cultural and liturgical response to the crises and challenges of post-modern social and religious life. The RCIA is as it were a bridge between the competing claims of post-modernity and the Christian ecclesial life. The RCIA therefore is a basic means of evangelisation. Basic to its ritual conception, the RCIA involves an inculturation that builds an intentional local church in a post-modern world. The church's fundamental response to the world is reflected in what is necessary for a local church to welcome, to educate, to reconcile, to differentiate, to incorporate and to sustain a newcomer in the faith. For examples we need to look around to the wider church for, as David Power says: "Innovations found serviceable in any church provide models for other churches as they endeavour to assess their own developments."[289] The study of the many innovations of inculturation throughout the world helps to raise significant questions about the dynamics of faith and culture in our own particular churches.

However it should be noted that the urgency for inculturation is felt less by those who belong to the dominant cultures of the West. Those who are disenfranchised in the West or who are outside North Atlantic societies are compelled more urgently to address the competing claims of faith and culture. Indeed inculturation can be interpreted as the work only of non-Western churches. The typical editions can be understood to be only in need of translation and then the norms of adaptation and integration are believed to apply only to local churches marginalised by the global world. However the challenge of observing and understanding contemporary cultural forces that affect faith and worship remains necessary for authentic Christian witness.

Challenges

The great pastoral and academic achievements in twentieth and early twenty-first century Catholicism can be seen as critical responses to a post-Enlightenment, subject centred, secular, scientific-empirical and technological life commonly referred to as modernity. More recently though there have arisen critiques of modern life that attempt to undermine the fundamental claims of the social and intellectual project itself. While the modern – post-modern debate has been heightened in the literary, artistic and social-scientific spheres, theological reflection now has to address the post-modern situation. While there remains a continuum of modern to post-modern thought and social practice, the church's projects of mission and evangelisation need to be situated within the new definitions of culture. The church is in daily encounter with post-modern concerns.

Post-modernism recognises that politically and economically the modern project continues to plunge ahead but in so doing renders it own demise as a social, philosophical and religious solution. An aggressive, methodical and ambiguous extension of modernity has created "hypermodernism." Political, social and economic globalisation efforts engender a "technologically sophisticated and glamorously unreal universe."[290] The super-modern (post-modern) world can extend the efforts of modernity to the entire world and compress time and space. National boundaries are ignored, capital is moved quickly and profit margins maximalised. A single world economy and new communication technologies create powerful homogenising forces that threaten local cultural and social identities. These forces are criticised for rendering individuals or societies either deeply pessimistic or overly confident about economic and technical advancement. The consequent joyless and artificial culture of aggressive individualism and feverish consumption threaten Christian ritual and symbol, morality and community. However another face of post-modernity offers alternatives to this frightening portrait of contemporary life.

Post-modern resistance to hyperactivity offers ways to assess critically the ways the church offers welcome, education, reconciliation and incorporation of the neophyte. Christian ecclesial realism can redeem the local culture. Post-modern culture remains a mixture of the perils and promises of an extremely complex social environment. The parable of sorting the weeds from the wheat is applicable here. The church's task is to resist the perils and integrate the promises. Borgmann's alternative categories of focal realism, patient vigour and communal celebration suggest a possible way of integrating the inculturation of faith and the post-modern condition.[291]

Critics of post-modern society complain that the computer and television have undermined our possibility for abstract discourse. They reconfigure what is considered real and true and subvert reasoned discourse by artificially sequenced bits of information and the titillation of entertainment. The crisis is not only epistemological (of knowledge) but ontological (of reality), like the child who being taken on the train to London for the first time and seeing the backs of rows of Victorian houses exclaimed: "It's just like Coronation Street!" The simulation of the real becomes the cause of what we know. Simulated information reorients symbolic knowing. Both the human appreciation and fear of metaphorical meanings are disoriented by the glamour of the hyper-real. The economic and technological highway leaves us reeling – time is an antique commodity and becomes compressed. The speed and frenzy of the task at hand transcends even the quickest human mind.

Simulation and technological accomplishment render time-consuming processes obsolete. What once could only be achieved through vigilance and patient endurance can now be simulated instantly.

Hyperactivity defies the underlying time and space needed for acquiring virtue, the moral vision that results from time and the rhythm of daily life. Hypermodernity's criteria for economic and technological life subvert the cycle, flow and even the monotony of time necessary for making ritual, narrative and the moral life. Supermarkets with a 24/7 service have destroyed the sense of the seasons; only the faith community struggles to observe the natural rhythms of nature. The timeless character of the global setting blurs the boundaries between work and leisure and transmutes the environment into a game. The hypermodern setting creates social infrastructures of hyperintelligence. Responsibility for passing on information and the methods of its dissemination are crucial for the well being of institutions; yet the means and methods by which we come to know and share these essentials are altered radically by the intelligent networks of computer and telephony.

The erasures of the public square and the public discourse that constitute the traditional means of social communication have fostered a detached and disconnected way of life. Picture the scene when a number of home-going students board a train, chatting merrily, only to sit down and talk on their mobile phones to others who are not there. As Borgmann observes: "This immobile attachment to the web of communication works a twofold deprivation on our lives. It cuts us off from the pleasure of seeing people in the round and from the instruction of being seen and judged by them. It robs us of the social resonance that invigorates our concentration and acumen when we listen to music or watch a play."[292] The traditional ways in which people were invited into the public arena to celebrate a common purpose and heritage are replaced by the web. Voyeurism stands in for presence. The danger is for the church, by embracing this outlook, to offer a continuity of these deprivations. How does the church respond to these challenges of hyper reality, hyperactivity and hyper intelligence? How do post-modern factors affect the catechumenate, the elect and the liturgies?

First, pastors and catechists and liturgists need to develop their role in the discernment of culture. One feature should be a certain resistance to culture, for not everything can be integrated into the rites and institutions of Christians. Some things are irremediably incompatible with the gospel. A simulated and virtual reality, a compression of time and space and an infrastructure of disembodied intelligence all undermine the realism, the morality and the praxis of the church community. Christian conversion requires the identification of cultural forces which are incompatible with the sacramental, moral and ecclesial imagination. Resistance to what is "real", "true" and "good" in post-modernity does not mean a simplistic rejection of post-modernity. Nor is Christian catechesis characterised by a romantic and naive return to pre-modern ecclesial inculturation.

Secondly, the task is to integrate what is compatible and good between church tradition and contemporary culture. Borgmann calls this approach "post-modern realism."[293] Calm, restrained and quiet voices offer interpretations of the post-modern condition that give new energy and strength to Christian claims. The categories of focal realism, patient vigour and communal celebration help us to make connections between Christian initiation and contemporary society. The eloquent reality of the post-modern environments and the interesting and unique associations of persons, ideas and things offer the opportunity to dialogue with a new social realism.

With a new focal realism the catechist makes connections between the curious and even daunting social forces and the mysteries of Christian salvation. The gospels reveal the truth through contrast and penetration. Sign and reality are correlated out of a sacramental realism that sees the power of God at work in the clefts and fissures of the post-modern environment.[294] The focal realism of those who teach and preach is embodied in a dangerous remembrance of Christian tradition – the Paschal Mystery and Lord's Prayer.

The patient endurance of post-modern Christian moral life believes that what is real and true will be revealed only over time. Moral virtues are constructed through unwearied staying power. The quick fix of post-modernity is "counterfeit vigour and joy"[295] and is antithetical to the habitual skills of concentration and contemplation which capture the realism that lies under the burden of complex situations. Morality is derived from constraint and not excess. Morality counters the temptation to trust in power over patience. Catechumens learn that it is possible to shape a moral life derived from the beauty and contradiction of the cross, to recognise the moral life in the lives of the great saints who endured the realism of the crucifixion.

The duress of post-modernity can be lightened by the fashioning of a new inclusive communal order. Eloquence will emerge from communities of resistance to dominant cultural forces. Religious communities are born out of patience and not of power. In celebration, reality, community and divinity are joined. The most unlikely associations of people gather for festive purposes. The RCIA becomes a nexus for those wearied by the post-modern solutions to contemporary life. Communities of catechumens are an unusual and eloquent assortment of people who reflect the social, economic and religious pluralism of today's world. Society's experience of radical shifts in the linguistic, ethnic and religious makeup of our lands offers many opportunities and challenges for inculturation. The RCIA as an instrument and locus for a dialogue between culture and faith is a precious gift.

Mystagogy

Anne Koester draws our attention to the period of post-baptismal catechesis or *mystagogy*, asking the question: "Is there life after the Triduum?"[296] She says: "Easter is appreciated and explained through the context of initiation. However the period after the Triduum tends to hobble to the finishing line. And the rite gives little direction. Attention to the Easter season can energise and inspire the newly initiated, the entire community and even the parish catechists." The Easter season is a time of mystagogy for all the faithful. In the second century, the period of the fifty days (Pentecost) of the Easter season was seen as a unity. However in the course of time, by the fourth century, the octave of Easter (or week *in albis*, in white garments) emerged as a time for the post-baptismal or mystagogical catechesis, after which the neophytes took their places in the congregation. The mystagogical teaching took place in the church in the context of the

Eucharist. The content of the teaching was substantially influenced by the experience of the Easter mysteries. In the fourth century too catechumenal formation was reduced from two or three years to the few weeks of Lent.[297]

Towards the end of the fourth century Pentecost no longer described the season but only the fiftieth day, the closing day of the season, now linked with the outpouring of the Holy Spirit. At the same time, in Jerusalem, the feast of the Ascension began to be celebrated on the fortieth day, thus fracturing the season further. By the end of the fifth century mystagogy faded into obscurity as the structure of the adult catechumenate disappeared, replaced by the practice of infant baptism. Since this practice diminished the attention to the role of the community in baptism, the catechetical periods after initiation were first shortened and then abandoned. This habit obtains today with periods of often frenetic preparation for the reception of sacraments followed afterwards by an almost complete abandonment of the recipients of grace.

The revision of the Liturgical Calendar in 1969 began the work of the retrieval of the Easter season. The RCIA, first published in 1972, in restoring the stages of the catechumenal process, provided that the mystagogical period should extend through the whole Easter season (RCIA 7.4). The period of mystagogy "is a time for the community and the neophytes together to grow in deepening their grasp of the paschal mystery and in making it part of their lives" (RCIA 244). The setting for mystagogy is to be the Sunday Masses because "the distinctive spirit and power of the period...derive from the new, personal experience of the sacraments and of the community" (RCIA 247). The neophytes, their godparents *and* "the entire local community should be invited to participate" in these Sunday liturgies (RCIA 248). The gospel and the experience of the Easter mysteries are the matter of the teaching for it is from "this experience, which belongs to Christians and increases as it is lived, [that] they derive a new perception of faith, of the church and of the world" (RCIA 245).

Experience is the keynote in the process. The rite says that the neophytes' participation in the sacraments "increases their contact with the rest of the faithful and has an impact on the *experience* of the community." Indeed the faithful "should derive from [welcoming the neophytes into the community] a renewal of inspiration and of outlook" (RCIA 246). The rite does not dictate the precise approach or specify the content of post-baptismal catechesis, but suggests three strategies for deepening the faithful's understanding of the paschal mystery – "through meditation on the gospel, sharing in the Eucharist and doing works of charity" (RCIA 244). The simplicity of the suggestions gives the flexibility needed to be creative in the approach to post-baptismal catechesis. It begins in *our* experience of the sights and sounds, the smells and tastes of the liturgical symbols. We need to foster in today's community a disposition towards symbols. We need to appreciate the early church's crucial linking of the concreteness of the human experience of ritual and symbol with the mystery of Christ's saving action. We must resist the temptation to explain and explain away the power laden symbols with wordy discourse. The symbols are the foundation of our exploration of the mysteries. There needs to be a balance between simply allowing the experience and providing the necessary guidance to understand meanings rooted in church tradition.

The primary symbol of the liturgy is the people. The neophytes are "Icons of God's continued presence in the community."[298] The rite encourages the neophytes and their godparents not only to "make an effort to take part" in the Sunday Masses during Eastertide but prescribes that they be assigned "special places in the congregation."[299] This recognition of the neophytes expresses how the sacraments bind the whole community to God in the paschal mystery of Christ. It reminds the faithful of the mystery of God's ongoing revelation and presence in our lives, of the continuous call to conversion, of the privilege of being church and of the demands and responsibilities of living a Christian life. *All* the faithful are symbols of new life to the newest members of the church and ultimately to the world. The faithful from the very beginning "are to provide an example which will help the catechumens to obey the Holy Spirit more generously."[300] During the period of mystagogy the neophytes should "[increase] their contact with" and "enter into close ties with the rest of the faithful,"[301] the better to appreciate the meaning of community. They should see the symbol of assembly and recognise their initiation into an authentic and vibrant faith community. This bond of unity helps all to embrace fully their identity as Christian people.

The Eucharist is the centre of the mystagogical process in which the neophytes and the faithful deepen their grasp of the mystery and make it part of their lives. It is often that in trying to understand and explain the meaning of our sharing in this mystery to others that we discover the deepest reality of our own lives and actions. The Easter people gather at Pentecost to celebrate the gift of the Spirit and to commit themselves to active participation in the ongoing mission of the church. After this special time of Eastertide mystagogy for the neophytes, their lives are now woven into the fabric of the larger faith community.

CHAPTER 13
Imagination

The contemporary catholic response to the post-modern world should include a review of *sacramental imagination*. Sacramental imagination looks beyond the two or seven formal sacraments of the church to the sacramentality of life, using normal and everyday elements, giving vision to those who partake and to those who stand far off and observe. Church is not the only place where the holy happens. Sacramental moments can occur at any moment, any place and to anybody.

Imagination and the cross

Mark Ravizza in a conference at Santa Clara University in 2002 asserted that one theme which regularly occurs, proposed by modernists attempting to challenge and refute the excess of post-modernism, is that of the imagination.[302] Responding to the historian Stephen Schloesser, he says that a twentieth-century Catholic imagination emerges in response to a particular challenge. Nineteenth-century naturalism had reduced reality to observable phenomena governed by causal laws and such a view left little room for the supernatural, for grace and for God. If a twentieth-century Catholic imagination developed specifically as an answer to the quite particular challenge of nineteenth-century naturalism, he asks if we face a similar challenge today. On the one hand, it might seem that we do. Certainly the quest for clarity and causal control that animated nineteenth-century naturalism continues to find expression in our own culture. Yet in a deeper sense, Schloesser reminds us that we live in a very different time and place. We post-moderns live in a world not of foundational explanations but of interpretations and perspectives. We struggle to understand chaos theory, not Newtonian determinism. We are haunted by randomness and contingency, not causal necessity. And this distances us quite a bit from our naturalist predecessors.

Ravizza wonders if we have not domesticated our contemporary Catholic imagination, turning it into precisely the sort of kitsch a sacramental vision once sought to avoid. He gives two examples where he believes that the sacramental imagination does not engage with our post-modern situation. In an article entitled "The Church Is 'Catholic' Because It's Sacramental," Richard McBrien asks what is distinctively Catholic about Catholicism. His answer is that it is the commitment to the principle of sacramentality – the view that the whole created order is sacred because it is a visible sign of the invisible reality of God. He waxes eloquently that "there is no limit to the principle's application. The whole of creation is a theatre of divine glory."[303] McBrien goes on to claim that although there may be long-faced Catholics, such sadness or sorrow is the result of a deficient sacramental imagination. Indeed, he insists, "There are no long faces where there is a truly sacramental faith."[304]

In a similar vein, Andrew Greeley contends in his book, *The Catholic Imagination*, that "Catholics live in an enchanted world, a world of statues and holy water, stained glass and votive candles, rosary beads, and holy pictures."[305] Greeley's work develops the theme of God's omnipresent closeness to our world in chapters with titles such as "The Enchanted Imagination", "Sacred Desire", and "The Mother Love of God". There is no mention of the Cross. Rather, Greeley focuses on how Catholics "tend to picture God, creation, the world, society, and themselves the way their great artists do – as drenched with grace."[306] Contemporary religious art continues to inspire us not only because it points to a transcendent reality, but also it provides Christic images for us, images of people who go through the finite, sacrifice for love, endure the Cross and, in so doing, ultimately give us hope.

There is something missing here. Any Catholic imagination has to grapple with the double gratuity of creation and incarnation. Yet given the "enchanted world" described by McBrien and Greeley, one wonders why the Paschal Mystery would even be necessary in such a grace-filled place. Who needs a saviour if "the whole of creation is [already] a theatre of divine glory?" Surely both these authors are correct to insist that grace abounds in creation. Creation is good. But creation also stands in need of redemption. And this poses a unique challenge for a Catholic imagination that wants to emphasise not the distance between God and the world, but the closeness – the presence of God in all things: How can such a sacramental vision duly accommodate the reality of suffering and evil? Ravizza suggests the answer may perhaps be found in Jesuit humanism, in the Ignatian tradition.

Ignatian spirituality is an approach to transcendence rooted in a staunch incarnationalism, where

> wisdom begins in recognition of divine enmeshment with the world, and a correlative human love for the world . . . But this very incarnationalism, shot through with a certain optimism about the human project . . . is also soberly realistic about the human condition and its involvement in the harsh realities of sin and death. The spirituality of Ignatius finds this realism only in a person's keen identification with the Cross, in an acquaintance with the suffering and death that mark the demise of every creaturely life . . . . In the tradition of Ignatian spirituality, transcendence is directly tied to a full-throttle encounter with the reality of life as it is, because this is the only authentic path to promise and hope.[307]

The truth of a sacramental imagination – that all reality is imbued with the hidden presence of God – needs to be complemented with what William Lynch has called a Christic imagination, an imagination that sees the life of Christ, especially the Cross, as a model of the fullest human life we can lead – a life poured out in love for one another. Such a Christic imagination urges us to imitate the lesson of the incarnation, to embrace the limited, finite reality of our lives, trusting that this will lead us to the salvation we seek.

Imagination and community

Mary Hilkert offers an alternative entry point.[308] Hilkert explores the preached word as it reflects the presence of God in nature and in the Scriptures of the church. A study of the "sacramental imagination," her book shifts focus away from the gap between the divine and the human and the sinfulness of humanity to the grace discovered in everyday life. Hilkert draws our attention to one of Friedrich Schleiermacher's lasting contributions to theology, that is, the identification of Christ's work with a new corporate existence. Contemporary theology, especially through the voices of phenomenological, liberation and feminist theologians, has sustained this fascination with communal existence. Hilkert underscores the authoritative and sacramental role of the Christian community. Questioning the traditional locations of authority, Hilkert encourages preachers, through the use of the "sacramental imagination", to discover "the word of God in the midst of their communities." The practical implication of her thesis, which is that "the gospel emerges from the life-experience of the community," is to give authority to both women and laity as preachers. Hilkert detects a decline in the quality of preaching. She argues that the reason for this decline is "our misunderstanding of where the word of God is located and who are the preachers of good news."

According to Hilkert, the misunderstanding springs from the influence of the Reformation traditions, usually through neo-orthodox categories. Using a distinction constructed by David Tracy[309], Hilkert argues that neo-orthodox categories portray a "dialectical imagination", in contrast to a Catholic spirituality that reflects the "sacramental imagination." The dialectical imagination emphasises the distance, hiddenness and absence of God, the sinfulness of human nature, the paradox of the cross, the imperfection of every human project and institution and the not-yet character of God's reign. The sacramental imagination asserts God's presence as self-communicating love, the goodness of creation, the incarnation, the divinising ability of grace and the foretaste of the reign of God now available in the community of the church.

Hilkert does value the dialectical imagination for its critique which tempers the sacramental imagination. She applauds neo-orthodoxy's rich theology of the word, which contributed to the rebirth of preaching in the Catholic tradition. However, when left to stand alone, says Hilkert, the neo-orthodox approach robs preachers of vitality, for it allows no point of contact between human experience and the preaching of the gospel. She presents Karl Barth as an extreme example of the attitude that rejects any continuity between revelation and creation or between revelation and religious experience, an attitude that becomes more flexible in those who follow him: Rudolf Bultmann, Ernst Fuchs, Gerhard Ebeling and Paul Tillich. Hilkert sees the "sacramental imagination" at play in the works of Karl Rahner, Edward Schillebeeckx and liberation theologians.

Hilkert proposes a theology of preaching and a theology of the word "that are rooted in the sacramental imagination but that also recognise the essential contribution of dialectical theology to the proclamation of the gospel."[310] The book's great irony is that the tradition Hilkert recommends as medicine for the church's future, the tradition of the sacramental imagination "which recognizes new imaging of the mystery of Christ," is also the tradition opposed to the sacramental authority of women. It is the tradition of the dialectical imagination that ordains women and opens its pulpits more readily to the laity. Perhaps that is because the "sacramental imagination" is alive and well in Reformation communities, communities that extol a strong theology of baptism coupled with a deep respect for the authority of the community: the communion of saints, the priesthood of believers, the word of consolation between brothers and sisters.

Imagination and liturgy

Nathan Mitchell writes of *liturgical* imagination. He makes a distinction between liturgical imagination and ceremonial imagination. He reminds us that Caravaggio "knew that in art the 'natural' is actually a composition, a medley, a work of imagination created conjointly by painter and viewer." Although artists often work with live models, the creation and enjoyment of a painting require of *us* the same intensity and work that dreaming requires. "The human imagination has to hunt and gather, compose and edit, with the same speed and anarchic freedom our slumbering bodies bring to dreams... Making the dream seem real was Caravaggio's goal as an artist." [311]

The bulk of "approved" counter-reformation painters – those who collected hefty fees from pleased papal patrons – produced *ceremonial art*, comforting familiar images to accompany "divine services"; Caravaggio produced *liturgical art* – images that demanded vigorous participation by viewers. The ceremonial embellishes; the liturgical establishes. Ceremonial stories are the kind obligatory at an office party for a retiring CEO; liturgical stories are the "lies" – the fictions – we create in order to arrive at the truth. "We look to fiction for self understanding, for analogies of encounter, discovery and decision that will help us contemplate and change our lives. And so it was for Jesus himself as he formulated his parables."[312] Fiction (in this sense) functions in liturgy the way darkness works in Caravaggio's paintings. Ceremonial imagination is literal; the liturgical imagination is not. Ceremonies take their pomp seriously; liturgies do not.

Mitchell asks if the entry of Jesus into Jerusalem is a parody of the pretensions of the Herodian client-king dynasty? Jesus' entry was a liturgy – that is why we can continue to celebrate it at the beginning of Holy Week, year after year. Was Jesus' cleansing of the Temple a strike at the cultic siphoning off of the resources belonging to the people who formed in Jesus' view a community based on Covenant renewal?

> By rejecting ceremonial pomposity in favour of liturgical "fiction", Jesus reclaimed those principles that grounded Israel's communal life of worship: 1) *divine initiative* (God's self-bestowal in creation and covenant); 2) *mutual responsibility* (a social-justice ethic based on Torah); 3) *faith* (trust in a God who lives wherever the people do, who wanders with them like a nomad, who guides them like a pillar of cloud); and 4) *service to the world* (since the human world is the place where

God is known and named in the most resolutely ordinary circumstances – in fuel, food, fire, flame, family, friend and faithful partners; in breath, bone, body, blood and bread).[313]

As a "liturgist", Jesus seems to have sensed that his job was not to give people answers, but to help them love the questions. The gospels present but do not explain. Ceremonialism demands "hands *off*"; liturgy demands "hands *on*". Jesus did not heal the leper at a safe distance; he touched the leper's rotting body and so *became* the sufferer's "uncleanness."

The ceremonial imagination separates; the liturgical imagination fuses and unites. The ceremonial imagination believes the lies it tells itself; the liturgical imagination does not. Easter is a liturgical mystery. The ordinary marginal Jewish layman becomes the Risen One who "shows up" not in feathers and flame but bearing our smudges and scars. Ceremonialism claims it has captured God's word, will and wisdom, while liturgy says that if you are not surprised when Jesus turns up, you have not been looking in the right places and you have not learned how to see in the dark. There is no ceremonialism about the post-resurrection appearances of Jesus.

Imagination in literature and art

Nina Butorac turns her attention to sacramental imagination in literature.[314] She explores sacramental imagination in Andrew Greeley's book, *The Catholic Myth*, which is a sociological study of American Catholic culture, behaviour and beliefs.[315] In the third chapter of his book, Greeley poses this question to his readers: "Do Catholics Imagine Differently?" He then proceeds to explain that, yes, indeed they do. "Religion...is imagination before it's anything else. The Catholic imagination is different from the Protestant imagination. You know that: Flannery O'Connor is not John Updike."

How might catholic and protestant approaches be different? Greeley says:

The central symbol (of religion) is God. One's "picture" of God is in fact a metaphorical narrative of God's relationship with the world and the self as part of the world... The Catholic "classics" assume a God who is present in the world, disclosing Himself in and through creation. The world and all its events, objects, and people tend to be somewhat like God. The Protestant classics, on the other hand, assume a God who is radically absent from the world, and who discloses (Himself) only on rare occasions (especially in Jesus Christ and Him crucified). The world and all its events, objects, and people tend to be radically different from God.[316]

Greeley defines this difference this way: "(T)he Catholic imagination is 'analogical' and the Protestant imagination is 'dialectical.'"[317] So what does Greeley mean by an "analogical imagination"? He means that our Catholic mind-set tends towards analogy, where one reality corresponds to another. From our earliest days, we recall churches filled with incense and candles, statues and flowers, bells, ashes, oils and fonts of holy water, each standing alone as natural objects of the world, yet each signifying a deeper mystery of faith. The sacraments themselves (with the exception of the Eucharist, which is the Sacrament of sacraments) are analogical. He quotes the New Catechism, that: "The visible rites by which the sacraments are celebrated signify and make present the grace proper to each sacrament."[318]

Literature, says Butorac, is not the natural domain of the Catholic imagination. The natural domain of the Catholic imagination is the visual or sensual arts. In an essay for the *New Art Examiner,* Eleanor Heartney examines the legacy of the Catholic Church and its influence on contemporary art. Presuming her audience might be hostile to such a claim, she supports her contention with a brief "delve into theology" and explains:

Catholic doctrine holds that the human body is the instrument through which the miracle of man's salvation from sin is accomplished. As a result, all the major mysteries of the Catholic faith – among them Christ's Incarnation, his Crucifixion and

Resurrection, the Resurrection of the faithful at the end of time, and the Transubstantiation of bread and wine into Christ's body and blood during the Mass – centre around the human body. Without Christ's assumption of human form, there could be no real sacrifice, and hence, no real salvation for mankind. The Catholic Church has traditionally relied upon visual imagery and sensual experience in order to convey these truths. The medieval cathedral, with its elaborate sculptural programs and stained-glass cycles provided a visual summary of both biblical tales and highly sophisticated theological disputes to a public that was largely illiterate. By the Renaissance, art had become an essential tool for the promulgation of religious doctrine...

All of this is of course in stark contrast to the Protestant emphasis on biblical revelation as the primary source of God's truth. Since the Reformation, Protestants have tended to regard Catholic practice of venerating Christ and the Saints through richly ornamented religious statuary as a form of idol worship. Sensual imagery and sensual language are seen as impediments, rather than aids to belief. The body and its experiences are things to be transcended...

The tension between Catholic and Protestant sensibilities outlined here can be summed up as a conflict between the Catholic culture of the image and the Protestant culture of the word. Catholicism values sensual experience and visual images as essential tools for bringing the faithful to God. By contrast, American Protestants depend for their salvation almost exclusively on God's Word as revealed through the Holy Bible...[319]

While it is possible that we may have lost much of our sacramental temperament to the secularised world view, or to a more abstract, transcendental expression so common in American Protestant literature, it is also possible that much of our Catholic sensibilities remain, lingering, so to speak, in the vaulted arches of our memory. Butorac suggests that Andrew Greeley would surely agree with such an assessment. He would state that it is there, it has always been there, and it needs only to be recognised and nurtured and named.

On the Way to Life

A recent study, "On the Way to Life" (OTWTL 2005), authored mainly by James Hanvey, seeks to provide a sound theological basis for the ongoing work of religious educators in the Catholic Church in England and Wales.[320] Part 1 is an interpretative essay. It examines significant data in the light of the "secularisation" thesis that characterises the culture of late-modernity/post-modernity. Two important models of interpretation are discussed, first, secularisation as the progressive diminution of religion and its public influence, and its confinement to the private sphere, and secondly, modernity as "the turn to the subject", in which "religion" is gradually superseded by "spirituality". Part II situates faith within its theological context.

A central proposition of the study is that that Vatican 2 opens up the possibility of a "Catholic Modernity":

> The ability to construct a Catholic modernity which can incorporate many of the central values of modernity – commitment to rational discourse, freedom, justice and equality, human rights, etc., – without weakening Catholic identity or the structures by which it is transmitted, lies in the strength and coherence of its central vision. A Catholic modernity is only possible because it is predicated on a sacramental vision of reality…this is grounded in the way in which the Incarnation overcomes the primal division of sin, and without compromising the distinctness of Creator and creation, refuses to let them be portrayed as antagonistic opposites. The sacramental vision can allow for plurality, variety, difference and differentiation.[321]

OTWL quotes David Tracy speaking of the Christian "analogical imagination", by which he means the ability to grasp "similarity-indifference" so that things are understood in ordered relationships. There is a sense in which the original "analogical relationship" is created by God in the act of creation itself. Its source lies within the Trinitarian life in the union and distinction of persons. It finds its complete expression in the Incarnation and the gift of the Spirit, whereby all things are reconciled in God without ceasing to be themselves. Indeed, we may speak here, says Hanvey, of the redemption of being in the sense that through participation in the grace of Christ and the Spirit all things are reordered to their own essence: they can genuinely become that which they are created to be by being ordered to that for whom they exist.

Through the grace of Christ and the Spirit our freedom is healed for it is "no longer the expression of 'self alone' or 'self over against' the perceived constraints of other existants." The unredeemed "freedom" is that of the tyrant realised in the destruction or seduction of all other freedoms. However, when freedom is "redeemed" from the "sovereign self" in Christ, then it becomes "a freedom to serve; it can 'assent' to other freedoms and facilitate them; it lives in communion." Thus freedom becomes an exercise of love that is "seeking the good of the other", the common good and ultimately the final good that is God's self.[322]

The Catholic sacramental vision of reality as a dynamic *communio*, says Hanvey, is one that has come more to the fore since Vatican 2. Its significance for the Church has also come to be emphasised. Vatican 2 placed the mystery of the Church itself at the centre of the process of developing a new way of engaging with secular cultures. In doing so it was developing a new "ecclesial apologetics", which, unlike the apologetics of the past, did not characterise the Church as a closed, complete world against a secular and atheistic culture, but instead allows the Church to contemplate the miracle of its own existence as the "first fruits" of Christ's work through the Spirit. The Church now becomes the open community and the visible sign of this redemptive freedom and healing of human existence. It is the sacrament of *communio*. Hanvey concludes:

> The retrieval of the Catholic sacramental imagination gives a coherent form to all the Church's discourse and it offers a cogent conceptualisation that can ground the educational and formational processes of the community. It is the essential vision of the Tradition and therefore allows a recovery of the community's history, hence its historical imagination. More importantly, its "retrieval" is not a return to the "past" but a re-centring on what is essentially a Catholic way of inhabiting all reality as the place where God dwells.[323]

At a Colloquium[324] organised to present OTWTL, Hanvey professed that there are profound philosophical and theological questions which the [Catholic] community needs to address, including how it finds a language which allows us to interpret contemporary culture, rather than being interpreted by that culture. But he claims a sense of optimism because of the enormous community resources which the Catholic community now has. These include the professional laity and theologians, as well as the community's traditions – one of the deepest in humanity – and the teachings of the Second Vatican Council. "This has led," he said, "to a creation of a Catholic modernity, which is rooted in its own beliefs, and seeks to work with the culture in which God is alive."

Theologian, and now bishop, Michael Campbell asked: "How do we retain a distinctively Catholic identity whilst remaining open to the modern world? Can a concept like 'Catholic modernity' be a useful guide to the way ahead?" The Gospel, the scriptures, Christian Initiation and the Paschal Mystery school the imagination. All of these sources are key for the educator and evangeliser. Catholic modernity needs to draw on all the resources available in order to provide answers to post-modernist questions.

Imagination and formation

Thomas Groome, in some notes in preparation for a Universities Meeting in 2004, provides some practical help in discerning the reality of sacramental imagination.[325] He explores the relationship between the faith of Catholic Christians and their world-view. He contends that the basis of the Catholic worldview is the human-divine covenant. Based on this covenant, a Catholic world-view recognises that life in the world is *good* and *gracious* as well as *meaningful* and *worthwhile*. All life created by God is essentially good; the world, therefore, is essentially good. Life is also essentially gracious because God's grace takes the initiative in the world. Catholic Christians contend that life is rooted in Ultimate Meaning, not random mishap, and that each life is worthwhile, not because of what an individual might possess or do, but simply because life is worthy *per se*. With this as a foundation, Groome emphasises the centrality of the sacramental in the Catholic imagination. A Catholic imagination cultivates an awareness of the extraordinary experiences of the ordinary, an awareness of the "more" in the hustle and bustle of daily life, in which we risk recognising the divine in the human and the human in the divine. Groome suggests three practices for encouraging a sacramental outlook: developing the habit of sacramental imagination through practices such as meditation and contemplation, acting as a good steward of the earth through an appreciation of the divine in nature and celebrating life through the Eucharist. Through the cultivation and activation of such a sacramental imagination, where we risk exploring possibilities and their potential consequences, we can best live out the human-divine covenant.

Orm Rush however suggests that, forty years on, one vital dimension of the liturgical reform envisaged by *Sacrosanctum Concilium* is still to be fully received: the need for the formation of a *sacramental imagination* as a necessary complement to well-performed liturgical ritual.[326] Although the Council distinguishes external and internal participation, they are interrelated. The effectiveness of the former depends on the latter. The shift to the vernacular was symbolic of the recognition by the council of their necessary interdependence. *External* participation is the structured involvement of the whole congregation in the act of worship through song, frequent sung and said responses, processions, kneeling, standing, proclamation of the readings, the sign of peace, lay ministers distributing the Eucharist, receiving communion in the hand, etc.

Internal participation can be defined as the imaginative engagement with the symbols and rituals of worship by each member of the liturgical assembly. This engagement can give rise to receptions of the sacramental moment as diverse as the number of participants. An essential dimension of such internal participation is what could be called "the sacramental imagination", or what many may still try to ignore as "distractions during Mass."

Symbols and rituals do not achieve their fullness *"ex opere operato"*. Each person who enters the church brings emotions still stirring from personal encounters of the previous hour, lingering memories about the unique joys and hopes, griefs and anxieties of their life at that moment. What salvation will mean for them, through encounter with Christ their Saviour in this particular liturgy, is determined by what it is they, as unique individuals, need to be saved from. The Holy Spirit is the go-between who enables sacramental encounter between the saving Christ and the needful individual.

The Holy Spirit ignites and enlightens the sacramental imagination, thereby making sacramental symbol effective. The *epiclesis*, that prayer for the enlightenment and empowerment of the Holy Spirit, can be seen as the significant liturgical moment (albeit within the whole liturgical event) marrying symbol and imagination. Here that Spirit, whom Jesus promised would enlighten the community to bring them to full knowledge of the truth, is received by the liturgical assembly, enabling them to participate fully, consciously and actively by igniting their sacramental imaginations.

The Vatican Council speaks of the importance of recognising this *de facto* diversity in reception: it speaks of taking into account the diversity in age, condition, way of life and standard of religious culture of each participant (SC 19). We all know of the great diversity of meanings that people make of homilies, beyond the intention of the homilist; prayerful engagement during the Easter vigil with the flickering Easter candle will bring forth Christ's healing presence in ways experienced quite differently by each individual. It is the sacramental imagination of each unique individual, schooled over time by the imaginative world of Scripture, tradition and the liturgy itself, which mediates their encounter, through the liturgical symbols, with the truly present and saving Christ.

Sacrosanctum Concilium needs to be interpreted in correlation with the Council's Dogmatic Constitution on Divine Revelation, *Dei Verbum*, promulgated two years later by the Council. There, in a significant shift from Vatican 1, revelation is conceived of as God's personal self-communication to humanity, offering salvation through Christ in the power of the Spirit. Faith is the personal reception of that divine outreach in love. Faith's loving response to revelation can be nowhere more intense than in liturgical ritual.

But both liturgy and life are schools of the sacramental imagination. It is the specifically Catholic vision of human life that sees the divine-human encounter being mediated *symbolically* – through people, objects, events. According to what has been called the Catholic principle of sacramentality, there is virtually nothing that cannot mediate the divine presence. For the Catholic imagination, the most ordinary in daily life can be sacramental of the extraordinary, the visible of the invisible, the tangible of the intangible. The symbolic mediation of revelation, however, requires the full, conscious and active involvement of human imagination. The child's thrill in candles on a birthday cake is the same thrill that will make *Christian* meaning of the Easter candle. It is this imagination that Catholics bring to the symbols and rituals of liturgy. It is this Catholic imagination that needs re-schooling.

It was the insight of the Council Fathers that, in the pre-Vatican 2 liturgy, with its emphasis on the priest as the sole mediator with God, the Catholic imagination had become ossified. The sense of mystery evoked in the Latin Mass, although deep and profound, was nevertheless confined to what the priest was doing. Furthermore, symbols were seen to mediate automatically, independent of faith's imaginative reception of them. A re-awakening of the active Catholic imagination was required.

Schooling in a sacramental imagination must include, as its primary art, the art of mystical attentiveness in daily life, a spirituality of the ordinary, a mysticism of the everyday. Whether in the workplace with its hardships and sense of achievement or at the family dinner table with its conflicts and its quiet joys, attention to God in the ordinary is a vital preparation for attending to the symbols and rituals of liturgy. In this area, the reception of SC has far to go.

CHAPTER 14
Sacraments

This chapter is devoted to the variety of applications of the sacrament of Confirmation, the development of the sacrament of marriage, the revision and restoration of the sacrament of Reconciliation and the invention of the ministry of consolation, all of which respond in their own way to the spiritual and communitarian needs of our time.

Confirmation

The rite of Confirmation has undergone many changes throughout its history and now we see not only diverse practices but diverse theological justifications for what we celebrate today. Paul Turner offers a useful exploration of this diversity. The elements of confirmation originated in the initiation process of the early church – anointing with chrism, imposition of the bishop's hand and prayer for the Holy Spirit, though the details varied in the different local churches.[327] These rites were not yet called "confirmation." By the fifth century bishops could no longer gather all the catechumens together at Easter; priests baptised, especially in rural areas, and bishops reserved the post-baptismal anointing with chrism to themselves at a later date. Contemporary documents speak of "confirming".

A further pastoral need was the reconciliation of heretics who had been baptised among heretics. The rite of reconciliation supplied elements missing from heretic baptisms, being the same elements that bishops had already reserved to themselves. In last century confirmation became part of the pastoral care of the dying. If the one near death had not been confirmed, any priest could offer the sacrament, even to babies in danger of death. Confirmation moved from initiation to commendation. In the last forty years or so many dioceses have offered confirmation to adolescents as a sacrament of Christian maturity. For centuries before this, first communion supplied the occasion for adolescents but when pope Pius X lowered the age for first communion to "the age of discretion" (canonically deemed to be around 7/8 years old) we were left without a rite of maturity (or of passage to adulthood). The popular appropriation of confirmation to meet this need has since provoked much theological debate.

Turner suggests three groupings of meaning for confirmation, initiation, maturity and reception.[328] The close link of confirmation with initiation applies when a catechumen is baptised at the Easter Vigil and is confirmed in the same liturgy, as also is a child of catechetical age (7 to 14 years) and in both cases the priest who baptises, confirms.

Canon Law speaks only of two categories of person for baptism, infants and adults. Six year olds may not be considered children and eight year olds not adult, but the terms describe not Christian maturity but canonical state. When a child is baptised, confirmation is deferred until the child reaches a more mature age. Canonically that age is about seven, unless the local conference of bishops decides otherwise. The age of confirmation now generally varies from seven to eighteen and the meaning (of the catechesis, if not of the sacrament) fluctuates within this range. Later ages stress the candidate's commitment; earlier ages stress the free gift of God's grace. In any case a degree of maturity is assumed. The most extreme case of maturity would be confirmation in danger of death – not an initiation so much as a conclusion. It constitutes a last desperate attempt to offer a rite of maturity deferred from the rites of initiation.[329]

The rite of reception into full communion of the Catholic Church calls for the confirmation of those who are not validly confirmed. This rite, a successor to the rite of reconciliation of heretics, has an implication that something was lacking in the baptism of those professing faith in the Catholic Church. It implies the need for reconciliation. It implies the guidance of the Holy Spirit to accomplish this communion. The rite does not simply note the spiritual progress of the individual but reinforces the ecclesiological assumption that the divided churches in the Christian family still need healing. The Catholic Church does not recognise the sacramentality of confirmations in churches descended from the Reformation, nor does it accept the validity of the ordination of the ministers who preside over the rite. Turner observes that confirmation is less a rite of initiation than a rite of transfer, a rite of communion or rite of reconciliation.

The coexistence of these different forms of confirmation in one family of faith causes some confusion. All manifest the one sacrament but signal very different human situations. Turner makes these observations about the catechesis.[330] Adults preparing for baptism benefit from extensive catechesis; no additional catechesis is required for confirmation. A child preparing for confirmation after infant baptism may have to prepare for years. One celebrating the rite of reception may receive very little catechesis on confirmation. A person in danger of death receives no catechesis at all.

Turner further analyses the references to confirmation in the Catechism of the Catholic Church (CCC). The Catechism assumes that confirmation will be celebrated by children some years after baptism. The catechism says little about the sacrament when celebrated with baptism, the rite of reception or in danger of death. Among the provisions (CCC 1310) the importance of celebrating reconciliation before confirmation is stressed, but catechumens would not do so until afterwards. Confirmation completes initiation if the one to be confirmed has already been receiving communion (CCC 1289); but this is not true for catechumens or candidates for reception. Confirmation should not be called a sacrament of maturity (CCC 1308); no one would say so at the Easter vigil. The preparation should lead to apostolic responsibilities (CCC 1309), but this will not follow when confirmation is administered in danger of death. Indeed not infrequently young people are required to perform apostolic service *before* confirmation – when it is the reception of the sacrament that should enable them to do so. The footnotes in the Catechism do not refer at all to the RCIA.

The Code of Canon Law reflects better than the Catechism the many modes of celebrating confirmation. The Code's requirements surface only because the Roman rite does not always celebrate baptism and confirmation together. While the church urges everyone to be confirmed, many do not seek the sacrament. To ensure its reception in the end, priests are permitted to administer confirmation in danger of death. Preparation is both demanded and excused. Infants in danger of death are not permitted to receive communion but may be confirmed. This fact relativises the importance of catechesis for confirmation. It may be waived under certain circumstances but catechesis is always expected for communion. In all cases the ritual remains the same.

Turner looks to the future, seeking some clarification of the applications to resolve the contradictions. The boldest move would be to move confirmation to baptism and replace it or dispense with it on other occasions. "This would eliminate the difficulties we face in applying the same catechetical explanations, canonical expectations and liturgical action to what are phenomenologically different experiences for the faithful."[331] Every baptism administered by a bishop or a priest should include confirmation. The requirement for catechesis should be eliminated. This would avoid large numbers of baptised but unconfirmed Catholics. The integrity of the rites would be restored. Greater unity between the eastern and western churches would be achieved. The urgent appeal to be confirmed would be replaced and the parents of reluctant adolescents would rejoice. The name of the sacrament might also be changed to "chrismation", the eastern term. Confirmation originally signified that the bishop confirmed what the priest had performed in baptism.

A second move for Turner would be the expansion of the repertory of rites to include a rite of reaffirmation for those wishing to reaffirm their commitment to the faith. The faithful regularly renew their baptismal promises at Easter and on other occasions. The desire to celebrate a rite of passage from child to adult is still a strong part of our culture. For many this is what the rite of confirmation currently achieves – that in confirmation they accept the faith affirmed by others for them in their infancy. Official teaching would say that baptism is not provisional; it bestows the life of Christ. However acceptance of faith deepens throughout life; to celebrate a once-in-a-lifetime sacrament would not match the spiritual journey. Many people recommit themselves to their faith at significant moments in their lives, and communities may do so too.

Thirdly, when baptised Christians celebrate the rite of reception into full communion of the Catholic Church, we add on confirmation. The main problem for the Catholic Church is the problem of the validity of orders in non-catholic churches. We strive for mutual acceptance of initiation rites among Christian churches, leading to a common table and a common priesthood. Finally the need for confirmation in cases of emergency should be eliminated.

Contemporary scholarship has raised questions about both the origins and the theology of confirmation. Aidan Kavanagh treats of the bishop's post-baptismal rites in the earliest versions of the so-called apostolic tradition (mid-fifth century) in which the gift of the spirit is not explicitly associated with these rites. He argues that these rites reflect only the traditional structure of what may be termed an episcopal *missa* or sending out. The bishop used such rites to dismiss various categories of people from the liturgical assembly, e.g. catechumens and penitents – a frequent practice in the early church. Such groups would go the bishop and receive, often by a hand-laying rite, his blessing. So the neophytes who had previously been dismissed from both catechetical instruction and from other liturgical gatherings were now, after baptism and anointing by the presbyter, dismissed from the baptismal bath to the Eucharistic table. Kavanagh suggests that while the rite would develop into a post-baptismal conferral of the Holy Spirit and ultimately be separated from baptism itself, the origins of what would later be "confirmation" are structural rather than theological.

Paul Turner questioned Kavanagh's interpretation of these acts as constituting an episcopal "dismissal" and suggested that they should be viewed as "the first public gesture of ratification for the bishop and the faithful who did not witness the pouring of water."[332] This would suggest a rite of "welcome" rather than dismissal, a rite by which those newly born of water and the spirit are now welcomed officially into the Eucharistic communion of the church. In its origins therefore what became "confirmation" through various historical accidents and developments was simply the way that the baptismal rite itself was concluded and the Eucharist begun in some communities. To separate it from baptism brings with it a whole host of theological and pastoral problems quite incongruent with its origins.

Another modern assumption has been that the Byzantine rite's post baptismal chrismation and "seal of the Holy Spirit" is the equivalent of the traditional "confirmation" hand-laying prayer for the sevenfold gift of the Spirit and consignation of the Roman tradition, and, as such, was to be preferred in the modern composition of initiation rites. The importation of the Byzantine formula "N. be sealed with the gift of the Holy Spirit" into the revised Roman rite has lead to the deletion of the classic post-baptismal anointing prayer known since the time of Ambrose of Milan where the imagery from John 3:5 and Titus 3:5 underscored that baptism is regeneration in water and the Holy Spirit.[333]

Gabriele Winkler in 1984 provided a compelling analysis of the eighth century liturgical documents (the *Missale Gallicanum Vetus*, the *Missale Gothicum* and the *Bobbio Missal*) and earlier (fifth century) decrees from the Gallican Tradition (the local councils of Rietz, Arles and Orange). Though the rites present an integral pattern of Christian initiation, there occurs the terminology of *confirmare* (confirm) and *perficere* (complete) to refer to something done by the bishop apart from the baptismal rite that serves to "complete" baptism. The practices do not appear to be regular parts of the rites of Christian initiation but episcopal actions done in extraordinary or irregular situations.[334]

In the same article Winkler raises serious doubts about the date and authorship of the famous Pentecost homily attributed to Faustus of Rietz in the late fifth century. Here for the first time the ultimately influential distinction is made between baptism as a "washing" and "birth" to new life and confirmation (as a hand-laying rite) interpreted as confirmation for "battle," a "strengthening" and a pneumatic "augment" of grace. Winkler believes this document, Gallican in origin, with a sophisticated theological interpretation, reflects a period later than the late fifth century.

In the Apostolic Constitution *Divinae consortium naturae* of 15th August 1971, Pope Paul VI decreed that, in its essence, "the Sacrament of Confirmation is conferred through the anointing with chrism on the forehead, which is done by the laying on of the hand, then through the words: Be sealed with the gift of the Holy Spirit." Paul VI, while referring to the dignity of the Roman formulary in use for the anointing with chrism since the twelfth century, chooses a presbyteral chrismation formula from the Byzantine Rite. The Roman tradition of the hand-laying prayer with its invocation of the sevenfold gifts of the Holy Spirit upon the newly baptised did the same for centuries in a legitimately distinct and at least more clearly biblical manner.

Johnson wonders if confirmation then is the rite of hand-laying with prayer or is it the chrismation.[335] In the medieval west did the ritual focus of confirmation shift away from the original pneumatic episcopal hand-laying prayer to the episcopal chrismation so that since 1971 no actual hand-laying occurs any more? Perhaps a hand-laying with prayer for the Spirit would be a better idea; the chrismation would be "an illustration for each candidate of that which the church prays for with imposition of hand and prayer."[336]

Frank Quinn notes a further anomaly that the first post-baptismal anointing and formula is regularly omitted in favour of confirmation in the initiation of adults in the Roman rite. Quinn continues: "Since the prayer accompanying the post-baptismal rite speaks so strongly of incorporation into the church, a principal focus of baptism, it is odd indeed that this rite can be omitted. Even odder is the addition of the image of prophet to the kingship and priesthood with which this rite has been associated for centuries."[337]

In Catholic circles there is a growing awareness that sacramental confirmation "is not a reaffirmation of a previous baptism; it is not the reutilisation of a key moment in the human life cycle. It is rather the gift of the spirit tied intimately to the water bath that prepares one for the reception of the body and blood of Christ as a full member of the church."[338] The implications of this realisation are two fold, that confirmation and first communion should be restored to baptism in all cases, whether the candidate is an infant, child or adult, or that at the very least the traditional canonical age of seven be the time at which those baptised in infancy are confirmed and receive first communion in that order. The first alternative is the preference of liturgists and the second is emerging as the practice in an increasing number of dioceses, no doubt linked to the desire for some catechesis for at least the sacrament of Eucharist. The restoration of confirmation to baptism is the preferred solution of Turner along with the development of other rites of affirmation or reaffirmation.

The author, in his time of working on the preparation of candidates for Confirmation, developed a device for the preparation of catechists (and parents, sponsors and others). Frequently questions about the sacrament would be raised only in terms of methodology though sometimes also structures were questioned. It was an important part of the preparation to try to answer the higher order questions relating to how Confirmation might be a strategy to implement a vision. The preparation seemed always to go more smoothly when some attempt had been made to answer these questions, which were originally framed in consultation with Herman Lombaerts, a theologian from Louvain, and some Diocesan adult education advisers.[339]

Catechists' meetings

Catechists have a particular part to play in the preparation of young people for Confirmation. "I did the planting, Apollos did the watering, but God made things grow" (1 Corinthians 3:6). Before beginning a programme the catechetical team would meet and discuss some of the following questions:

The vision

> Look first at the society in which we live and function as a Church:
>
> What kind of society are we creating?

With which groups of people do we identify and share our vision?

What are the conflicts we face today?

What is our purpose in being Christians in our society?

What is our vision of the role of the Church in today's world?

The strategy

Look at where Confirmation fits into our strategy for the Church:

Why do we have Confirmation?

What are we aiming for in our Confirmation programme?

What is the place of young adults in the Church?

Where does Confirmation fit into the pastoral strategy of our local Church?

The structures

Look at the current practice of the Church:

Why does the Bishop normally confirm?

What criteria do we use for belonging to the Church?

What kind of community are the candidates being initiated into?

What do we understand by the terms "freedom" and "commitment"?

What do we understand by the call to be "disciples of Christ"?

What concern do we show for the minority groups, the un-churched, the spiritually poor and the disillusioned?

The method

> Consider what methods are best to bring about what you hope to achieve:
>
> Why should we use the catechumenate model (Rite of Christian Initiation of Adults)?
>
> What is the role of the catechist?
>
> Who will appoint the catechist?
>
> Who will train and support the catechist?
>
> To whom are the catechists responsible?
>
> What is the role of the Catholic school?

These questions raise not only an interest in the theology of the sacrament of Confirmation and indeed in the whole process of Initiation but the opportunity to reflect also on authority and service. Not infrequently the most common questions initially raised are confined the third and last sections above. If applied properly this process may have helped the author to avoid the presumption of asking parents what they were most looking forward to at Christmas and being greeted by one parent saying that the last thing he looked forward to was Christmas and then explaining why.[340]

Marriage

The RCIA has influenced the renewal of the Rites of Marriage. In the Order of Christian Marriage (OCM) proposed for England and Wales in 1992, in addition to the rite of marriage itself, we find material relating to the period of preparation for marriage and provision for various events throughout the course married life. In Part I there are prayers for a celebration on the occasion of an engagement, and blessings for the period of engagement. There are the domestic rites of the blessing of the food and drink at the wedding and the blessing of the new home. Later there are rites for celebrating anniversaries. In Part II there are rites and pastoral notes for particular circumstances, that is for weddings of an inter-church nature, weddings of the elderly, the regularisation of marriage, weddings for Catholics who do not participate in the public life of the church, weddings of catechumens, inter-faith weddings and weddings involving non-believers.

The author was greeted one day by a young lady enquiring about getting married in the church. Unfortunately, she said, her fiancé was not keen on a church wedding as he was an atheist. The couple came to visit the priest and the fiancé lead the priest to understand that that he could not lose face with his atheist friends by appearing in a church. The priest followed the lines of the pastoral advice in the Order for such a situation and shared this with the atheist. After provisionally saying that he might come to church but only as long as God was not mentioned, he finally married with full rites and to the full satisfaction of all parties because his outlook as a non-believer was respected.[341]

Some points in the Pastoral Notes which were helpful to the fiancé were: "The non-believer should be encouraged to participate as far as may be appropriate in the planning and the catholic partner should always be sensitive to the other's lack of belief" (OCM 606); "A careful choice of scripture texts will manifest the theme of mutual love and respect and other aspects of Christian teaching on marriage, especially those which attract general consent" (OCM 608); "Care is needed lest the non-believers present should be alienated through an excessive emphasis on moral or dogmatic positions. Rather, the minister should show how marriage is related to the economy of divine and human love. He should seek common ground between the values of non-believers and the teaching of the church, with an emphasis on interpersonal commitment and fidelity in the relationship of marriage" (OCM 611).

Part III offers additional texts including prayers of the couple, prayers of the parents and families and further alternative prayers and blessings. By the application of these suggestions, many more people at a celebration are enabled to play a significant part. There is a considerable amount of newly-composed material in the Order and the Pastoral Notes are excellent throughout. The Order offers an opportunity for the ministry of the church and its members from an early stage of a relationship through to the wedding and beyond throughout the married life. The involvement of the local ecclesial community is encouraged. Marriage is seen not just as a private and convenient arrangement but as an entry into the covenant of God with his people and a participation in the Paschal Mystery through the sacrifices of love made by a couple to one another and mutually by the couple and the community.

Ministry of reconciliation

The revised Rite of Penance (RP) was published in English in 1974.[342] It was called (the Rite of) Penance rather than (the Rite of) Reconciliation by which name is has since become better known. Even small children can use the name and understand its meaning in their lives.

The theology of this sacrament is briefly reviewed in the first two paragraphs of the Introduction. Paragraph 1 reveals that the reconciliation brought by Jesus is for all people:

> The Father has shown forth his mercy by reconciling the world to himself in Christ and by making peace for all things on earth and in heaven by the blood of Christ on the cross. The Son of God made man lived among men in order to free them from the slavery of sin and to call them out of darkness into his wonderful light… Jesus, however, not only exhorted men to repentance so that they should abandon their sins and turn wholeheartedly to the Lord, but he also welcomed sinners and reconciled them with the Father.

Paragraph 2 reflects a particular concern for the faithful – those who are baptised. The rite itself is concerned only with the practice of the sacrament and not with the implications of the Paschal Mystery for the whole human race.

An important innovation was the restoration of the community dimension of the sacrament, particularly in Rites B and C for reconciliation with the community present; Rite A is reconciliation for a single penitent with the priest.

Communal celebration shows more clearly the ecclesial nature of penance. The faithful listen together to the word of God, which proclaims his mercy and invites them to conversion; at the same time they examine the conformity of their lives with that word of God and help each other through common prayer. After each person has confessed his sins and received absolution, all praise God together for his wonderful deeds on behalf of the people he has gained for himself through the blood of his Son (RP 22).

Rite C is the celebration of reconciliation with General Absolution. For the paragraph on *The Discipline of General Absolution* (RP 31) the translations of the Latin text for England and Wales and for Ireland show a considerable difference in tone and emphasis. Here are the two texts.

England and Wales version:

31 An individual, complete confession and the receiving of absolution *constitute* the sole, ordinary means for a member of the faithful *who is conscious of serious sin* to be reconciled with God and the Church. Physical or moral impossibility alone excuses from this kind of confession; in the case of such impossibility, reconciliation is *possible* in other ways.

Absolution without prior, individual confession *cannot be given* collectively to a number of penitents *unless*:

a) the danger of death is imminent and there is no time for a priest or priests to hear the confessions of the individual penitents;

b) a serious need is present.

Ireland version:

31 Individual, integral confession and absolution *remain* the only ordinary way for the faithful to reconcile themselves with

God and the Church, unless physical or moral impossibility excuses from this kind of confession.

Particular, occasional circumstances may render it *lawful and even necessary to give* general absolution to a number of penitents without their previous individual confession. In addition to cases involving danger of death, it is lawful to give sacramental absolution to several of the faithful at the same time, after they have made only a generic confession but have been *suitably called to repentance*, if there is grave need.[343]

The English/Welsh version seems to be more legalistic in tone than the Irish version – *constitute* vs. *remain*. The former also emphasises *conscious of serious sin*. General Absolution in England/Wales is *possible* but *cannot be given unless* one of two conditions is fulfilled. Ireland notes that *particular, occasional circumstances may render it lawful and necessary* to give general absolution; a requirement is that the faithful *suitably called to repentance*.

In the time after the publication of the Rite, when its provisions began to be explored, there was an enthusiastic response from the laity. For example, a community service with general absolution would be offered in Lent, sometimes with the bishop presiding at a station church, and crowds would flock in. One bishop in a pastoral letter called this opportunity for reconciliation an "amnesty." This author, in recommending the application of these new Rites, was accused of making things too easy for the faithful! However the frequency of Rite C declined and the acceptance and use of Rite B has become general practice.

In the spirit of Vatican 2, adaptation of the Rite is commended:

In preparing particular rituals the conferences of bishops may adapt the rite of penance to the needs of individual regions so that after confirmation by the Apostolic See the rituals may be used in the respective regions. It is the responsibility of the conferences of bishops in this matter.

a) to establish regulations for the discipline of the sacrament of penance, particularly those affecting the ministry of priests;

b) to determine more precisely regulations about the confessional for the ordinary celebration of the sacrament of penance (RP 12) and about the signs of repentance to be shown by the faithful before general absolution (RP 35);

c) to prepare translations of texts adapted to the character and language of each people and also to compose new texts for the prayers of the faithful and the minister, keeping intact the sacramental form.

The inculturation of signs of repentance is deemed a possibility. Respect for a people's language and character shown through adapted and new texts. However a warning note is sounded by the requirement of confirmation by the Apostolic See. The Vatican 2 recognition of a place for the legitimate authority and autonomy of the local bishop in matters of liturgy is here circumscribed.

John Celichowski, looking for an entry point to a contemporary understanding of reconciliation, explores the value and implementation of the rites of Reconciliation through a reflection on the process of Alternative Dispute Resolution.[344] He quotes a moving reflection on the need for reconciliation that is starkly evident in our criminal justice system:

> We want (prisoners) to have self-worth...So we destroy their self-worth.
>
> We want them to be responsible...So we take away all responsibilities.
>
> We want them to be positive and constructive...So we degrade them and make them useless.
>
> We want them to be non-violent...So we put them where there is violence all around.[345]

He informs us that in the last twenty five years the Alternative Dispute Resolution (ADR) movement has emerged which includes negotiation, mediation, arbitration and various hybrid forms and has given parties in conflict a broader array of processes through which they can resolve their differences and even become reconciled. At the same time the international arena has seen a growing use of "truth and reconciliation" commissions, e.g. in post-apartheid South Africa and in El Salvador in the wake of decades of civil war.

Celichowski observes that while the ADR movement is relatively recent, forms of ADR heave been around for a long time. The Bible tells the story of Abraham negotiating with God in his ultimately unsuccessful attempt to save Sodom and Gomorrah from destruction (Gen 18:16-33). It also portrays Solomon as a wise arbitrator of the competing claims of two women over the same child, literally employing an offer to "split the difference" not as an end in itself but as an instrument to achieve true justice (1 Kings 3:16-28). The Letter to the Hebrews portrays Jesus as the mediator of a new covenant effecting through his self-sacrifice reconciliation between God and his people (Hebrews 8:6, 9:15, 12.24). Since early times the Church has had its own form of "dispute resolution": the sacrament of penance or reconciliation. There is a danger that this sacrament may become a relic of isotropy through disuse, particularly in the industrialised West.

Celichowski lists possible reasons for a decline in the practice of sacramental reconciliation: shortage of priests, separation of reconciliation from the reception of communion, negative or indifferent experiences of the faithful and a variety of cultural changes. We can observe too a lessening of a sense of sin, boundaries of accepted or tolerated behaviour becoming enlarged, narrower and relativised definitions of sin. The original understanding of private confession and its confidentiality has lost credence and people will go elsewhere to confession rather than remain in their own community while in community services many people seem to be willing to approach a priest who knows them well.

Celichowski believes that a catholic culture with a capacity for honest self-critique, the ability to name its demons and to experience guilt and the desire and will to change for the better is not in decline. Daytime TV public confessions, he says, seem designed for the purpose of spectacle and ratings points rather than for enlightenment and transformation. ADR sees sin more as breaking a covenant than a criminal act, and is itself a movement away from a rush to judgment to a more intimate, deliberative and collaborative experience. ADR helps us to see sin as a dispute where we think differently from others. Reconciliation can be seen as a move to reuniting people with one another in a community and with God. The sacrament can be seen as a sacred and profound process of conflict resolution.

We can see the mystery of reconciliation unfolded in the ministry of Jesus, in word and deed and in his Paschal Mystery. It is a ministry of service with no shadow of power or control. The attitude of professional service can rest on a presumption of dominance and techniques of control. "The confessor is not the master of God's forgiveness but its servant" (CCC 1466). A disposition towards mutuality, collaboration and a participatory attitude acknowledges that people do have a capacity for confronting reality especially when risks of avoiding reality are made clear to them.

Ministry of consolation

The Order for Christian Funerals (OCF) was published in 1990.[346] The Order focuses on the centrality of the Paschal Mystery – the funeral is celebrated during the Eucharist, the paschal candle and holy water speak of Easter, the grains of incense on the paschal candle allude to wounds of the Christ who died and rose for us. "The rite for the burial of the dead should express more clearly the paschal character of Christian death, and should correspond more closely to the circumstances and traditions found in various regions" (SC 81). This holds good also for the liturgical colour to be used. There are many opportunities to express faith in the Paschal Mystery. Appropriate adaptations can be made, for example, in the recent use, at the celebration of the funeral of a 15 year old girl, of her original infant baptismal robe as the pall, placed on the coffin, and the lighting of her baptismal candle.

Funeral services are undergoing a process of inculturation by the inclusion of secular poetry, songs and readings. Non-religious funerals show signs of becoming secular liturgy; people will frequently copy the individual ideas of a previous funeral which can become *the* way to do a funeral.

One of the insights of the new Order has been in the promotion of the *Ministry of Consolation*. This author went to take up pastoral duties at a new parish. At weekday Mass there was generally a good crowd of regulars, but on a day when a funeral was announced, the people stayed away. When asked why, the reply was that they did not want to intrude on what was a private occasion. The response was that on such an occasion it would be proper to have even more parishioners attending than usual! So the people began to come, and then to minister by welcoming, giving out leaflets and performing necessary liturgical ministries, for example lector and minister of the Eucharist.

This liturgical ministry then developed into a ministry of supporting the bereaved family with visits, prayer, practical help and moral support. The ministers who took Eucharist to the sick saw their ministry in a new light and began to draw in others to provide companionship and support to the bereaved. Hence the ministry of consolation grew in this parish even before the publication of the new Order of Christian Funerals in 1990.

The General Introduction to the Order of Christian Funerals gives a succinct summary of the ministry of consolation (OCF 8). The ministry of the whole community is described (OCF 9-13) and the liturgical ministries (OCF 14-15). The ministry to mourners and the deceased is described (OCF 16-20); the whole ministry is summed up as follows:

> "If one member suffers in the body of Christ which is the Church, all the members suffer with that member" (1 Corinthians 12:26). For this reason, those who are baptised into Christ and nourished at the same table of the Lord are responsible for one another. When Christians are sick, their brothers and sisters share a ministry of mutual charity and "do all that they can to help the sick return to health, by showing

love for the sick, and by celebrating the sacraments with them." So too when a member of Christ's Body dies, the faithful are called to a ministry of consolation to those who have suffered the loss of one whom they love. Christian consolation is rooted in that hope that comes from faith in the saving death and resurrection of the Lord Jesus Christ. Christian hope faces the reality of death and the anguish of grief but trusts confidently that the power of sin and death has been vanquished by the risen Lord. The Church calls each member of Christ's Body – priest, deacon, layperson – to participate in the ministry of consolation: to care for the dying, to pray for the dead, to comfort those who mourn.[347]

The General Introduction gives us, first, the theology underpinning the liturgy and the ministry. Our unity through our baptism and the Eucharist makes us responsible for one another. In the case of sickness we share a ministry of mutual charity. So too when a member of Christ's body dies, the faithful are called to a ministry of consolation to those who have suffered the loss of one whom they love.

The theological virtues are at the heart of the ministry of consolation. "Christian consolation is rooted in that hope that comes from faith in the saving death and resurrection of the Lord Jesus Christ" (OCF 8). Faith therefore is the spring to the ministry and faith leads to hope and therefore the possibility of help and reassurance to those who have suffered a loss of a loved one. The nature of hope is that it faces the reality of death and the anguish of grief, but trusts that the power of sin and death has been overcome by the risen Lord. The church calls each member of Christ's Body to participate in the ministry of consolation, and summarises the ministry as "care for the dying, prayer for the dead and comfort for those who mourn."

The ministry of consolation does not just happen. The General Introduction reminds us (OCF 9) that teaching is needed for the community to understand and take up its ministry to the bereaved. The responsibility for care of the bereaved lies with the community, and the General Introduction adduces the Beatitudes in support of its argument – "Blessed are they who mourn; they shall be consoled"

(Matthew 5:3). We are reminded that there are different gifts and offices within the community. From this principle, the parish community needs to understand the Christian meaning of death, and then the purpose and significance of the Church's liturgical rites for the dead. The teaching further includes information on how the parish community assists families in preparing for funerals. The parish's response to the event of death may well be to the anguish as voiced by Martha in John 11:25-26; however the community's faith in the resurrection of the dead brings support and strength to those who suffer the loss of those whom they love.

The ministry of consolation is not a momentary or transitory occurrence (OCF 10). Members of the community may not only console the mourners with words of faith but also they may comfort them with acts of kindness, for example with some of the routine tasks of daily living, shopping, providing meals, taking children to school, meeting relatives and arranging for their accommodation. This help enables the mourners to plan the funeral and to devote some time to prayer and mutual support. A major part of the ministry of consolation is allotted to the celebration of the rites and the funeral liturgy (OCF 11). Some teaching on full, active and conscious participation can be discerned here. It recommends that the rites take place at a time which permits as many of the community as possible to be present. In particular the Vigil and the Rite of Committal are singled out with the funeral liturgy.

The proper exercise of the ministries celebrates in full the paschal mystery and enables both the bereaved and the community to come to terms with the experience of suffering and death. The ministry of consolation is a happy outcome of reflection on the celebration of the funeral liturgy and the role of the community which enables the celebration of the various rites of the Order of Christian funerals to be effective and hopeful.

PART 4: MINISTRY

CHAPTER 15
Presence

The scriptures offer a variety of expressions of the presence of Christ. In the feeding of the 5000, Christ offers to the people a prophetic experience of Eucharistic presence (Mk 4:34-52); this passage opens with the preaching of the word leading directly to the feeding. Immediately following this episode is the calming of the storm when Jesus appears and astounds the disciples by the power of his presence over the elements: "Who is this man that the winds and the sea obey him?" In the cleansing of the temple, Christ offers a prophetic and eschatological glimpse of his identity: Whose house is the temple? (Mk 11:15-18) and his body as the temple (Jn 2:14-22).

Power

In the light of recent scholarly studies, we may understand the presence of Christ in fresh ways. The story of the healing of the man possessed by a Legion of Demons and the loss of a herd of pigs into the lake is well known (Mk 5:1-20) but difficult to interpret and to integrate into a robustly post-modern situation. Markus Lau examines recent historical research and enables us to enter more deeply into the kind of presence Jesus exerted in his day.[348] The military background of this passage points, says Lau, to the *Legio X Fretensis*, which had been active in the

Jewish War and whose ensign, a boar, matches the pigs mentioned in Mk 5:1-20. However, the figure 2000, which is mentioned to give the size of the herd, does not correspond to this context. Roman legions consisted of about 5000-6000 soldiers. This contradiction can only be resolved, when the history of the *Legio X* is taken into consideration. In 66 AD a *vexillatio* (detachment) of this *Legio X*, consisting of 2000 soldiers, was involved in fights with Jewish insurgents.[349] These details fit well with the allusions in Mk 5:1-20 to the *Legio X* and can explain the figure 2000.

Along with the military vocabulary and the imperial-roman background a clear allusion is to be found in the self-designation of demons as *legion* (v. 9). The Demons use the ancient faith, language and terms of their original homeland, that is from the Roman milieu. The desire of the legion of demons not to leave the country (v.10) but to be allowed to remain fits the military context, inasmuch Roman legions of course occupy the conquered land and do not want give it away. The demons seem like soldiers. They are waiting for the command to march out against the supposed "enemy". The behaviour of the herd of pigs (v.13), their collective "mass suicide", is puzzling. Pigs are not herd animals but in view of their behaviour in v. 13 they are implicitly assumed to be. The herd of swine behaves not like pigs but in a very military fashion. Certain Roman legions had the emblem of a pig, more precisely a boar and one of these was the *Legio X Fretensis*. The relationship between Jesus and the demons is one of opposites. Jesus appears as a kind of "anti-Demon", or an untypical warlord.

In v. 14, a new group of actors appears on the stage. It is the residents of the area. The legion of demons possesses and controls their environment, so the residents of the area from v. 14 interact with Jesus. Nobody could subdue the man possessed in spite of the use of chains and shackles. All experiments of this nature have obviously failed (vv. 3-5). The Legion of demons is the real occupier and troublemaker in the area, a very similar experience to that of the occupying presence of the *Legio X* in the Jewish war. Then there is the contrast between the Legion of demons and Jesus. It is clear from the outset that the demons do not have Jesus' power. They feel "near the end" (vv. 6-7). The demonic brigade defends itself against Jesus but in the event Jesus is the winner. He is mightier than the demonic occupying power, so he can expel it from the land. This frees both the possessed victim from his immediate disastrous situation and the whole environment of an unsustainable, disturbing presence. How will such a liberated person and a liberated people behave towards this new winner, in the context of the Roman occupation, as he turns out to be a highly successful Warlord?

The Gerasene locals reacted surprisingly, with fear and dread, to Jesus and his deed (v. 15). For the locals, the new champion is not necessarily a Liberator. Rather, there is a more pressing question: Is the winner over the enemy Legion rather only a new occupier, as it would usually be seen in the 1st Century AD? Will he – similarly to the Legion of demons (v. 10) – not leave the country subject? So "they began to beg him to leave from their area" (v. 17) even as the Legion begged Jesus earlier (vv. 10, 12). But the difference is that the Legion of Demons will hold on to the bitter end in the occupied land; Jesus, without further ado, leaves the area (v. 18). The winner is not a new occupier. Ironically at the end of the Gerasene story (vv. 18-20) the announcement of his liberating work is in the hands of the healed man, an outsider set free, now at home in the land. The occupiers were not effective, but Jesus is and remains a presence and obviously with sustained success. The next stay of Jesus in the area of Decapolis (Mk 7, 31-37) testifies to the positive effect of the announcement of the healing. Without any fear a sick man is brought to Jesus, because he obviously has some trust in his capabilities. From this perspective of the passage, Mark's Jesus is portrayed as a powerful warlord and liberator rather than an occupier.

We have previously examined *presence* in other scripture passages, in the prophet (Nehemiah 8:1-8), in Jesus on the road to Emmaus (Lk 24: 13-35) and in the community and its representative Philip (Acts 8:27-39). The Constitution on the Sacred Liturgy points to a specific presence of Jesus in the Liturgy in which the church accomplishes what Jesus proclaimed through his ministry and above all in the paschal Mystery:

> Just as Christ was sent by the Father, so also He sent the apostles, filled with the Holy Spirit. This He did that, by preaching the gospel to every creature, they might proclaim that the Son

of God, by His death and resurrection, had freed us from
the power of Satan and from death, and brought us into the
kingdom of His Father. His purpose also was that they might
accomplish the work of salvation which they had proclaimed,
by means of sacrifice and sacraments, around which the entire
liturgical life revolves. (SC 6)

It is clear that this work is accomplished in our time by the specific
presence and action of Christ (author's italics to indicate the variety
of presence):

> To accomplish so great a work, Christ is always *present in His
> Church*, especially in her liturgical celebrations. He is *present in the
> sacrifice of the Mass*, not *only in the person of His minister*, "the same
> now offering, through the ministry of priests, who formerly
> offered himself on the cross", *but especially under the Eucharistic
> species*. By His power He is *present in the sacraments*, so that when
> a man baptizes it is really Christ Himself who baptizes. He is
> *present in His word*, since it is He Himself who speaks when the
> holy scriptures are read in the Church. He is *present, lastly, when
> the Church prays and sings*, for He promised: "Where two or three
> are gathered together in my name, there am I in the midst of
> them" (Matt. 18:20).[350]

The theme of presence resonates in situations of preaching, celebration
and adult faith formation where faith is in dialogue with contemporary
culture. Nathan Mitchell asks how we make a "connection between
the presence of Christ with what congregations actually *do* at liturgy…
[this presence of Christ] has been far easier to assert than to verify."[351]
Paul famously addressed this problem in his correspondence, sternly
accusing the Corinthian Christians of *not* eating the Lord's Supper,
despite their "coming together in one place" and their performance
of the proper rite (1 Cor 11:20). As Jerome Murphy-O'Connor has
written: "Even though the ritual words (1 Cor 11:24-25) were said,
the lack of love (1 Cor 11:21-22) meant that in reality there was no
Eucharist."[352]

Mystery

Mitchell says: "Presence is one thing; its discernment and verification another." Scholastic theologians spoke of sacramental cause and effect but by the twentieth century theologians had begun to ask not only how Christ acts in the sacraments, but how his presence in liturgical celebrations is disclosed in and by the participating assembly.

Dom Odo Casel asserted that "for the sacramental celebration to conform the Christian to Christ's dying and rising, *it must make present the passion itself,* for the passion contains the mystery of redemption."[353] It is Christ's Pasch – or better, *Christ himself present in this mystery* – who is fully, really active and available in the church's liturgical celebrations. Hence Casel says: "Mystery means the heart of the action...the redeeming work of the risen Lord," while liturgy corresponds to "its original sense of 'people's work', service; . . . *the action of the church in conjunction with this saving action of Christ's."*

Casel's view is that the *mysterium* has become, in the sacramental economy, "a holy ritual action, in which the [originating] redemptive event becomes present under the rite"; thus when "the community of worship performs the rite, it takes part in the redemptive act and by that acquires salvation."[354] Mitchell observes however that here Casel's theology of "mystery presence" *(Mysteriengegenwart)* is unconvincing as Christ's "redemptive act" was, after all, an *historical* one, inextricably linked to particularities of time and space, culture and context.

So the narrative of God's saving deeds in Christ is neither a timeless myth, nor an endlessly repeated loop that regularly returns and renews itself like the natural cycle of seasons. Jesus' resurrection was emphatically *not* resuscitation, the mere return to a *past* life; it was his breaking through to a *new* life, one nobody had ever lived before. "Easter innovates, and does so radically", writes Jean-Luc Marion. "Since the Resurrection of Christ, we must relearn everything, like children (or rather . . . like an old person, overcome by newness).... We are thrown forward in a world too new for us."[355]

Thrown *forward*, says Mitchell, not back. If Christ's passion and death were real historical events, and if Easter is a radically disruptive innovation that throws us forward into "a world *too* new for us", then the relationship between "Jesus' historical deeds and the Christian assembly's liturgical celebration" is more complex than first meets the eye.

Mitchell asks: How can Christ's deeds be lifted from history and "relocated" to liturgical celebrations? More precisely, *how* is Christ "present" in the worshiping assembly? It is not sufficient to say that his presence is guaranteed by grace or "effected by the signifying power of the sacraments." The problem lies in the notion of presence itself.

If we ask what new "presence" arrives from the empty tomb, we are stung by the gospels' discourse of disappearance, absence, distance, and emptiness. The "gardener's" first instruction to Mary in John 21:17 is "Don't touch; stop clinging!" Even at table on the road to Emmaus, the bread-breaking Stranger *disappears* the very moment a glimmer of recognition dawns on the disciples (Luke 24:31). Easter seems to redefine presence as absence – or at least as an unrecognisable presence that breaks beyond the scope of human perception, consciousness and action.

Assembly

When post-conciliar theologians attempted to move beyond the implicit impasse of Casel's "mystery presence", they turned toward the agency of the assembly itself as the central symbol within the liturgical act. To speak of the assembly as *subject* of the liturgical action (and not merely as passive recipient of benefits dispensed by the presiding minister) is not a denial, demotion, or displacement of Christ's agency in the sacraments. On the contrary, it is to affirm "the presence of Christ in the assembly" as "the central liturgical symbol."

The Dutch theologian Piet Schoonenberg argued in 1964 that: "The Eucharistic celebration already begins with a *praesentia realis*, a real presence of the Lord among us [cf. SC 7], and its aim is to make this presence more inward. And this takes place in the signs of the word and the bread and the wine.... The latter presence is called *praesentia realis*, 'real presence', and rightly so. But not rightly when it alone is so called, or so called as the primary example." For Schoonenberg, therefore, "what is more important than the presence of Christ under the *species* is the whole presence of the Lord in his Church, namely as she celebrates the Eucharist."[356]

Hence, though it is true to say that "the Eucharist makes the church,"[357] we cannot derive Christ's presence in the liturgical assembly from Christ's Eucharistic presence in the holy gifts. "By Christ's eucharistic presence we do not mean in the first instance his presence under the eucharistic species; we mean his presence in the community that is celebrating the Eucharist. That is where we assemble, to hear his word and to shew forth his death in the holy meal. The Lord is then among us, even though no consecrated hosts are there in the place."[358]

The views of Schoonenberg were endorsed by many Roman Catholic theologians working in the conciliar and post-conciliar periods. As early as 1962, for example, the American Jesuit Edward J. Kilmartin came to similar conclusions in his *Sacraments, Signs of Christ,* a study that, as Jerome M. Hall observes, "introduces central themes that are found throughout his later work."[359]

Among these is Kilmartin's conviction that sacraments, as "signs of the relationship between Christ, the Church, and the Father," achieve their "salvific effect ... precisely in their interpersonal character."[360] Hence, "the encounter between worshiping Christians and the divine Persons is signified by the interpersonal relationships among the members of the liturgical assembly. Since the sacraments are constituted precisely in the interpersonal relationships of the members of the Church at prayer, the active participation of the members of the liturgical assembly in the event of worship is not merely desirable but is essential for the communication of the sacramental grace."[361]

This is the radical reason why, to use Schoonenberg's formula, liturgical celebrations, of the Eucharist especially, already begin with a real presence of the Lord among us, and its aim is to make this presence more inward, more intense. It is also the reason why Edward Kilmartin insisted that the assembly's worship "can be understood only in terms of the relationship of Christ and the Church", since that church's ultimate nature can be seen only in the celebration of the liturgy, where Christ's ecclesial body enacts itself as "a community of prayer, of thankful memory and petition for covenant faithfulness expressed in proclamation of God's word, songs of praise, and common action."[362] Hence, Kilmartin concluded, the faith that the church's members share

> does not obliterate their personal uniqueness but is expressed through diverse and interdependent ministries… and all the modes of Christ's presence in the liturgy point to essential characteristics of the Church instituted by Christ in the Holy Spirit, no one of which should be emphasized to the exclusion of another. Fundamental to all these presences … and underlying the distinctiveness of each is the presence of Christ in the Spirit by faith in the liturgical assembly: the Church is above all an event of faith, praising God in the prayer of memory and in the epicletic petition for its transformation and the transformation of all the world.[363]

Idolatry

Jerome Hall's summary of Kilmartin's theology reflects a widely held consensus among those for whom SC 7's clear endorsement of Christ's presence in the singing and praying church affirms the assembly's centrality as "primary symbol" in liturgical celebrations. Nevertheless, over the past twenty-five to thirty years, this view has come under fire from post-modern theologians of both the right and the left. In his essay "The Present and the Gift", for example, Jean-Luc Marion rejects what he regards as two equally odious "idolatries" – one which seeks to limit and localise Christ's presence in *bread*, the other, which seems to subordinate Christ's presence to the conscious attention of the celebrating *community*.[364]

The first "idolatry", which results from an imperfectly understood theology of transubstantiation, "fixes and freezes the person of Christ in an available, permanent, handy, and delimited thing."[365] Of this "God made thing", writes Marion, "one would expect precisely nothing but real presence: presence reduced to the dimensions of a thing, a thing that is as much disposed to 'honor by its presence' the liturgies where the community celebrates its own power."[366] The result is a "God packaged in the tabernacle, exhibited like a museum attraction, and 'brandished like a banner' in processions."[367]

The other "idolatry," Marion argues, arises from exaggerated attention to the celebrating community – its consciousness, acts and intentions. Marion refutes the suggestion that at the Eucharist, "communion with God passes by way of the communion of men among themselves," thereby making the sharing among participants "the sign of communion with God."[368] Christ's presence is simply displaced from an object (bread) to a community. The idolatry of community confuses *presence* with *"the* present," where *"the* present" is determined by the community's own experience of time, duration, history, and self-awareness.

For thinkers like Marion, the only way out of this dilemma lies in a fundamental reinterpretation of "presence" – and this requires an even more radical revision in our language about God. Traditional theology speaks of God as *being*, indeed as "Supreme Being." But being, Marion argues, is a human category, one based on humanly devised strategies of perception and predication. The alternative, Marion suggests, is to understand God as love (charity, *agape)*. Love is simply given; indeed, it gives itself *from* itself, *in* itself, unconditionally. Only love keeps its "otherness" in the very act of giving itself away. Seen from this perspective, the Eucharist is the place where God's love announces itself (its "presence") most surely and most purely. Far from confining God to "object"(bread) or community, the holy gifts of Eucharist become the ultimate way love arrives, "gives itself from and in itself" and so "delivers itself body and soul."[369]

Marion thus wants to re-read presence starting neither from bread, nor from community, but from its Trinitarian source. For the persons in God constitute themselves precisely through loving acts of self-surrender, self-giving, *kenosis*.

Thus the celebrating assembly – the church – is itself the creation of God's unconditional love in the Spirit of Christ, giving itself *in* and *from* itself. To speak of Christ "present when the church prays and sings" is not to limit God's self-gift idolatrously, for the church does not create its own identity (from its "present", its own "here and now"), but receives it from an Other.

So "presence" is best understood as *an open space of passage/transit* rather than as delimiting boundary. It belongs to the definition of all real presence to be limitless, like love. We can affirm Christ's always arriving "presence" in the celebrating community precisely because his coming – ever new – displaces our emptiness, making us truly the embodied site where love "delivers itself body and soul."

Presence

Mitchell suggests that if we are to expand and deepen our understanding of how sacraments "speak" presence, new approaches will be required on three fronts.[370]

> First, our interpretation of the sources and strategies of language; as Jesus before his death was the Word of God in the flesh of this world, so the sacraments of the church are the language of the future in the language of our world.

> Secondly, our view of the incarnation and its abiding relation to human history; the incarnation is an ongoing reality; therefore worship is, as the body of Christ, the primary speech of our kinship with God. Worship is not the action of those who have managed to transcend their human condition but of those "whose humanity is restored."

> Thirdly, our analysis of Christian liturgy as an act of anamnesis (memory, remembering); keeping in mind both the Paschal Mystery and Jesus' coming in glory, the language of memorial is less about our remembering God rather than about God's remembering us.[371]

Remembering is offering. We can only verify remembering in ethical practice, in the liturgy of the neighbour. Our liturgical action does not render present Christ and his saving work but rather that we enter newly into the presence of his person and saving work in the medium of ritual cultic activity.

Language of presence

Easter "innovates, and does so radically," writes Marion.[372] This innovation has a name – the risen Christ – that renames everything else. As a result, nothing can remain the same as it was before; we must relearn everything, we must learn anew how to speak. We become persons "overcome by newness...thrown forward in a world too new for us."[373]

Easter redefines presence and does so radically. This presence manifests itself by sight and touch. Touch is our most tangible proof of presence and God's eschatological promise to be with us always finds flesh in the risen Christ. Yet the risen one tells Mary of Magdala not to touch (Jn 20:17). Easter seems to define presence as non-presence.

Christ's body does not belong to the past. It affirms that while ordinary modes of presence do not apply (touch, sight), Christ's bodily presence is not erased by the resurrection.[374] Easter makes us come to terms with a presence that *looks* and *feels* like *absence*, but in fact is a more radical affirmation of bodily presence. For the risen Christ reveals that our body – in all its fleshliness, including its death – has entered the space of God's presence once for all. Death and resurrection mean a revolutionary transformation and hence intensification of this bodily life.

Word and sacrament

After Easter Christ thus give himself to the world in and as a real (though glorified) *body* that speaks in signs, whose *structure* is that of a pre-Easter world, but whose *content* is post-Paschal and revolutionary. SC 56 sees unity of word and Eucharist as one table since the two are "so closely connected with each other" that together they "form but one single act of worship."

The unity of word and sacrament is an ancient patristic theme found in the fathers, especially in the works of Origen:

> This bread which God the Word declares is His body is the word which feeds souls, word proceeding from God the Word, and bread from Heavenly Bread... And this drink which God the Word declares is His blood is the word which gives drink and wonderfully intoxicates the hearts of those who drink. You who are accustomed to attend the divine mysteries know how, when you receive the body of the Lord, you keep it with all caution and reverence, lest any part of it fall, lest anything of the consecrated gift slip away. For you believe, and rightly so, that you are guilty, if anything of it fall away through your negligence. But if you employ such caution, quite properly, in keeping the body of Christ, how can you think that it is less of a sin to have treated the word of God with negligence than to treat His body with negligence?[375]

Vatican 2 echoed this thought: "The church has always venerated the divine Scriptures as she venerated the Body of the Lord, in so far as she never ceases, particularly in the sacred liturgy, to partake of the bread of life and to offer it to the faithful from the one table of the Word of God and the Body of Christ" (DV21).

Post-modern theologians speak of sacraments as "language events" – in so doing they are neither excluding the body nor reducing Christ's self-gift in the Eucharist to the status of a spiritualised memory, a less-than-real presence. David Power argues that language as event is better able to accommodate the reigning criteria of liberative inclusivity and diversity which now challenge classic interpretations of sacrament that maintained institutional order in society and church. Thus, sacraments are no longer means of grace conveyed or indicated by the celebrant to the laity through word and action but rather communal celebratory events of the gift of God's grace in Jesus Christ. As with every corrective, there is loss here as well, perhaps most pointedly the danger that what is celebrated may become the community itself.[376]

Our anamnesis in the Eucharist is our faith-formed recognition of a living relationship initiated by God in the paschal mystery of Christ, whose bodily presence is deepened and intensified, not erased, through the post-Easter speech of signs. As Eucharistic Prayer 4 reveals, it is *because* we "celebrate this memorial of our redemption…recall[ing] Christ's death, his descent among the dead, his resurrection…his ascension…and looking forward to his coming in glory" that we can "offer…his body and blood, the acceptable sacrifice which brings salvation to the whole world."[377]

David Power points out that such language is neither mythical nor metaphysical. "This narrative remembrance effects a rupture with mythical and metaphysical thinking, captured best perhaps in the symbol of the burning bush and the cross as they represent the implication of God's manifestation to Moses and in Christ."[378]

In Luke's Emmaus story we see that Easter transforms Christ's bodily presence from empirical fact (now absent) to divine gift. As Marion puts it: "The ascension does not signify the disappearance of Christ into the closed heavens but the opening of heaven by a retreat that remains a mode of return."[379]

Real presence

For centuries, Roman Catholics have quoted the Council of Trent's affirmation that Christ is present in the Eucharistic species "whole and entire, body and blood, soul and divinity,"[380] and have insisted that this presence is best called *real presence*. Mitchell sums up what he sees as the key issues about sacramental presence in the debates of modern and post-modern theology.

1) Although "real presence" has the status as shorthand for the orthodox Catholic understanding of Christ's self-gift in the Eucharistic species, the phrase itself *(praesentia realis)* appears only in the later medieval period. It is absent from liturgical texts, from the classic creeds, and from most papal and conciliar formulas. Even the Council of Trent preferred to use the adverbial phrase *"vere, realiter ac substantialiter"* to speak of Christ's presence in the consecrated bread and wine.[381]

Ironically, perhaps, some of the most explicit uses of the phrase "real presence" in the sixteenth century come from reformers. We meet it, for instance, in a 1537 letter of Archbishop Cranmer, who asserted that "this catholic faith which we hold respecting the real presence has been declared to the church from the beginning." We meet *praesentia realis,* as well, in orthodox Lutheran theology. Vatican 2's *Constitution on the Liturgy* spoke of the many presences of Christ in the church, affirming that he is *"praesens... tum maxime"* (present...especially in the Eucharistic species) (SC 7), but *praesentia realis* appears verbatim only in post-conciliar texts such as Paul VI's 1965 encyclical *Mysterium Fide* (no.39), his 1968 *"Credo of the People of God"* and the 1967 instruction *Eucharisticum Mysterium* (no. 49). While belief in Christ's presence is found from the beginning, the phrase "real presence" develops much more slowly and unevenly within the tradition.

2) Christ's Eucharistic presence is real, but not exclusive. Not only are there many presences of Christ within the church and its liturgy (SC 7), but the adjective "real" does not aim to deny, negate, or exclude: "This presence is called 'real' – by which is not intended to exclude the other types of presence as if they could not be 'real' too, but because it is presence in the fullest sense: that is to say, it is a substantial presence by which Christ, God and man, makes himself wholly and entirely present."[382]

3) Christ's real presence in the Eucharistic species must always be understood in relation to Christ's real presence in the Word, not only because this is a patristic theme (found, as noted earlier, in the work of Origen), but because SC 56 and DV 21 affirm that Word of God and Body of Christ together form *one* table, one act of worship, and that the church thus "venerates the divine Scriptures as she venerates the Body of the Lord."

4) The goal of Eucharistic celebration is not Christ's real presence in the sacramental species, but the church's. For in this sacrament, the reality (Christ's body and blood) disclosed by the signs of bread and wine itself becomes the sign of a further reality (the unity of Christ's body, the assembled church).

5) There is, then, a radically kenotic ('self-emptying' of one's own will and becoming entirely receptive to God and his perfect will) aspect

to Christ's real presence in the Eucharist. This should not surprise us, since the mystery of the Eucharist is itself rooted in the self-surrender of One who "emptied himself, taking the form of a slave" (Phil 2:7) and indeed, in the mutual self-surrender that constitutes the persons of the Trinity. Such self-giving creates a real presence whose conditions of possibility we cannot determine; we can only receive it as gift, as "present." Everywhere, at every Eucharistic table, the same glorified body and blood of Christ becomes available as food and drink to each and to all.

Mitchell concludes: "The risen Christ is present but not confined, in a meal eaten but never fully consumed, in bread broken and a cup shared but never diminished. It is a presence *not* of this world made available – *giving itself* – in signs that belong *only* to this world. It is a presence that lasts as long as the signs of that presence last, a presence that changes us into it, not it into us."[383]

CHAPTER 16
Catechesis

In 1555, in a time of great turbulence and change, we find an interesting example of catechesis in the town of Hadley in Suffolk. The preaching and teaching of Thomas Bilney had a profound influence on the whole town that it seemed to Doctour Rowland Tailour to be rather "a university of the learned than a town of Clothmaking, or labouring people":

> The towne of Hadley was one of the firste that recevued the woorde of God in al England at the preachynge of Mayster Thomas Bylney: and suche gracious successe had it, that a great number of that parishe became excedyng well learned in the holy scriptures, as wel women as men, so that a man myghte have founde amonge them many that had often red the whole Bible thorow, and that could have sayde a great part of S. Paules Epistles by hart, and verye wel and readely have geven a godlye learned sentence in any matter of controuersy. Their Children and servauntes were also broughte up, and trayned so diligentlye in the ryghte knowledge of Gods woorde, that the whole towne seemed rather an Vniversitye of the learned, then a towne of Clothmaking, or laboring people. And that moste is to be commended, they were for the more part faithfull followers of Gods woord in their lyvyng.[384]

If we understand evangelisation as *kerygma* or the primary proclamation of the Gospel to non-believers which stirs up faith, and if catechesis is understood in its specific sense as a maturing of faith and incorporation into the Christian community, then evangelisation is rightly regarded as the founding principle and general presupposition of catechesis.[385] The end of catechising is not knowledge, but practice, as exemplified in the people of Hadley who "were for the more part faithful followers of God's word in their living."

The term catechesis originates in the Greek verb *echein* which has a variety of meanings with an underlying understanding of *to have*; originally the form was *sechein*, but initial letters *s* and *w* were lost from many verbs before classical times. *Katechein, echein* with addition of the prefix *kata*, literally meaning onto/downwards, means to *pin down* and in general usage has come to be translated as teach. Therefore recent attempts to explain the process of teaching in terms of "echo" (? the disciple "echoes" words of the master) seem unhelpful as a robust explanation of the process of the giving and receiving of the word of God, as suggested in the following story. In Greek mythology, *Echo* was a mountain nymph transformed into a disembodied voice; according to Ovid, her chatter distracted Hera from the infidelities of Zeus, and the goddess punished her by depriving her of independent speech, rendering her able only to repeat the last words spoken by another. When Narcissus failed to requite her love, she faded away into a voice (*echo*) only. This explanation seems to have little to do with understanding catechesis as a dialogue of believers.

Principles

The Constitution on the Sacred Liturgy put into words what had been conveyed ritually at the Vatican Council's opening liturgy.

> Sacred Scripture is of the greatest importance in the celebration of the liturgy... it is from the Scriptures that actions and signs derive their meaning. Thus to achieve the reform, progress and adaptation of the liturgy, it is essential to promote that warm

and living love of Scripture to which the venerable tradition of both eastern and western rites gives testimony (SC 24).

Some still seem to view the Liturgy of the Word as a time of instruction rather than as an act of worship in its own right. The purpose of the Liturgy of the Word is not education so much as formation. We gather to encounter God, not to learn about God. We listen to the readings to hear Christ speaking to us, not to learn about Christ.

The liturgy is the summit toward which the activity of the Church is directed; at the same time it is the font from which all her power flows. The liturgy in its turn moves the faithful, filled with "the paschal sacraments", to be "one in holiness"; it prays that "they may hold fast in their lives to what they have grasped by their faith" (SC 10). Liturgy has a catechetical dimension and "contains rich instruction for the faithful" (SC 33). "It is not enough for catechists to propose and explain dogmatic statements and moral principles; it is necessary that they elucidate as well how the church lives its faith when it celebrates the liturgy" (SC10).

In 1974 the Apostolic Exhortation *Evangelii Nuntiandi* spoke of the three means of evangelisation. The first means is the witness of an authentically Christian life, given over to God in a communion that nothing should destroy and at the same time given to one's neighbour with limitless zeal. As the Pope had said recently to a group of lay people, "Modern man listens more willingly to witnesses than to teachers, and if he does listen to teachers, it is because they are witnesses" (EN 41).

The second means is preaching the Gospel. "And how are they to believe in him of whom they have never heard? And how are they to hear without a preacher?... So faith comes from what is heard and what is heard comes by the preaching of Christ" (*Rom* 10:14, 17). This law once laid down by the Apostle Paul maintains its full force today. Preaching, the verbal proclamation of a message, is indeed always indispensable. "We are well aware that modern man is sated by talk; he is obviously often tired of listening and, what is worse, impervious to words. We are also aware that many psychologists and sociologists express the view that modern man has passed beyond the civilization of the word, which is now ineffective and useless, and that today he lives in the civilisation of the image" (EN 42).

Anscar Chupungco agrees that we must move from a culture of the word to the culture of the image. Words, he says, often lack the power to evoke images from life; the message they communicate is not relevant – that is to say not related to people's cultural life and traditions. The message of the liturgical texts and rites often does not leave any lasting impression because it has no bearing on the concrete life of the listeners.

The third means is catechetical instruction [in] "the living content of the truth which God has wished to convey to us and which the Church has sought to express in an ever richer fashion during the course of her long history …without neglecting in any way the training of children, one sees that present conditions render ever more urgent catechetical instruction, under the form of the catechumenate, for innumerable young people and adults who, touched by grace, discover little by little the face of Christ and feel the need of giving themselves to Him"(EN 44).

Adults

The definitive aim of catechesis is to "put people not only in touch but in communion, in intimacy, with Jesus Christ" CT 5). Catechesis has a threefold character. It is "the process of transmitting the Gospel, as the Christian community has received it, understands it, celebrates it, lives it and communicates it in many ways" (GDC 105).

"Catechesis always has been and always will be a work for which the whole Church must feel responsible and must wish to be responsible" (CT 16). A culturally conditioned warning appears, showing concern over a perceived flight from ordered catechesis to a privatised message: "It is also quite useless to campaign for the abandonment of serious and orderly study of the message of Christ in the name of a method concentrating on life experience. No one can arrive at the whole truth on the basis solely of some simple private experience, that is to say, without an adequate explanation of the message of Christ, who is 'the way, and the truth and the life' (Jn 14:6)"(CT 22).

However it must be recalled that "those to be evangelised are '*concrete and historical persons*,' rooted in a given situation and always influenced by pedagogical, social, cultural, and religious conditioning. They may or may not be aware of this. In the catechetical process, the recipient must be an active subject, conscious and co-responsible, and not merely a silent and passive recipient" (GDC 167).

By 1990 a clear option for adult catechesis is revealed in a little booklet from the International Council for Catechesis.[386] The first principle is to recognise the situation of adults as adults. "A catechesis of adults will be acutely sensitive to *men and women insofar as they are adults*. It will approach them in their adult situation, which is for the most part the lay state, and will be attentive to their problems and experiences. It will make use of their spiritual and cultural resources, always respecting the differences among them. Finally, adult catechesis will stimulate the active collaboration of adults in the catechesis which involves them" (ACCC 26).

Secondly it is important to accept adults where they are: "It is essential to keep in mind the specific adults with whom one is working, their cultural background, human and religious needs, their expectations, faith experiences, and their potential. It is also important to be attentive to their marital and professional status" (ACCC 56).

The third principle of fundamental importance is the *dialogical approach* which, while recognising that all are called to the obedience of faith (Rom 1:5), "respects the basic freedom and autonomy of adults and encourages them to engage in an open and cordial dialogue" (ACCC 57). In this way, adults can make known their needs and can participate, as they should, as subjects or agents in their own catechesis and in that of others.

Dialogue of believers

The situation, somewhat gloomily outlined in the GDC in 1997, recognised the importance of science and technology for the birth and development of modern culture. Furthermore "the scientific mentality, which derives from them, profoundly modifies 'culture and ways of thinking', with consequent human and religious repercussions" (GDC 20). "The widespread influence of the communications media... out of economic or ideological interest often imposes a vision of life which does not respect the cultural distinctiveness of the peoples whom they address. The Church is also obliged to take into account the extent to which Christians have been shaped by the climate of secularism and ethical relativism" GDC 25). The church has to examine the situation of the "many people who have been baptised but lead lives entirely divorced from Christianity...Re-awakening these to the faith" whether they are "the simple people...or [the] numerous other Christians, often highly educated, whose religious formation amounts solely to that which they received in childhood" (GDC 27).

A different challenge rises from those who have "difficulties about the acceptance of the Council" whose sense of belonging to the Church has weakened and "a certain disaffection towards the Church is frequently noted." Thus the Church is often regarded in a one-dimensional way as a mere institution and deprived of her mystery. "In some instances tendentious positions have been adopted and set in opposition to the interpretation and application of the renewal sought in the Church by the Second Vatican Council" (GDC 28).

While it is affirmed that: "Catechesis is intrinsically bound to every liturgical and sacramental action" frequently the practice of catechetics testifies to a weak and fragmentary link with the liturgy: limited attention to liturgical symbols and rites, scant use of the liturgical sources, catechetical courses with little or no connection with the liturgical year and the marginalisation of liturgical celebrations in catechetical programs.

Formation for the apostolate and for mission is one of the fundamental tasks of catechesis. Nevertheless while there is a new sensitivity to the formation of the laity for Christian witness, for inter religious dialogue, and for their secular obligations, education for missionary activity "*ad gentes*" still seems weak and inadequate. Frequently, ordinary catechesis gives only marginal and inconsistent attention to the missions (GDC 30).

Gospel and adaptation

The gospel message cannot be isolated from the culture in which it was first inserted (the biblical world or, more concretely, the cultural milieu in which Jesus of Nazareth lived). Nor can it be isolated from the cultures in which it has already been expressed down the centuries; it does not spring spontaneously from any cultural soil; it has always been transmitted "by means of an apostolic dialogue which inevitably becomes part of a certain dialogue of cultures" (CT 53).

The gospel itself is the model of inculturation. The Word of God became man, a concrete man, in space and time and rooted in a specific culture: "Christ by his incarnation committed himself to the particular social and cultural circumstances of the men among whom he lived" (GDC 109).

Inculturation of the faith is a profound and global process and a slow journey. It is not simply an external adaptation designed to make the Christian message more attractive or superficially decorative. On the contrary, it means the penetration of the deepest strata of persons and peoples by the Gospel which touches them deeply, "going to the very centre and roots" of their cultures. The relationship between the Christian message and human experience is not a simple methodological question. It springs from the very end of catechesis, which seeks to put the human person in communion with Jesus Christ (GDC 116).

The model for the catechist is Jesus himself. "Jesus made himself a *catechist* of the Kingdom of God for all categories of persons, great and small, rich and poor, healthy and sick, near and far, Jews and pagans, men and women, righteous and sinners, rulers and subjects, individuals and groups. He is available to all. He is interested in the needs of every person, body and soul. He heals and forgives, corrects and encourages, with words and deeds. Jesus concluded his earthly life by sending his disciples to do the same, to preach the Gospel to every creature on earth 'to all nations' (Mt 28:19; Lk 24:47) 'to the end of the earth' (Acts 1:8), for all time, 'to the close of the age' (Mt 28:20)" (GDC 163).

The adaptation of the preaching of the revealed word must always remain a law for all evangelisation. "There is an intrinsic theological motivation for this in the Incarnation. It corresponds to the elementary, pedagogical demands of healthy human communications and reflects the practice of the Church throughout the centuries…the Gospel is transmitted as genuine, satisfying, healthy and adequate food. All particular initiatives must therefore be inspired by this criterion and the creativity and talent of the catechist must bow to it" (GDC 169).

We live in a pluralistic and secularised world, in which forms of unbelief and religious indifference may be encountered together with vibrant expressions of religious and cultural pluralism. In many individuals the search for certainty and for values appears strong. Spurious forms of religion, however, are also evident as well as dubious adherence to the faith. In the face of such diversity, some Christians are confused or lost. They become incapable of knowing how to confront situations or to judge the messages which they receive. They may abandon regular practice of the faith and end by living as though there were no God – often resorting to surrogate or pseudo-religions. Their faith is exposed to trials. When threatened it risks being extinguished altogether, unless it is constantly nourished and sustained (GDC 193).

Catechesis enables believers "to give the reasons for the hope that is theirs" (cf. 1 Pet 3:15). When properly inculturated, catechesis will respect and value the language proper to the message, enter into dialogue with forms and terms proper to the culture of those to whom it is addressed and stimulate new expressions of the Gospel in the culture in which it has been planted. In the process of inculturating the Gospel, catechesis should not be afraid to use traditional formulae and the technical language of the faith, but it must express its meaning and demonstrate its existential importance.

Initiatory catechesis

The Rite of Christian Initiation of Adults (RCIA) provides the most useful and inspirational text for catechist and catechumens and community.[387] Here we highlight those points which refer to or are counter to the post-modern world. The catechesis is to be "gradual and complete in its coverage" which means to say that hurrying the process and cutting corners is not part of the vision. It is to be "accommodated to the liturgical year" which means that no catechesis is isolated from its context of the celebration of the sacred liturgy. It is to be "supported by celebrations of the word" which are occasions where the word is not simply taught but proclaimed, received and welcomed at a much deeper personal level in the heart of the community gathered in communion with Jesus. The catechumens are in this way lead to "acquaintance with dogmas and precepts and to a profound sense of the mystery of salvation in which they desire to participate" (RCIA 75).

In the process of initiatory catechesis, the catechumens "learn

- to turn more readily to God in prayer,
- to bear witness to the faith,
- in all things to keep their hope set on Christ,
- to follow supernatural inspiration in their deeds and
- to practise love of neighbour, even at the cost of self-renunciation."

The final learning point hints at the Paschal Mystery. This is a spiritual journey in which "they pass from the old to a new nature made perfect in Christ." This transition should be "manifest by means of its social consequences." A further reference to the Paschal Mystery is revealed in the observation that "since the Lord in whom they believe is a sign of contradiction, the newly converted often experience divisions and separations, but they also taste the joy that God gives without measure."

The Rite tells us that "the instruction that the catechumens receive during this period should be of a kind that…

- enlightens faith,

- directs the heart towards God, foster participation in the liturgy,

- inspires apostolic activity and

- nurtures a life completely in accord with the spirit of Christ."

These little lists, common in this document, offer not only a chance to check the content and progress of catechesis but act as a stimulus to fulfilling the vision of a life lived in a gospel community (RCIA 78). After all catechesis is a dialogue of believers.

Through their participation in the Paschal Mystery at Easter, the neophytes "derive a new perception of the faith, of the church and of the world" (RCIA 235). Mystagogy, which follows the celebration of the Easter sacraments, has two aspects, paschal and general. The general aspect is that the participation of the *neophytes*, the newly initiated, "increases their contact with the rest of the faithful and has an impact on the experience of the community." Interaction is made easier and more beneficial for during this period the neophytes experience a "full and joyful welcome into the community and enter into closer ties with the other faithful. The faithful, in turn, should derive from it a renewal of inspiration and of outlook" (236).

Crisis of transmission

A catechetical conference in France (2002) examined the current hypothesis that there is a crisis of transmission in all institutions in the field of education in homes, youth organisations, sports clubs and so on, situations in which authority comes under fire. The French bishops in a Letter in 1996 had identified their concerns about the challenge of proclaiming the faith where there is a decline of religious practice, the loss of Christian memory and the difficulties of change. They said that this crisis was not specifically religious and that it was due for the most part to a range of social and cultural changes which are swift, deep and global. Catechesis is not spared from this crisis. Catechesis of children and young people in France has declined in recent years though there has been a growth in the number of adults seeking catechesis and Christian formation. This growth is in direct competition with the activities of other religious or pseudo-religious bodies who offer a pathway into transcendence. The old forms of catechesis had fallen in to desuetude. The inventiveness of new forms of catechesis has attracted derision and has been seen to fall short of the methods of new cultural forms.

Denis Villepelet suggests that this crisis is not so much of transmission but there is a profound and radical questioning of the value and legitimacy of what is transmitted. The rapidly changing world has become cold, indifferent and deaf to the reasons for hope offered by Christianity. It is not so much a rejection or hostility as indifference: Christianity does not seem to answer the real and critical questions of our contemporaries. What is offered simply does not make sense. Villepelet sees it as a good and useful and genuine task of the church to look again at the crisis in Christian faith if it conceives faith as a permanent journey of conversion.[388]

Catechesis in the socio-cultural context

Inculturation takes place in concrete and specific circumstances. Episcopal Conferences, in many places, are proposing Catechetical Directories (and analogous instruments), catechisms and aids, workshops and centres of formation. In the light of what has been expressed in the General Directory, an updating and revision of local directories also becomes necessary (GDC 213).

The catechetical directory of the Ukrainian Catholic Church was published in 2000.[389] It situates catechesis in the evangelising mission of the church, defines the specifics of catechesis in the eastern Catholic Church and traces historically the roots of catechesis in the Ukrainian Catholic Church (3). Many Ukrainians emigrated and took with them to other countries the faith of their church expressed in the customs, rituals and traditions of their culture. "It is in these new countries that catechesis must be faithful to the Eastern catholic traditions and to their church while adapting to the cultures of these countries" (9).

In addition to community and scripture, the directory notes the importance of iconography, hagiography and the cosmic dimension of eastern theology and spirituality as sources of catechesis (28). In its relationships with other churches the Ukrainian catholic church has two dimensions, the particularity of its own tradition which is to be researched, deepened and developed and the drive for the re-establishment of full communion between the churches of the East and West (48).

Theologically the tradition of Deification or Theosis expressed in liturgical life and church law describes "the process of transforming and returning to the original gift of being like God and growing in God." Deification is the goal of human life. This was God's plan from the moment of the creation of the world (51). The liturgy is the source of spirituality of Eastern Christians. The liturgy is the place of theophany and transfiguration. Wherever the liturgy is celebrated, that place becomes "heaven on earth" (62). Light is one of the main themes of the liturgy and it is permeated with the resurrection (63-4). Mary was named Mother of God, the Theotokos, at the Third Ecumenical Council of Ephesus in 431 A.D. She is the mother of the incarnate Logos. The name Theotokos proclaims the unity of Christ as both God and man (70). Of all God's creatures, Mary is the example, par excellence, of synergy or cooperation between God's will and human freedom (71). Teachings concerning Mary should be part of any total catechetical programme, because she is a "living catechism" and "the mother and model of catechists" (72).[390] Holy icons reveal to the eyes of the faithful the life and miracles of the Incarnate Word, the saints and the Church. Looking at an icon and discerning in it the image of Christ, one discovers one's own dignity. Communing with an icon teaches one to penetrate to the depths of one's being, so that one may be changed and transformed. In this way, the icon helps to form a mature Christian (73).

The Directory concludes with some practical points: Today the Church needs to find new ways of transmitting the faith through evangelisation and catechisation, taking into account the milieu in which she finds herself (75). Catechesis begins from the one God and leads back to Him, but cannot be the same for each individual because each is unique. To ensure an appropriate and satisfactory catechesis, the Church formulates directives and guides for catechising people in groups, usually differentiated by age (99). The model for all catechesis, even if organised by age groups, is Christ the Teacher. We are called to teach as Jesus taught. When he taught the people he took account of their situation, their needs, and their capacity for learning (100). Life is a pilgrimage in which we cooperate with God in order to arrive at the future kingdom. With our limited abilities, we can never know or love God enough. As St. Gregory says: "Christian perfection has but one limit, that of having none" (110).[391]

Liturgical catechesis and culture

St Basil said: "The ability to adapt oneself to contemporary circumstances is a sign of a mature person."[392] In a ground-breaking book in 1976 John Westerhoff asked: "Will our children have faith?" He said that there was no shortage of religion but as for faith... Because socialisation processes had been largely ignored, Westerhoff says, we were unaware of the hidden curriculum that dominated our efforts, namely that our educational programmes were aimed at institutional incorporation rather than at the mature Christian life of faith. The next generation will have faith if the present generation in the Church is faithful in living the life of faith with them. [393]

Why is there often a passive lack of understanding, lack of engagement, above all a rare experience of the power of the rite? Without catechesis the programme of reform would not have got off the ground. In the absence of catechesis early interest would have waned, the novelty factor worn off. Changes always require explanation. The relationship between liturgy and culture is not always clear. The Council's exhortation was that the rites should not as a rule require much explanation (SC34) yet people need to be enlightened on spiritual and cultural aspects of the liturgical celebration. "Catechesis is an indispensable companion of liturgical renewal."[394] Catechists provide a bridge and a link for theologians and liturgists and exercise a pastoral role leading their listeners to a more profound appreciation of the liturgical celebrations, so that "they may hold fast in their lives to what they have grasped by their faith."[395]

In baptism by immersion, an abundance of signs – running water, flowing baptismal oil – speaks eloquently and ungrudgingly. Yet some frown on excessive realism and graphic ritualisation of the liturgy. But the other extreme can be disorienting and distressing – a few drops of water at baptism, a smudge of sacred oil and then the white wafer at Eucharist. Hospitality, vibrant ministry and a welcoming environment are a good foundation for inculturating the gospel in the local culture.

Acculturation

Not to be confused with inculturation, acculturation is "the exchange of cultural features that results when groups of individuals having different cultures come into continuous first hand contact; the original cultural patterns of either or both groups may be altered, but the groups remain distinct."[396]

Early written codes of law, for example, the Old Testament Law of Moses, or the Babylonian law of Hammurabi, acted to stabilise cultural practices and reduce acculturative changes. Cultural appropriation is the adoption of some specific elements of one culture by a different cultural group. It can also include the introduction of forms of dress or personal adornment, music and art, religion, language, or behaviour. These elements are typically imported into the existing culture, and may have wildly different meanings or lack the subtleties of their original cultural context. Because of this, cultural appropriation is sometimes viewed negatively, and has been called "cultural theft."

Acculturation is the adaptation or borrowing of traits from another culture. So the failure to inculturate liturgy occurs when catechists adopt an experiential approach to the sacraments but do not draw material from the liturgical rites and fail to show the relationship between liturgy and life experience. Acculturation can occur when the liturgy of the local church is lifted directly from the pages of the typical edition published by Rome. For example at the rite of reception for children for baptism the typical edition directs the minister to sign the child on the forehead as an expression of welcome into the Christian community. While the English translation elaborates the Latin text by describing the sign of the cross as the church's act of "claiming the child for Christ", the meaning of the gesture is more usually assumed to be one of welcome. Applying the method of cultural evocation however in explaining the sign of the cross as a gesture of welcome, it cannot be said that the cross is a symbol of the great joy the community experiences in welcoming a child. The rite of clothing a child in a white garment as an "outward sign of Christian dignity" seems to have little or no connection with prevailing culture. Indeed in modern society clothing rarely indicates the dignity of the person but rather the peculiarity of the occasion.

A similar discrepancy maybe noted with regard to church buildings. Is the church the house of God, that is, the temple where God dwells, or is it the house of the church, that is the building designed for welcoming the gathering of the assembly of the people of God? It is both of course but undue reference to one over the other can lead to difficult if not insoluble conflict within the community. Similarly with regard to the central symbol in the church; is it a table or an altar? The rite of the dedication of an altar has neatly combined the two ideas by saying that: "the altar is the table for a sacrifice and for a banquet."[397] However a catechist may have difficultly linking the reality of an imposing block of marble to the concept of the Eucharist as the intimate meal of the family gathered round the table. For catechesis to succeed, the liturgy must first be inculturated. When liturgy fails catechists they are left to their own devices. Chupungco observes: "the effect on catechesis can be lamentable. The use for instance of true-life but often unrelated or irrelevant anecdotes, far-fetched images and remote social values does nothing but throw a heavy mantle of obscurity upon the nature and purpose of the sacraments. The doctrine or the substance of the sacraments is thus often lost in the maze of evoked personal experiences, which do not always attain the desired faith dimension of the liturgical celebration."[398]

Challenges

Veronica Rosier offers thoughts on three areas for development in the catechetical field. "The model for all catechesis is the baptismal catechumenate."[399] The baptismal catechumenate is the process by which the church transmits the gospel in a threefold way: it is *known* in scripture and tradition, *celebrated* by the assembly in its liturgy, especially in the Eucharist, and *lived* by the Christian community in terms of the moral conversion and social consequences demanded by discipleship of Christ. After initiation, ongoing catechesis is necessary to develop and bring to fruition these three different dimensions of the faith of the ecclesial community: word, memory and witness. Rosier notes a first challenge in the use of the baptismal catechumenate as a model for other forms of catechesis.[400] Rosier quotes Catherine Dooley who "warns against the danger of the use of the so-called 'RCIA model' in which the RCIA is adapted and applied to a whole variety of life experiences such as confirmation preparation, formation for religious life and for marriage preparation."[401] There is, says Rosier, a real danger of the distortion of the rites intended for the un-baptised being applied to the baptised who need fuller catechesis. While the vision of the church is being realised gradually in many communities, there is a second danger, referred to also by Thomas Morris, that of trying to fit the new vision into older existing structures; there is need of a clearer articulation of the distinction between an educational model and a liturgical-formational model of catechesis.[402]

A second challenge is to strengthen "the weak and fragmentary link" frequently found between catechesis and liturgy in which there is "limited attention to liturgical symbols and rites, scant use of the liturgical sources, catechetical courses with little or no connection with the liturgical year [and] the marginalisation of liturgical celebrations in the catechetical programmes."[403] This concern is serious as "catechesis is intrinsically bound to every liturgical and sacramental action" and the liturgy is the privileged place for catechesis. For here the liturgy is not perceived as the primary source of theology or as the source from which the church's power flows.

The duration of the preparation either for reception of the integral sacraments of initiation or for the completion of baptism by confirmation and Eucharist always respects each individual's spiritual journey; the time spent should be "long enough" for the conversion and faith to become strong (RCIA 76). On occasion this process may be deemed untidy, unmanageable or impractical when parents are preparing their children for Eucharist or confirmation when both parents and children may be at different stages of conversion in their spiritual journey. Further indeed some parishes are tempted to accommodate the periods of the catechumenate determined not to the needs of their spiritual journey but to a set time frame or schedule governed more by the parameters of formal education, holidays or the civil calendar.

The RCIA does not simply make a distinction between catechumens and uncatechised adults. The rite reveals and opens up "a directive to penetrate the theological, socio-religious and socio-cultural dimensions of the particular situation of uncatechised initiated adults, to which the liturgy must speak and which liturgy should reflect truthfully."[404] Too often the rites are used for the purposes of teaching about the Christian life. Catechists may not fully understand that catechesis is a "school of faith, an initiation and apprenticeship into entire Christian life" (GDC 30). Liturgical rites are foremost worship of God by God's people and are never didactic in intent even though they contain much instruction for the faithful (GDC 71).

The third challenge is for a correct understanding of mystagogy. The General Directory and the Catechism refer little to the church's liturgical rites as sources for catechesis and theology, especially in the season of Easter. The Catechism's exposé on "The Sacramental Celebration of the Paschal Mystery" notes the close relationship between catechesis and liturgy as mystagogy. But the following section on the seven sacraments, apart from baptism, does not start from the liturgical rites, symbols, prayers and actions. There is a distinctive shift of approach that commences with theological and doctrinal formulations of the church and the *Code of Canon Law*.[405]

The focus on the baptismal catechumenate in the early church and in the RCIA demands a paschal spirituality. Baptismal spirituality is fundamentally liturgical.[406] For the revitalisation of the faith of lapsed Catholics, non-practising Catholics, sociological Catholics and others in need of a new evangelisation there is a need for a deeper understanding of mystagogy. "Proposing a catechumenate perhaps many years after baptism is not necessarily the most satisfactory way of addressing the needs of indifferent Catholics. The formation of catechists who are genuine mystagogues is a real priority."[407] Ron Lewinski argues for a recovery of Christian mystagogy for the contemporary church when he says that: "mystagogy is a careful blend of the imagination and experience together with critical reflection."[408]

CHAPTER 17
Ministry

Paul's letter to the Ephesians (perhaps an early teaching on baptism) affirms the centrality of ministry in the early Christian community:

> He who descended gave...his gifts to equip the saints for the work of ministry, for building up the body of Christ, until we all attain to the unity of the faith and of the knowledge of the Son of God...so that we may no longer be children, tossed to and fro and carried about with every wind of doctrine, by the cunning of men, by their craftiness in deceitful wiles (Eph 11-14).

The burgeoning awareness of the vocation of the laity as apostles to the secular world and stewards of the church's mission as an evangeliser has given rise to the popular term "lay ministry" to describe the active vocation of all the baptised. This general ministry of the laity has at times also been called the "lay apostolate" (LG 33) and the "lay vocation" (CF 23, 56). Included in this general lay ministry are several specific ministries designed to support the church community, such as lector/reader, extraordinary minister of communion, catechist, sponsor/godparent, etc. There are a number of non-ordained people who have undertaken roles that immediately prior to Vatican 2 belonged entirely to the ordained, including parish pastoral and catechetical staff, hospital and prison chaplains, campus ministers and diocesan leadership roles.

Vatican 2 began its description of the church in Lumen Gentium (LG 9 -17) with the People of God, moving on to the Hierarchical Structure (LG 18ff). The common priesthood of the faithful through baptism and the anointing of the Holy Spirit is affirmed (LG 10). The whole people share in Christ's prophetic office. This people are called to a fellowship of life in Christ the King (LG 13). The laity are all those not in the ordained ministry or in religious life, and they carry out for their own part the mission of the whole Christian people in the Church and in the world.

What specifically characterises the laity is their secular nature. The laity, by their very vocation, seek the kingdom of God by engaging in temporal affairs and by ordering them according to the plan of God. They live in the world in each and in all of the secular professions and occupations. They live in the ordinary circumstances of family and social life from which the very web of their existence is woven. They are called there by God that led by the spirit of the Gospel they may work for the sanctification of the world from within as a leaven. In this way they may make Christ known to others, especially by the testimony of a life resplendent in faith, hope and charity. All are called to holiness, to walk unhesitatingly according to their own personal gifts and duties in the path of living faith which arouses hope and works through charity (LG 41).

The foundation of the apostolic activity of the laity is their sharing in the priestly, prophetic and royal office of Christ and therefore they have their own share in the mission of the whole people of God in the Church and in the world (AA 2). The laity's right and duty to the apostolate is derived from their union with Christ the head; incorporated into Christ's Mystical Body through Baptism and strengthened by the power of the Holy Spirit through Confirmation, they are assigned to the apostolate by the Lord Himself. They are consecrated for the royal priesthood and the holy people (cf. 1 Peter 2:4-10) not only that they may offer spiritual sacrifices in everything they do but also that they may witness to Christ throughout the world (AA 3). Perhaps it should be noted in passing that rarely do individual laity (let alone ordained clergy) manage to perform fully and equally all three tasks allotted by baptism, the priestly, prophetic and pastoral. There will frequently be an interest or a calling in a particular direction – a penchant for engaging in worship, a zeal for justice and peace, a concern for helping those in any kind of need. The use of the term "lapsed" applied to anyone who falls short in any of these three areas, particularly the first, seems somewhat churlish and narrow-minded.

It is the Holy Spirit who sanctifies the people of God and gives the faithful special gifts also (cf. 1 Cor 12:7), "allotting them to everyone according as He wills" (1 Cor 12:11) in order that individuals, administering grace to others just as they have received it, may also be "good stewards of the manifold grace of God" (1 Peter 4:10), to build up the whole body in charity (cf. Eph 4:16). From the acceptance of these charisms, including those which are more elementary, there arise for each believer the right and duty to use them in the Church and in the world for the good of men and the building up of the Church, in the freedom of the Holy Spirit who "breathes where He wills" (John 3:8).

Only by the light of faith and by meditation on the word of God can one always and everywhere see Christ in everyone whether he be a relative or a stranger, and make correct judgments about the true meaning and value of temporal things both in themselves and in their relation to man's final goal (AA 4). So the laity carry out their apostolate both in the Church and in the world. "In both areas there are various opportunities for apostolic activity. Since in our times women have an ever more active shale in the whole life of society, it is very important that they participate more widely also in the various fields of the Church's apostolate" (AA 9).

Language and translation sometimes offer a moment of reflection. In a later version of AA we find that: "As sharers in the role of Christ as priest, prophet, and king, the laity have their work cut out for them in the life and activity of the Church" (AA 10). The original Latin says: *"laici suas partes activas habent in Ecclesiae vita et actione."* Abbott's earlier translation is more benign: "The laity have an active part to play in the life and activity of the church." An apologetic note is struck here too where: "Their activity is so necessary within the Church communities that without it the apostolate of the pastors is often unable to achieve its full effectiveness."[409]

In a little triad of thoughts, we are assured that the laity, firstly, bring to the Church people who perhaps are far removed from it, secondly, earnestly cooperate in presenting the word of God especially by means of catechetical instruction, and thirdly, offer their special skills to make the care of souls and the administration of the temporalities of the Church more efficient and effective. In the parish, which offers an obvious example of the apostolate on the community level, they bring to the Church community their own and the world's problems as well as questions concerning human salvation, all of which they should examine and resolve by deliberating in common. This activity has more recently been dubbed "collaborative ministry".

Ministry – part of evangelisation

The Apostolic Exhortation *Evangelii Nuntiandi* show us *ministry* as one part of evangelisation. "Those who have received the Good News and who have been gathered by it into the community of salvation can and must communicate and spread it" (EN 13). For the task of evangelising all people constitutes the essential mission of the Church. It is a task and mission which the vast and profound changes of present-day society make all the more urgent (EN 14). The, by now, classic definition of evangelisation is that it means "bringing the Good News into all the strata of humanity, and through its influence transforming humanity from within and making it new: 'Now I am making the whole of creation new'"(EN 18). The essence of ministry is first of all: "to bear witness… to God revealed by Jesus Christ, in the Holy Spirit, to bear witness that in His Son God has loved the world – that in His Incarnate Word He has given being to all things and has called men to eternal life" (EN 26).

In a lyrical passage (EN21), the Exhortation engages in a rhetorical vision of the effect of witness in the wider world:

Take a Christian or a handful of Christians
who, in the midst of their own community,
show their capacity for understanding and acceptance,
their sharing of life and destiny with other people,
their solidarity with the efforts of all
for whatever is noble and good.

Let us suppose that, in addition,
they radiate in an altogether simple and unaffected way
their faith in values that go beyond current values,
and their hope in something that is not seen
and that one would not dare to imagine.

Through this wordless witness
these Christians stir up irresistible questions
in the hearts of those who see how they live:
Why are they like this?
Why do they live in this way?
What or who is it that inspires them?
Why are they in our midst?

Such a witness is already a silent proclamation of the Good News and a very powerful and effective one. Here we have an initial act of evangelisation. It will address many, whether they are people to whom Christ has never been proclaimed, or baptised people who do not practice, or people who live as nominal Christians but according to principles that are in no way Christian, or people who are seeking, and not without suffering, something or 'someone' whom they sense but cannot name. Other questions will arise, deeper and more demanding ones, questions evoked by this witness which involves presence, sharing, solidarity, and which is an essential element, and generally the first one, in evangelization" (EN 21). This witness is person-to-person, one-to-one. "In the long run, is there any other way of handing on the Gospel than by transmitting to another person one's personal experience of faith?" (EN 46).

In the course of history, evangelisation has not been with out difficulties. Evangelisers have had the temptation for various reasons to narrow down the field of their missionary activity. There has been the often humanly insurmountable resistance of the people being addressed by the evangeliser. The evangelising work of the Church is strongly opposed, if not prevented, by certain public powers. Preachers of God's Word are deprived of their rights, persecuted, threatened or eliminated solely for preaching Jesus Christ and His Gospel. "But we are confident that despite these painful trials the activity of these apostles will never meet final failure in any part of the world" (EN 50).

The active presence of the laity in the temporal realities is important. The laity are called to work in the service of the ecclesial community for its growth and life by exercising a great variety of ministries according to the grace and charisms which the Lord is pleased to give them.

> A glance at the origins of the Church is very illuminating, and gives the benefit of an early experience in the matter of ministries. It was an experience which was all the more valuable in that it enabled the Church to consolidate herself and to grow and spread. Attention to the sources however has to be complemented by attention to the present needs of mankind and of the Church. To drink at these ever inspiring sources without sacrificing anything of their values, and at the same time to know how to adapt oneself to the demands and needs of today – these are the criteria which will make it possible to seek wisely and to discover the ministries which the Church needs and which many of her members will gladly embrace for the sake of ensuring greater vitality in the ecclesial community (EN 73).

A serious preparation is needed for all workers for evangelisation, but is all the more necessary for those who devote themselves to the ministry of the Word. "We earnestly desire that in each individual Church the bishops should be vigilant concerning the adequate formation of all the ministers of the Word. This serious preparation will increase in them the indispensable assurance and also the enthusiasm to proclaim today Jesus Christ (EN 73). At the end of the day, evangelisation will never be possible without the action of the Holy Spirit. Techniques of evangelisation are good, but even the most advanced ones could not replace the gentle action of the Spirit" (EN 75).

Hospitality

While witness can often be an individual occupation, ministry always belongs to the community, especially in and through the liturgy. The prime ministry, as Nathan Mitchell suggests, is that of hospitality. Liturgy, he says, is always "an act of hospitality and pastoral care, of making room and making welcome."[410]

This is not to reduce worship to a social occasion or a cosy group but is to root it in the very life of God. For God's life is "a communion not of colliding egos, but of self-emptying persons who 'make room' for one another'. God is a communion of persons forever in a condition of giving themselves away, freely, to each other."[411]

The divine persons very identity is constituted by giving (*donatio*), by self-emptying (*kenosis*), by mutual outpouring. God is a community of persons forever "caught in the act" of surrendering, in love to each other and to us. "Thus to be made 'in the image and likeness of God' is to be created for community, for partnership, for life with others, for an existence that enacts and embodies itself as *self-surrender*, a life bestowed on behalf of others. Ours is a God who 'makes room' opens up space for the stranger, welcomes the 'other'."[412]

Mitchell reminds us of the Hebrew poems in the first chapters of Genesis where God created a world for humankind by creating a rich *diversity* of living things; God created community by creating *difference*. "Difference introduces strangeness into familiarity, and triggers our inextinguishable longing for the 'other'. The mystery of strangeness and familiarity – of communion within difference and unity within diversity – encamps at the very heart of our sacramental symbols."[413]

The liturgy is the place par excellence where our hospitable God "makes room", opening a space where communion can flourish *in* and *as* difference and diversity. Our desire for the other in a world where strangeness and familiarity play side-by-side is the human root of our desire to come together as church. Our identity as church is thus as much a meeting of strangers as a meeting of familiars. That is why the responsibility to welcome the stranger lies at the heart of Christian hospitality.

At Vatican 2 *Sacrosanctum Concilium* affirmed that: "the liturgy daily builds up those who are in the church, making of them a holy temple of the Lord, a dwelling-place for God in the Spirit" (SC 2). Vatican 2 repeats the traditional view that baptism assimilates believers to the one priesthood of Christ.[414] When ancient baptismal liturgies called chrismated Christians priests, they were not making "priesthood" a metaphor for ministry. They meant to affirm *baptism* as the radical sacrament of priesthood in the church; they were not seeking to derive the "priesthood of the laity" from the "priesthood of the ordained." That is why we sometimes refer to the *ministerial* priesthood of the ordained, the implication being that the Christian's radical identity as "priest" has already been bestowed in baptism.

In the aftermath of the Council, the approach to lay (liturgical) ministries needed time to mature. As Hahnenberg puts it: "Early attempts to recover an active ministry for the non-ordained in the liturgy perhaps erred in this direction: they based their view of the common priesthood on the model of the ordained priesthood," seeking to extend the ordination franchise, as it were, by "granting the laity a 'priesthood' of their own."[415]

Aidan Kavanagh drew our attention to this point (and to a potential problem) more than a quarter-century ago. In his memorable essay, *Unfinished and Unbegun: The Rite of Christian Initiation of Adults*, Kavanagh wrote: "[T]he Church baptises to priesthood: it ordains only to executive exercise of that priesthood in the major orders of ministry. . . . While every presbyter and bishop is therefore a sacerdotal person, not every sacerdotal person in the Church is a presbyter or bishop. Nor does sacerdotality come upon one for the first time, so to speak, at one's ordination. In constant genesis in the font, the Church is born there as a sacerdotal assembly by the Spirit of the Anointed One himself."[416]

Communion

Richard Gaillardetz develops a theological foundation for ministry grounded in the central doctrinal symbol of our Christian tradition, the doctrine of the Trinity. In response to important questions raised regarding the distinction between ministry and Christian service, on the one hand, and the distinction between ordained and non-ordained ministry on the other. The growth of ministry, he says, has effectively pared off many traditional tasks once reserved for the priest while demanding from him new skills and a new vision of collaborative ministry.[417]

Today, says Gaillardetz, "Trinitarian doctrine is remarkable for its clarity, and regrettable for its pastoral irrelevance." God exists as "being-in-communion". For humankind this life of communion takes on a partially personal form and involves the capacity for full, active and reciprocal participation in the life of communion. We are called to realise our personhood in the life of communion patterned on the triune life of God. The personal, relational being of God is devoid of any relations characterised by domination, manipulation or subordination, so too is the human person called to reject these kinds of relationships and to realise his or her personal being in relationships which are fundamentally reciprocal, mutual and life-giving.

Gaillardetz asks: "Do we need to distinguish our life of communion with God from our communion with one another?" The earliest intuitions of the Christian community were that these are two different dimensions of the same fundamental orientation. Jesus emphasises the primacy and inseparability of the first two commandments demanding love of God and of neighbour (Mk 11:28-34; Luke 10:25-28; Matt 22:34-40). From a completely different tradition connected with the Johannine community, we find the conviction that the love of God and love of neighbour are inseparable (1 Jn 4:8, 20). Again from a third biblical tradition, that found in the Letter of James, we see the integral connection between faith in God and human commitment to the welfare of others (James 2:14-17). Each tradition confirms the connection between communion with God and communion with neighbour.

We see this life of communion signified and effected in the life of the church. "The church, in Christ, is a kind of sacrament or sign and instrument of intimate union with God and the unity of the whole human race" (LG 1). We of course do not find the full realisation of this communion, even within the church, in human history. The church itself journeys toward the final consummation of God's offer of divine communion.

Gaillardetz suggests a model of Christian ministry which can be derived from a Trinitarian foundation. The minister is a servant of communion. We are beings who realise ourselves fully only in communion. The various manifestations of ministry will find their root meaning in the proclamation and/or restoration of the life of communion. "The life of communion is realised within the fabric of ordinary existence. If we hold fast to the conviction of the inseparability of communion with God and communion with neighbour, then every event of communion, whether explicitly religious in character or not, is a graced event. The mystagogical task of Christian ministry is first to recognise the basic events of communion which are woven into ordinary human existence, and second to name those events of communion as graced events, as encounters with nothing less than the God of Jesus Christ."[418] Too often, Gaillardetz believes, people today isolate religious experience from their daily lives and compartmentalise it, relegating the experience of God to church and moments of explicit prayer. Daily acts of love and compassion must be reclaimed as a participation in the mystery of God.

The minister needs to recognise human experiences of brokenness where the capacity for communion is inhibited and sometimes destroyed. Social sciences can recognise root causes. But prophetic ministry has its foundation in the ministry of Jesus Christ who was fearless in his condemnation of every world power which quenched the human spirit. Often too the minister is broken. Gaillardetz warns that: "Christian ministry is particularly attractive to people with co-dependent tendencies whose professed desire to 'help others' masks a more fundamental need to control others in service of his or her own personal needs."[419] Social institutions like the family and even the church can reward and perpetuate co-dependent or addictive behaviours. The very woundedness of the minister may become strength. Knowing what can impede progress towards communion can be for a minister a source of support and strength. Out of a humble recognition of personal brokenness the minister may become a "wounded healer."[420]

Jesus' ministry of reconciliation brought freedom from the power of those forces which could distort the human movement toward another in the life of communion. Too often the healing ministry of Jesus has been focused on the miraculous. But perhaps "the greatest healing which Jesus offered came not in the regeneration of withered limbs or blind eyes but in Jesus' offer of fundamental acceptance extended toward each person he met. Jesus' relationships were characterised by a probing, perceptive presence to the other person."[421] Jesus wrought healing as much by his personal presence to others as by dramatic acts.

Above all the minister is a person of hope for every minister will come to the point of questioning the effectiveness of their work. What is lacking is an appreciation of the eschatological character of the life of communion. The fullness of life will always elude us. Humankind travels through history leaving a rich narrative of human triumph and defeat. "Our survival depends on our possession of an eschatological hope, grounded in prayer and nurtured in Christian community, which looks to the fulfilment of the life of communion in God's time."[422]

Diaconate

Kenan Osborne, in reviewing the major changes in ministry put into place by Vatican 2, notes first the establishment of the ministry and mission of all the baptised as foundational for all institutional church ministry.[423] He says that from this it follows that the sacraments of Christian initiation rather than holy orders are really the most important sacraments in the Christian church on a ministerial level; they provide the foundation on which all considerations of church ministry should be based.

Osborne observes the minimal emphasis on this development in the *Catechism of the Catholic Church* where the stress is on the pope, bishops, priests and deacons but only to a limited degree on baptised lay men and women. The permanent diaconate is derived from priesthood of the faithful. The re-establishment of the permanent diaconate has brought blessings to the church and to those who have been ordained. Permanent deacons have moved into various ministries that have often not been taken on by presbyters as an essential part of their ministry. Nevertheless Gaillardetz believes that permanent deacons are often confused about their personal identity as clerics in the Catholic Church, especially since qualified lay men and women have already taken on many of the ministries assumed by deacons.

Osborne stresses his view that the central image of the deacon's ministry "remains the icon of Jesus washing the feet of the disciples, and the central call is that of Jesus which came to serve and not to be served. The icon of the foot washing and the New Testament word of the Lord on service remains the foundational source for the spiritual and theological growth of all Christian ministries… The very name deacon reminds the permanent deacon to be a servant-minister."[424] However this functional definition of the deacon does not help in clarifying his identity since all ecclesial ministers, including the bishop, presbyter and lay ecclesial minister, are called to be servant-ministers.

John Collins suggests that *diakonia* developed from the concept of functionalism of the eighteenth century as a way to describe the ministry, where deacon was defined not from an ecclesiological foundation based on the church as diakonia, but inductively from the sum of the functions performed.[425] The diaconate was revived in a charitable, social form in northern Europe in the nineteenth century, particularly in the Lutheran church. The tendency to think of diakonia as a kind of Christian social work made its way into the Christian understanding of ministry by way of early twentieth century German biblical scholarship. Collins insists that diakonia in the New Testament describes a form of ministry distinguished by the fact that one has been sent or commissioned on behalf of another. Gaillardetz has applied Collins' findings explicitly to the life and the ministry of the permanent deacon. He sees the deacon as one sent by the bishop in service of the needs of the church. The bishop is responsible for the oversight of the local church; the ministry of the deacon is both ordered by the bishop who is responsible for apostolic oversight and is explicitly placed at the service of the bishop's ministry of oversight. Formation programmes for the diaconate vary widely but the most common seem to be weekend courses over a four year period. Very few dioceses insist on a degree in pastoral theology or ministry. As a result lay ministers are often better educated than permanent deacons.

Deacons tend to bring the traits of their former life into the ministry of the diaconate. If they have been "successful", ministerially, in their previous life then they will tend to be "successful" in diaconate, that is to say they continue to exercise their spiritual gifts as before. Do they allow themselves to undergo conversion during their preparation for a new ministry? "If they begin with an open mind they will continue with an even more open mind," said one Seminary Rector. Owen Cummings warns that: "Recognisable traits such as ritualism, clericalism, anti-intellectualism, crusadism and negativism can impede diakonia… other traits such as messianism and exemplarism can damage the deacon's important relationship with his family."[426] There is still room for considerable theological and pastoral reflection on the identity and role of the permanent deacon.

Formation

Osborne notes that the official expansion of lay ministry and the recognition of ministry have become an important dimension of the church's life. Since Vatican 2 many lay men and women have prepared themselves by intensive study, some even progressing to the level of doctorate. They play essential roles as religious educators, faith formation leaders, ministers in hospitals and nursing homes, as well as prisons, directors of liturgy and educators and chaplains in schools, colleges and universities. Lay ecclesial ministry is of course nothing new in the church. Lay men and women as brothers and sisters in institutes of religious life have ministered as lay people in the church for centuries and have made enormous contributions above all in education and nursing institutions. No one doubts the contribution made by lay people; nonetheless they are often not taken seriously by church authorities, are declared redundant when priests and deacons are available, are often poorly remunerated, not given adequate benefits and are not provided with job security.

Some Bishops' Conferences and many dioceses in recent years have initiated and supported a number of initiatives for the training and support of lay ministry. In the United States the Bishops' Conference has considered the formation of lay ministers. The four areas of formation – human, spiritual, intellectual, and pastoral – that provide a framework for the formation of deacons and priests provide also a framework for lay ecclesial ministers as well. Lay ecclesial ministers therefore need:

- Human qualities that are critical to form wholesome relationships and necessary to be apt instruments of God's love and compassion,

- A spirituality and practice of prayer that root them in God's Trinitarian life, grounding and animating all they do in ministry,

- Adequate knowledge in theological and pastoral studies, along with the intellectual skill to use it among the people and cultures of our country,

- The practical pastoral abilities called for in their particular ministry.[427]

The same *Resource* speaks of the authorisation of ministers. Authorisation is the process by which properly prepared lay men and women are given responsibilities for ecclesial ministry by competent Church authority. This process includes the following elements: "acknowledgment of the competence of an individual for a specific ministerial role (often called 'certification'); appointment of an individual to a specific position (in some dioceses called 'commissioning'), along with a delineation of the obligations, responsibilities, and authority of that position (and length of term, if specified); and finally an announcement of the appointment to the community that will be served by the lay ecclesial minister."[428]

In a different vein, "Preparing together" was an initiative of the Arundel and Brighton diocese in Advent 2002. 6000 people took part in a consultation. One of the consistent "themes" across all the responses was that of "participation". In the very first session the small groups had focused on what our Baptism means to us. Reflecting on scripture, and on a particular paragraph from *The Catechism of the Catholic Church* too, discussions were centred on the gifts each has been given so that each might contribute more fully as members of Christ's body to the building of the kingdom here on earth. Significant numbers of people said that they wanted to participate, to make a difference, to be active in their communities and share responsibilities. Numerous suggestions were made for possible developments, training and support so that there was "a recognition of the dignity and responsibility of all baptised" in participating in the mission of Christ through the Church.[429]

A discrepancy emerged in the weary, heartfelt cries from some priests and other parish leaders about people saying they want all these things but "when you ask for volunteers to make things happen it all goes very quiet!" "It's the same faithful few who do everything." "People are too busy these days – they don't have the time." There were also exasperated cries from those who said they wanted to make a contribution but they "weren't allowed to" or their offer of support was "never taken up." The solution to this dilemma, says the report, might be to explore the additional knowledge, understanding and skills that might be necessary to bridge the gap between those who want to volunteer and those who manage them.

So, the Diocese asked, what can priests and parish leaders gain from examining successful organisations in the voluntary sector? The proposal was to explore the programme of "Volunteer Management" in a Christian context. This was not solely about matching people to particular jobs. It was fundamentally about enabling individuals to recognise and celebrate their gifts. It would provide some answers to these questions: How can the leaders in our communities invite, support and affirm those who actively participate in our communities? What source of support and encouragement can our parish communities provide for those who also witness their love of God and neighbour at home, at work and in the local community?

1. *Clovis I was king of the Franks from 481 to 511. In 496 he, and all his subjects, converted to Christianity, which gained him the support of the Church for his conquests of other tribes in western and central Europe. (Les Chroniques de France 14th Century.)*

2. Mario Botta's Cathedral, Evry, France (1988-1995)

3. Notre-Dame de l'Arche de l'Alliance, Paris (1998)

4. *Notre-Dame de l'Arche de l'Alliance, Paris –*
Baptistery (1998) (Architecture-Studio)

5. Notre-Dame de l'Arche de l'Alliance, Paris —
David dancing before the Ark (1998)

6. Notre-Dame de l'Arche de l'Alliance, Paris – The Visitation (1998)

7. Notre-Dame de Pentecôte, La Défense, Paris –
Ambo evoking the Burning Bush (2001)

8. Notre-Dame de Pentecôte, La Défense, Paris – the Angel accompanies Tobias and the pilgrim who leaves the church (2001)

9. Holy Redeemer Church, Bangkok – pagoda-like exterior

*10. Holy Redeemer Church, Bangkok – image of the
Risen Christ evoking imagery of Buddha*

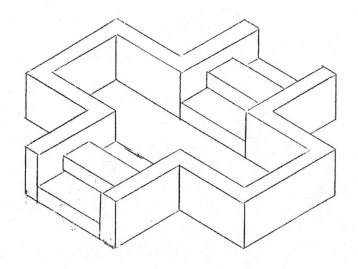

*11. St Joseph's, Guildford – design based on an
early Christian cruciform font (1999)*

CHAPTER 18
Sacred Space

In recent times the hierarchies of the United States,[430] Canada[431] and England and Wales[432] have issued or re-issued guidance on places of worship. The English and Welsh text, *Consecrated for Worship*, speaks of the visionary theme of Vatican 2 that "under divine grace the Church is created and sustained by its liturgical life. The Church assembles at the font to enact its birth in the person of new members. It is gathered and schooled by the Word proclaimed at the ambo in its midst. It centres its life on the altar where the Eucharist, the source and summit of all its activity, is offered. The sacred space of a church building is given shape by the rites of the Church" (CFW 2).

The document quotes Paul's Letter to the Ephesians:

> *You are no longer strangers and aliens, but you are citizens with the saints and also members of the household of God, built upon the foundation of the apostles and prophets, with Christ Jesus himself as the cornerstone. In him the whole structure is joined together and grows into a holy temple in the Lord; in whom you also are built together spiritually into a dwelling place for God* (Ephesians 2:19-22).

It continues: "The witness of the New Testament is that the Christian Temple is not so much a building of stone, as a building of living stones. The Christian Temple is the Christian people built on the foundation of Christ, the living cornerstone" (CFW 25). It points out that, even though the community saw itself as "a holy temple, a dwelling place of God, it became commonplace to speak of where the church gathered, the house of the Church (*domus ecclesiae*) as being also the house of God (*domus Dei*)." Recognising a division between these two ideas which has become apparent, it continues: "It is important to recognise that both of these understandings have found a firm place in the Catholic Christian tradition. Both inform the Rite of Dedication of a Church, and both need to be respected in contemporary use and design of churches" (CFW 26).

Joseph Keenan writes on temples and churches, noting that the temple is a phenomenon in many religions past and present, and that "the early church's worship places unwittingly evolved from buildings which housed the Christian liturgical communities into sacred buildings which functioned as temples."[433] Speaking of temples, he says that:

> the space on the other side of the railing is more sacred than the "laity's" section of the temple-room. When focussing on the space where the statue is, the worshipper should experience most intensely the presence of the Buddha or the one to whom the temple is dedicated, or at least experience more intensely the presence of mystery and the holy. The services are...ritual chanting, the ritualised presentation of offerings... the laity are passive observers of the rituals one by the priest. Kyoto and Jerusalem separate the profane world from the sacred. ..Lines of demarcation are clearly made. Selectivity in admission of people to holier spots is also done by Jewish and Buddhist temples...early Christian house churches were ordinary domestic dwellings prior to their taking on temple characteristics.[434]

It is important for present day discussions to have a sense of history. Keenan notes the historical development over succeeding centuries, that gradually only the clergy could read and write and they kept that in the Latin language. "As romance languages emerged and as the church expanded into lands where the vernacular was vastly different from the Latin, the uneducated laity automatically had verbal participation taken away from them....seeing themselves as more and more unworthy to receive the Eucharist, even their non-verbal participation dwindled... the laity were passive bystanders who paid the clergy to offer prayers and sacrifices for them."[435] By the eleventh century the building began to function much more like a temple; it was no longer the *domus ecclesiae*; it was the *domus Dei*. Other developments in history further accented the holiness of the clergy and the sanctuary in which they presided, namely, mandatory celibacy, Eucharistic reservation practices and absolute ordination.

Keenan contrasts the temple and the church in this way: "The temple had many functions; the *domus ecclesiae* simply houses the church." The temple sacralises space, expresses the meaning of the society using it, localises the presence of God, creates a sense of the sacred and more. The *domus ecclesiae* provides shelter; everything else must come from the interaction of the worshipping community; this is very demanding. He continues:

> The failure of Christian communities to meet this demand has led them to say that the new liturgy has failed and that we have lost a sense of the sacred. Temples are often very alluring and very beautiful, and can be very efficacious in many ways, but the price one pays for such an allurement is the demeaning of the laity who are an integral part of the body of Christ.[436]

The time and space where Christians gather for worship has become an important dimension of post-conciliar architecture and liturgical theology. Gathering is not a merely utilitarian act; it is a theological principle. As the Canadian Catholic bishops note in their 1999 document, *Our Place of Worship*: "[T]he assembly of believers is the starting point for developing a house for the Church," precisely because the "full, conscious, active participation called for by the Council and demanded by the liturgical rites requires that liturgical space be developed to support this ideal."[437] The bishops of the United States build on this in their 2000 document *Built of Living Stones: Art, Architecture, and Worship*:

"Every church building is a gathering place for the assembly, a resting place, a place of encounter with God, as well as a point of departure on the Church's unfinished journey toward the reign of God."[438]

Therefore decisions about church art and architecture should always be based upon "the theology of the Eucharistic assembly and its liturgical action and the understanding of the Church as the house of God on earth."[439] Consequently, "the fundamental prerequisite for those engaged in the building or renovation of a church is familiarity with the rites to be celebrated there."[440]

Processions

When Western church architecture created gathering spaces for stations and processions, it was implicitly affirming the assembly's acts of gathering, greeting, and welcome as the living icon of the hospitable God who "makes room and makes welcome," who gathers people from age to age and unites them as a "holy nation, a royal priesthood." This, after all, is what liturgies and sacraments do: they open our eyes to see in human deeds – the washing of a body, the eating and drinking of a meal – the gracious arrival of One who is both strangely familiar and familiarly strange. We cannot forget that on the road to Emmaus, it was a *Stranger* whom the disciples "recognised in the breaking of the bread" (Lk 24:35).

The modern Roman rite is still punctuated by processions: during the entrance rite, at the proclamation of the gospel, at the presentation and preparation of gifts (for the Eucharistic table and for the poor) and at communion. Much of the time, modern liturgical catechesis is content to explain processions as either *utilitarian* (getting the assembly and/ or ministers from one place to another), *educative* (ritual choreography that teaches us about the feast or season) or *honorific* (e.g. the use of lights, incense, and movement to accompany proclamation of the gospel).

When we interpret processions in this way we implicitly privilege rational thought over ambiguous action. Our assumption is that a procession means what *we* say it means, that we are serenely, supremely, and self-consciously in charge of the proceedings. As Romano Guardini observed, our well-meant explanations may actually prevent our grasping "how the act of walking [itself] becomes a religious act, a retinue for the Lord progressing through his land, so that an 'epiphany' may take place."[441] The epiphany in question is not always a consoling one – and it may well defy every expectation. As Martha Graham once replied to a questioner who asked what her dances "meant": "Darling, if I knew what they meant, I wouldn't dance them." We are well advised, then, to let our symbols be roomy and our explanations spare.

Andrew Ciferni has observed: "All liturgical reform is based on some model of celebration which largely determines the details of revised rites."[442] A key clue to the model at work in the Missal of Paul VI can be found in the most recent version of the General Instruction of the Roman Missal.[443] GIRM 47 states: "After the people have gathered, the Entrance chant begins as the priest enters with the deacon and ministers. The purpose of this chant is to open the celebration, foster the unity of those who have been gathered, introduce their thoughts to the mystery of the liturgical season or festivity, and accompany the procession of the priests and ministers." The focus is on *the assembled people,* whose singing "opens . . . fosters . . . introduces…accompanies."

The action and space of gathering, the entrance procession and its music – all these exemplify what Andrew Ciferni calls "Vatican II ecclesiology made flesh."[444] Their significance is not merely pastoral, strategic, utilitarian or logistical. Nor are "gathering spaces" and "entrance rites" invented by post-conciliar enthusiasts who seek to "exalt" the assembly at the expense of the ordained. Nor does the importance of the assembly's place for gathering somehow rival or reduce the significance of the "sanctuary" space. Although some traditionalists see the "sanctuary" as a strictly clerical preserve, the Canadian bishops wisely remind us that "The Rite of Dedication of a Church speaks of the whole assembly space as 'sanctuary',," and that "[i]n the Roman tradition, placement of the Eucharistic table in the midst of the assembly has ancient precedent."[445] Surely it goes without saying that the purpose of the sanctuary is to unite, not to divide. As *Consecrated for Worship* says: "The sanctuary is an integrated part of the whole sacred space."[446]

Peter Humfrey

Worship space

Nathan Mitchell reflects on church architecture. He sees a fear of the vernacular – the vernacular, he says, draws power away from the centre and towards the margins. Vernacular empowers – in speech or on art – the marginalised and discomforts the elite. "Power-holders and power-brokers are thus rightly nervous about any art, dialect, local or regional variation that threatens the ancient dream of a common language – a mother speech spoken by all, whose meanings can be meticulously controlled and defined." [447] Art and architecture, he says, like music and liturgy, have become largely the work of specialists and professionals. A space is sacred after all because of what is done there, discovered there. Those who serve congregations in matters of "environment and art" have a mystagogical ministry to help an assembly negotiate its meeting with the Mystery. "Faith flows not from the pretension that evil, death, darkness and anguish are unreal, but from the conviction that one may still 'see wonders' in the midst of suffering."[448]

Narrative

Richard Vosko explores ways of bringing tradition and vision together. He says: "Our homes and our holy edifices can express infinite possibilities when they reflect who we are and what we might be."[449] For some, churches have lost their familiar look. For others the appearance of church is less important that what goes on inside.

Vosko maintains that possession of a narrative is an important aspect of every person's life. He quotes Neil Postman: "When people do not have a satisfactory narrative to generate a sense of purpose and continuity, a kind of psychic disorientation takes hold, followed by a frantic search for something to believe in or, probably worse, a resigned conclusion that there us nothing to find."[450]

Vosko says that we can easily lose a sense of purpose in the face of the many distractions of today – that acts of rudeness and incivility are symptoms of this confusion. For Catholics the church has almost always provided a sanctuary in times of local and global trials, so some Catholics say this is why they are upset and angry over the reform

320

taking place in the church. He says: "The older reliable narrative has been transformed and is now expressed in a different manner. For many the perceived unswerving uniformity of yesterday's church served as a rampart against all odds, personal and public. The bastion has been replaced by a rich diversity that for some has weakened the image of the church."[451] Church buildings have become a scapegoat for this ire because they are the most visible expressions of these mutations.

The problem is understanding the evolving role of the church in a modern age, and appreciating the contribution of the liturgical movement to that role. This is why the age old narrative acclaimed by the church must not be forsaken but given a new focus. "The purpose of narrative is to give meaning to the world and not to describe it scientifically; the measure of a narrative's truth is in its consequences. Does it provide a sense of hope, ideals, personal identity, a basis of moral conduct, explanation of that which cannot be known?"[452]

The narrative celebrated in the Eucharistic liturgy is about the birth, the journey, the suffering, death and resurrection of Jesus Christ. The paschal event is still a solid foundation for faith and remains the keystone of the church. The manner in which it is remembered and enacted needs ongoing resuscitation. This was the purpose of Vatican 2, to breathe new life into the old narrative – here tradition and vision were bridged.

Building or renovating public structures is a daunting task. On the one hand this is because there is pressure to honour the traditional narrative because it is vivid in the minds of many people. On the other hand a well designed space can make it possible for the narrative to be enacted in ways that are more indigenous to contemporary faith communities. Vosko offers these two proposals: "First the space should be shaped to accommodate the public rites that allow the story or myth to be remembered in a festive atmosphere. The building is a metaphor not just a container for ritual furnishings or art. Second, the place of worship should be planned to stir the imagination. The sacred setting for the ritual enactment of the paschal event must enable the participants to envisage possibilities for the future without compromising the basic storyline...the environment must bear inspiring and meaningful messages."[453]

Good, older buildings must be properly adapted to accommodate the reformed rituals without taking away their innate artistic and architectural beauty. Newer places must be shaped with beauty and grace in mind. In either case the traditional myth should not be discarded. The traditional story is used as the cornerstone from which new expressions of the narrative can rise up. The challenge is that: "Liturgical practices and church designs which belong to a bygone era of the church's history…are simply too familiar and too comforting to let go of in a society that is reeling from an unrelenting onslaught of information spewed out by every electronic medium possible. Mass culture is a by-product of the whimsical and fickle tastes of consumers which are shaped by advertising, opinion polls, standardised products, the proliferation of shopping malls, mass marketing and the commercialisation of organised entertainment."[454]

Setting for public worship

Dealing with the questions and problems pertaining to the environment for worship is not an easy task. It is one that requires dialogue that is marked by understanding and not just opinions, civility and certainly not hostility. Some people disagree with the authority of the church's ritual books. They have even less respect for liturgical scholarship. Vosko believes: "Attention must be paid to education and communication; people are often simply uninformed. Personal opinion and rage are not helpful to the dialogue when they are not rooted in a solid understanding of the issues."[455] Otherwise this approach will turn the issues into political ones that produce winners and losers. Such a contest can only fracture the body of Christ. The current directives are based on the principles that guide the liturgical practice of the church and should be honoured.

Many new churches do not resemble the house of God but look more like civic buildings or sports venues or supermarkets. As Vosko says: "Some Catholics are opposed to anything that is contemporary."[456] Vosko offers this insight from Thomas Merton on anti-modernism: "One of the big problems for an architect in our time is that for a hundred and fifty years men [sic] have been building churches as if a church could not belong to our time. A church has to look as if it were left over from some other age. I think that such an assumption is based on an implicit confession of atheism – as if God did not belong to all ages and as if religion were only a pleasant, necessary social formality, preserved from past times in order to give our society an air of respectability."[457] The appropriate setting for worship is one that is based on ecclesiology and liturgy. The settings for public worship must accommodate the reformed rites.

The church has managed to celebrate the paschal mystery for 2000 years in so many different environments, each reflecting the region, the culture, and the politics of the time. Here are some examples of new build and re-ordering, which demonstrate some of the principles we have outlined above.

Cathedral of the Resurrection at Evry, France

The Cathedral of the Resurrection at Evry in France was designed by Mario Botta and built betwen1988 and 1995. The powerful structure of the building emphasises the strength of resistance required in a building designed to cope with the brutal forces of nature (see picture 2). In its insistence upon its own geometrical axis in the replacement of the former old church, this building boldly declares a historical heritage that is enriched by geometrical invention. The architect spelled out his vision in this way:

> I thought of the design for the "House of God" in the hope of making a house for Man. The city is Man's house. It is where he lives, works and communicates with other people. It is a collective space where history and memory reside, where work, the strains of work and people's hopes are accumulated. To build a cathedral today is an extraordinary opportunity to create and enrich the environment in which we live. It is a new sign, awaited by Man. It offers a moment of silence, of reflection and prayer and speaks of Man in relation to the rapid changes and contradictions of life today. Building a cathedral is not just a bishop's see; it is above all an affirmation that the

deepest of forces are still present. It is the will to create a place where the spirit is tightly woven into the urban fabric, a place which can help us face the everyday challenges and struggles of life. A cathedral today is a symbol of man's new attitude toward the environment in which he lives. For the architect this means working and building in the hope of meeting the need for eternity that is present in each of us.[458]

Notre-Dame de l'Arche d'Alliance, Paris

The second example is conceived in completely different way. The church of Notre-Dame de l'Arche d'Alliance (Our Lady of the Ark of the Covenant) was built in the high rise suburbs south of Montparnasse in Paris and opened in 1998. The Ark of the Covenant was the wooden box made of acacia and covered in gold leaf which contained the Tables of the Law given by God at Mount Sinaï. The building is in the form a cube placed on twelve pillars over a public garden. The exterior is clothed in a tubular lattice (see picture 3). Internally the altar is a cube of white Tassos marble, the tabernacle is made of cedar wood and replicates the Ark of the Covenant. The font is below the main body of the church and can be seen through glass panels in the floor; it is accessed by a flight of stairs up to the church (see picture 4). There are two large stained glass windows, one depicting David dancing before the Ark and the other the Visitation (see pictures 5-6). The church is an eloquent and harmonious presentation of a vital theme for post-modernity, that of God's Covenant with his people.[459]

Older church buildings have throughout history become unsuitable for worship for practical or liturgical reasons. It was not uncommon in the past to demolish an old church and build anew. The crusaders were quite revolutionary as were those who built the cathedrals of the early Middle Ages. Another famous example would be the rebuilding, in the 4th and 15th centuries, of St Peter's Basilica in Rome. Since Vatican 2 there have been often three stages of rapid change, first the moving forward of the altar for the priest to stand behind and face the people, second, the re-ordering of all the sanctuary furniture and thirdly the re-ordering again of the whole church (rarely) or of the sanctuary and perhaps baptistery either with a forward looking arrangement in line with recent church documents or with a reversion to what was there some time before. Sadly and frequently, it is only the furniture which has been renewed while the assembly has remained static, even, as one liturgist observed, "waist-high in wood." Before the renewal of the furniture, it seems better to attend to the renewal of the community, through catechesis and prayer. Successful church building is then a marriage of architect and liturgist and community.

Cathedral of St Anne, Leeds

In the third example, Paul Walker discusses the re-ordering of the Cathedral of St Anne in Leeds:

> The design was intended to fulfil the desire to have a clear, unimpeded view of an altar, says Walker, "a desideratum of the Liturgical Movement. It has also been a desideratum that the worship assembly should be gathered around and close to, rather than assembled before and distanced from, the altar. The sanctuary is the focal area of the whole reordered setting and of what should really be most prominent with it, the altar and ambo."

> The ambulatory screen of the 1963 reordering "has been removed but not replaced, opening up the chancel space laterally, and easing the interruption and compression of space in the chancel caused by the forward central positioning of the cathedra and its solid backing screen, a consequence that might have been mitigated by not setting the cathedra quite so high, reducing the unfortunate effect of it seeming *dominant* rather than *prominent.*"

> The sandstone Gothic font is from the cathedral's demolished 19th century predecessor, "and though artfully converted to have running water, both its size and new location seem hardly suited to its being used for adult baptism. Presumably there were good reasons for not including some designed provision for generous affusion if not immersion, and not placing it elsewhere."[460]

Notre Dame de Pentecôte, Paris

A fourth example is the attractive church of Notre Dame de Pentecôte. The church was designed by Paris-based architect Franck Hammoutène and completed in 2001. It is built in the heart of the business community at La Défense in Paris. The giant translucent glass wall at the front of the church is 115-feet tall but only 31 inches thick and can be seen from 2 km away. On entering the church the visitor is welcomed by an inviting mural depicting Joshua inviting the people to enter the Promised Land; on the way out the visible and encouraging mural is of Tobias and the Angel (see picture 8). All the liturgical furnishings speak of the Holy Spirit and Pentecost. Of particular note is the ambo which evokes the Burning Bush (see picture 7). The architect explains a little of his vision thus:

> ### Une architecture en harmonie avec son lieu et son temps
>
> *Nous sommes nombreux à aimer le quartier de La Défense. Son architecture qui reflète le ciel et le visage des hommes; sa foule bigarrée venue de tous les lieux où se lève le soleil. Ruche laborieuse où chacun rejoint le centre d'intérêt qui est le sien pour construire, inventer, créer, exporter, acheter, traduire, financer...les verbes ne suffissent pas pour décrire tout le mystère de cette humanité en marche.*
>
> *En contemplant cette foule, vous ajouterez quelques verbes essentiels à tout chrétien pour vivre sa foi : prier, réconcilier, louer, célébrer, rendre grâce, demander pardon, réfléchir à l'avenir de l'homme...*
>
> *Il faut une église à la Défense. Elle ne sera ni une cathédrale, ni un monastère, mais une "Maison" où il fera bon célébrer l'Eucharistie et entendre la parole de Dieu, où il sera possible de rechercher la meilleure manière possible d'être témoin de Jésus-Christ dans le monde de l'économie, du travail, du service.*
>
> *Et pour en parler aux hommes de toutes langues.*[461]

Holy Redeemer Church, Bangkok

A distant example of inculturation may be found in Bangkok where most of the Catholic churches are firmly in the European style of the 18th and

19th centuries. There is however one "Thai" church, Holy Redeemer. The exterior is in pagoda style (see picture 9). Inside, the golden risen Christ evokes the Buddhist culture, and the altar furnishings are all Thai except for the two western statues (see picture 10). On the sanctuary may be seen a set of chairs, a gift from the nearby Buddhist temple. When asked how the architecture and furnishings had been received, the parish priest replied that some Buddhists had said he had stolen their heritage and some Catholics said that he had sold out to the Buddhists.

St Joseph's, Guildford

A final example is the plan for the full immersion font for St Joseph's, Guildford. It is designed to be at the main entrance, the faithful pass either side of it on entry, the elect step down into it from the narthex and rise from the water to proceed to the altar. The cruciform shape evokes fonts from the earliest days of Christianity (see picture 11). The Directory on Church Building, *Consecrated for Worship,* says the following:

> In the celebration of baptism the washing with water should take on its full importance as the sign of that mystical sharing in Christ's death and resurrection through which those who believe in his name die to sin and rise to eternal life (RCIA 206) (CFW 229).

> In the baptismal Liturgy preference is given to baptism by immersion (that is either by full immersion, or standing or kneeling in water while water is poured over the head and whole body) rather than by infusion (that is, leaning over a font or bowl as water is poured over the head) (see picture 1). New fonts should be designed and sited to enable both methods to take place for both adults and children from any side (CFW 231).[462]

Conclusion

A TV news reporter, commenting on the celebration of the Way of the Cross at the Colosseo in Rome one Good Friday evening, said: "The crowds have gathered to watch the ceremony." The dialogue of faith and culture however is not a spectator sport. The dialogue between faith and culture must grow and develop so that the Gospel can take root in post-modern culture to reveal more fully the glory of God and engage all peoples in the pursuit of the common good and the salvation of their souls. It is not a hard task; it simply requires an open mind and heart, a sense of purpose and an insatiable curiosity about what more is be discovered. This book, it is to be hoped, has served that curiosity as a guide and a stimulus. The Vatican Council's *Dogmatic Constitution on the Church* offers this encouragement to persevere, in pilgrim spirit, in the dialogue of cultures until the end of time:

> The Church, like a pilgrim in a foreign land, presses forward amid the persecutions of the world and the consolations of God, "announcing the cross and death of the Lord until He comes" (cf. 1 Cor 11:26). By the power of the risen Lord, she is given strength to overcome patiently and lovingly the afflictions and the hardships which assail her from within and without, and to show forth in the world the mystery of the Lord in a faithful though shadowed way, until at the last it will be manifested in total splendour.[463]

Bibliography

ALBERICH, Emilio SDB and VALLABARAJ, Jerome SDB. *Communicating a Faith That Transforms.* (Bangalore: Kristu Jyoti Publications 2004).

ANTONIO, David William. *An Inculturation Model of the Catholic Marriage Ritual.* (Collegeville: Liturgical Press 2002).

AUSTIN, G. *Anointing with the Spirit* (Collegeville, MN: Pueblo 1985).

BARNA, George, quoted in *Tim Stafford (August 5, 2002). "The Third Coming of George Barna". Christianity Today Magazine.*

BAUMAN, Zygmunt. "A Sociological Theory of Post-modernity" in *Intimations of Post-modernity.* (London: Routledge, 1992).

BAUMAN, Zygmunt. 'A Sociological Theory of Post-modernity' in *The Postmodern Reader* ed. Drolet, Michael. (London: Routledge 2003).

BAUMAN, Zygmunt. *Liquid Modernity* (Cambridge: Polity Press 2000).

BAUMAN, Zygmunt. Community: Seeking Safety in an Insecure World (Themes for the 21st Century Series) (Cambridge: Polity Press 2000).

BEAUDUIN, Lambert. *Liturgy the Life of the Church*, trans. Virgil Michel (Collegeville MN: The Liturgical Press 1926).

329

BEDE the Venerable. *History of the English Church and People.*

BENTLEY, T. *Learning beyond the Classroom: Education for a changing world.* (London: Routledge 1998).

BERGER, Arthur Asa. *The Portable Postmodernist.* (Walnut Creek: Altamira Press 2003).

BERGER, Peter L., LUCKMANN, Thomas. *The Social Construction of Reality: A Treatise in the Sociology of Knowledge.* (London: Penguin Social Sciences 1991).

BONHOEFFER, Dietrich. *Letters and Papers from Prison,* (first English translation 1953 by SCM Press). This edition translated by Reginald H. Fuller and Frank Clark from *Widerstand und Ergebung: Briefe und Aufzeichnungen aus der Haft.* (Munich: Christian Kaiser Verlag 1970. Touchstone 1997).

BORGMANN, Albert. *Crossing the Postmodern Divide,* (Chicago: University of Chicago Press 1992).

BOTTERY, Mike, "Education and Globalisation: Redefining the Role of the Educational Professional". *Educational Review* 58.1 February 2006. 95-113.

BOULDING, Maria. *The Coming of God.* (London: SPCK 1982).

BOYS, Mary. *Maps and visions: educating in faith.* (Lima, Ohio: Academic Renewal Press 1989).

BOXALL, Ian. *The Books of the New Testament.* (London: SCM Press 2008).

BROWN, Raymond E. et al., eds., *The New Jerome Biblical Commentary* (Englewood Cliffs NJ: Prentice-Hall 1990).

BRUEGGEMANN, Walther. *Texts under Negotiation: The Bible and Postmodern Imagination* (Minneapolis: Fortress Press 1993).

BUGNINI, Annibale. *The Reform of the Liturgy 1948-1975* (Collegeville, MN: The Liturgical Press 1990).

CATECHETICAL COMMISSION OF THE UKRAINIAN CATHOLIC CHURCH. *Catechetical Directory of the Ukrainian Catholic Church.* (Lviv: Svichado Publishers 2000).

CCCB. Canadian Conference of Catholic Bishops. *Our Place in Worship.* (Ottawa, ON: Publications Service CCCB 1999).

CASEL, Odo. *Das Christliche Kultmysterium*, 3rd ed. (Regensburg: Pustet 1948) 102; cited in Hall, *We Have the Mind of Christ.*

CASEL, Odo. *Das christliche Kultmysterium*, 4th revised and expanded ed. by B. Neunheuser (Regensberg: Pustet, 1960), 29; English translation: *The Mystery of Christian Worship* (Westminster, Md.: Newman, 1962).

CASEL, Odo. "The Mystery of Worship," an excerpt from *The Mystery of Christian Worship and Other Writings,* in Vogel, Dwight W. ed., *Primary Sources of Liturgical Theology: A Reader* (Collegeville, MN: Liturgical Press 2000).

CATHOLIC BISHOPS' CONFERENCE OF ENGLAND AND WALES. *The Parish Church: principles of liturgical design and reordering.* (London: Catholic Truth Service, 1984).

CATHOLIC BISHOPS' CONFERENCE OF ENGLAND AND WALES. *Order of Christian Marriage.* (London: Pastoral Liturgy Committee, Bishops' Conference of England and Wales 1992).

CATHOLIC BISHOPS' CONFERENCE OF ENGLAND AND WALES. *The Sign We Give: Report from the Working Party on Collaborative Ministry.* (Chelmsford: Matthew James Publishing 1995).

CATHOLIC BISHOPS' CONFERENCE OF ENGLAND AND WALES. *Religious Education Curriculum Directory.* (Chelmsford: Matthew James. 1996).

CATHOLIC BISHOPS' CONFERENCE OF ENGLAND AND WALES. *On The Threshold.* The Report of the Bishops' Conference Working Party on Sacramental Initiation. (Chelmsford: Matthew James 2000).

CATHOLIC BISHOPS' CONFERENCE OF ENGLAND AND WALES. *Consecrated for Worship. A Directory on Church Building.* (London: Catholic Truth Society 2006).

CATHOLIC EDUCATION SERVICE. *The Common Good in Education.* (London: CES 1997).

CATHOLIC EDUCATION SERVICE. *The Catholic Partnership for Lifelong Learning.* (Chelmsford: Matthew James. 1999).

CATHOLIC EDUCATION SERVICE. *On the Way to Life: Contemporary Culture and Theological Development as a Framework for Catholic Education, Catechesis and Formation.* A Study by The Heythrop Institute for Religion, Ethics and Public Life. (London: CES 2005).

CHALLEEN, Dennis. *Making It Right: A Common Sense Approach to Criminal Justice* (New York: Melius & Peterson 1986).

CHAUVET, Louis-Marie. *Symbol and Sacrament. A Sacramental Reinterpretation of Christian Existence*, trans. Patrick Madigan and Madeleine Beaumont (Collegeville MN: Liturgical Press/A Pueblo Book 1995).

CHUPUNGCO, Anscar J. *Liturgies of the Future: The Process and Methods of Inculturation* (New York: Paulist 1989).

CHUPUNGCO, Anscar J. "Baptism, Marriage and Funeral Rites: Principles and Criteria for Inculturation," in *Baptism, Rites of Passage and Culture*, edited by S. Anita Stauffer (Geneva: Lutheran World Federation 1998).

CHUPUNGCO, Anscar J. *Liturgical Inculturation: Sacramentals, Religiosity and Catechesis* (Collegeville: The Liturgical Press 1992)

CHUPUNGCO, Anscar J. "The Theological Principle of Adaptation," Dwight Vogel. Ed., *Primary Sources of Liturgical Theology: A Reader* (Collegeville, MN: Liturgical Press 2000)

COLLINS, John N., *Deacons and the Church: Making Connections Between Old and New.* (Leominster: Gracewing 2008).

CONFERENCE DES ÉVEQUES DE FRANCE. *Proposer la foi dans la société actuelle, III. Lettres aux catholiques de France.* (Paris : Les Editions du Cerf 1996).

COOMBS, P. H. and AHMED, M. *Attacking Rural Poverty. How non-formal education can help*, (Baltimore: John Hopkins University Press 1974).

CUMMINGS, Owen. *Deacons and the Church.* (Mahwah NJ: Paulist Press 2004).

DENZINGER, H. and SCHÖNMETZER A. *Enchiridion Symbolorum Definitionum Et Declarationum De Rebus Fidei Et Morum.* (DS) (New York: Herder 1957).

DERRIDA, Jacques. "Letter to a Japanese Friend" *Derrida and Différance*, ed. David Wood and Robert Bernasconi, (Warwick: Parousia 1985).

DERRIDA, Jacques. "Deconstruction and the Other," in Richard Kearney, *Dialogues with Contemporary Continental thinkers: The Phenomenological Heritage* (Manchester: Manchester University Press, 1984).

DIOCESE OF ARUNDEL & BRIGHTON. *Preparing Together; A Reflection and Discussion Programme Offered to Parish Communities in November 2002.* Diocese of Arundel & Brighton Pastoral Service. www.dabnet. org/docs.htm

DRUCKER, P. *The Age of Discontinuity; Guidelines to Our Changing Society.* (New York: Harper and Row 1969).

DRUCKER, Peter F. *Managing for the Future.* (Oxford: Butterworth-Heinemann 1993)

DUJARIER, Michel. *A History of the Catechumenate: The First Six Centuries.* (New York: William H Sadlier 1979).

DUJARIER, Michael. *The Rites of Christian Initiation.* (New York: Wm H Sadlier, Inc 1979).

ELIOT, T. S. Collected Poems 1909-1962. (New York: Harcourt, Brace & World 1970).

ERAUT, M. 'Non-formal learning, implicit learning and tacit knowledge in professional work' in Coffield F. *The Necessity of Informal Learning*, (Bristol: The Policy Press 2000).

FAIST, Thomas. 'Social Citizenship in the European Union: Nested Membership.' *Journal of Common Market Studies*. (Oxford: Blackwell Publishers 2001).

FINGARETTE, Herbert. *Confucius -The Secular as Sacred* (New York: Harper Torchbooks 1972).

FOXE, John. The historye of Doctour Rowland Tailour, whiche suffred for the truth of Gods woord, vnder the tiranny of the Romayne Byshop. Anno. 1555. the. 9. day of February in *Book of Martyrs*. Book 11 p.1693 in 1570 edition. (*Foxe's Book of Martyrs Variorum Edition: Online version 1.1 – Summer 2006*). http://www.hrionline.ac.uk/johnfoxe/

FREIRE, Paulo. Education, Liberation and the Church. *Theological Perspectives on Christian Education. A Reader on Theology and Christian Education*. Ed. Jeff Astley, Leslie J. Francis and Colin Crowder (Grand Rapids, Michigan: Gracewing 1996).

FREIRE, Paulo. *Pedagogy of the Oppressed*. (London: Continuum 2001).

GAILLARDETZ, Richard R. "In Service of Communion: A Trinitarian Foundation for Christian Ministry" *Worship* 67.5 (1993).

GALLAGHER, James, SDB. *Soil for the Seed*. (Great Wakering: McCrimmons 2001).

GORRINGE, Timothy. *God's Just Vengeance*. (New York: Cambridge University Press 1996).

GREELEY, Andrew. *The Catholic Myth*. (New York; Macmillan Publishing Company, 1990).

GREELEY, Andrew M. *The Catholic Imagination*. (Berkeley: University of California Press, 2000).

GROOME, Thomas H. *Christian Religious Education: Sharing Our Story and Vision.* (San Francisco: Jossey Bass 1999).

GUARDINI, Romano. *The Spirit of the Liturgy,* trans. Ada Lane (New York: Crossroad Publishing Company 1998) First published in German in 1918.

HAHNENBERG, Edward P. *Ministry: A Relational Approach* (New York: Crossroad Publishing Company 2003).

HALL, M. Jerome. *We Have the Mind of Christ: The Holy Spirit and Liturgical Memory in The Thought of Edward J. Kilmartin.* (Collegeville, MN: Liturgical Press 2001).

HAUGHTON, Rosemary. *Images for change: The Transformation of Society.* (New York: Paulist 1997).

HEBBLETHWAITE, Peter. *Paul VI: The First Modern Pope* (New York: Paulist Press 1993).

HILKERT. Mary Catherine. *Naming Grace: Preaching and the Sacramental Imagination.* (Continuum 1997).

HOFINGER, Johannes. *The art of teaching Christian doctrine.* (Notre Dame: University of Notre Dame Press 1957).

HUMFREY, Peter. *Confirmation: A Community Preparation.* (London: Geoffrey Chapman 1985).

INTERNATIONAL COMMISSION ON ENGLISH IN THE LITURGY (ICEL). *The Rite of Penance.* (London: J F Neale 1974).

INTERNATIONAL COMMITTEE ON ENGLISH IN THE LITURGY (ICEL). General Instruction of the Roman Missal (*Institutio Generalis Missalis Romani. 2002)* (London: Catholic Truth Society 2005).

IRISH BISHOPS' CONFERENCE. *Rite of Penance.* (Dublin: Veritas 1976).

IRWIN, Kevin W. *Models of the Eucharist.* (New York/Mahwah, NJ: Paulist Press 2005).

ISPC. *Catéchèse en Mutation I et II*, Les Actes du Colloque de l'ISPC in Catéchèse: Revue de pastorale et de formation 172 3/2003, 173 4/2003. (Paris: CNER 2003).

JAMESON, Fredric. "Postmodernism and Consumer Society," in Foster, Hal, ed., *Postmodern Culture* (London: Bay Press 1985).

JARVIS, P. *The Sociology of Adult and Continuing Education*, (Beckenham: Croom Helm 1985).

JOHNSON, Barbara. *The Critical Difference*. (Baltimore: John Hopkins University Press 1981).

JOSEPHUS, Titus Flavius. *The Jewish War*.

KAVANAGH, Aidan. *The Shape of Baptism: The Rite of Christian Initiation* (Collegeville, MN: The Liturgical Press 1978/1991).

KELLNER, Douglas. *Globalization and the Postmodern Turn*. Graduate School of Education & Information Studies. (Los Angeles: University of California 1998).

KIDD, J. R. *How Adults Learn* (Englewood Cliffs, N.J.: Prentice Hall Regents 1978).

KLIEBART, H. M. *The Struggle for the American Curriculum 1893-1958*, (New York: Routledge 1987).

KNOWLES, Malcolm. *History, philosophy, and nature of adult education*. (Fort Lauderdale: Nova University, Center for Higher Education 1980).

KOTTAK, Conrad Phillip. *Windows on Humanity*. (New York: McGraw Hill 2005).

LAKELAND, Paul. *Post-modernity: Christian Identity in a Fragmented Age*. (Minneapolis: Fortress Press 1997).

LEADBEATER, Charles. *Living on Thin Air. The new economy*. (London: Penguin 2000).

LEWINSKI, Ron. "Recovering Christian Mystagogy for Contemporary Churches," in *Before and After Baptism*, ed. James A. Wilde (Chicago: Liturgy Training Publications 1988).

LEWIS, Bernard. *Islam and the West*. (New York: Oxford University Press, 1993).

LUCEY-ROPER, Michelle M. *The Visio Baronti in its early medieval context*. (Oxford: University of Oxford 2000).

LYNCH, William F. *Christ and Apollo: The Dimensions of the Literary Imagination* (New York: New American Library 1960).

MANNION, Gerard. *Ecclesiology and Post-modernity: Questions for the Church in Our Time*. (Collegeville, Minnesota: the Liturgical Press 1989).

MARION, Jean-Luc. "The Present and the Gift," in *God Without Being*, trans. Thomas A. Carlson (Chicago: University of Chicago Press 1991).

MARION, Jean-Luc. "The Gift of a Presence," in *Prolegomena to Charity*, trans. Stephen Lewis (New York: Fordham University Press 2002)

MARTIMORT, A.G. *The Church at Prayer, Vol. 1 Principles of the Liturgy* (London Geoffrey Chapman 1983).

MERTON, Thomas. *Sign of Jonas* (New York: Harcourt and Brace 1979).

MILLER, Vincent J. *Consuming Religion: Christian Faith and Practice in a Consumer Culture*. (New York: Continuum 2004).

MINISTRY OF RECONSTRUCTION (1919) *Final Report of the Adult Education Committee*, London: HMSO. 410 pages. Republished by University of Nottingham Department of Adult Education. Abridged version with an introduction by R. D. Waller published (1956) as *A Design for Democracy*. (London: Max Parrish 1919).

MOHRMAN, C. "*Sacramentum* dans les plus anciens textes chrétiens," in her *Etudes sur le latin des chrétiens* 1 (Storia e letteratura 65; Rome: Edizioni di storia e letteratura. 1958).

MOLTMANN, Jurgen. *Religion, Revolution and the Future,* (New York, Charles Scribner's Sons, 1969).

MORRIS, Thomas H. *The RCIA: Transforming the Church – A Resource for Pastoral Implementation.* (New York: Paulist Press 1997).

MURPHY-O'CONNOR, Jerome. Commentary on I Corinthians, 11:17-34 in Brown, Raymond E. et al., eds., *The New Jerome Biblical Commentary* (Englewood Cliffs NJ: Prentice-Hall 1990).

NIDA, Eugene. *Message and Mission.* (New York: Harper & Brothers 1960).

NIDA, Eugene. *Theory and Practice of Translation.* (Leiden: Brill 1969).

NORBERG, Dag. Medieval Latin After the Year 1000. *Manuel pratique de latin médiéval* (Paris, 1980), English translation by R.H.Johnson.

NOUWEN, Henri J. M. *The Wounded Healer* (Garden City: Image Books 1972).

O'MEARA, Thomas F. Foreword to Karl Rahner and Karl Lehmann, *Kerygma and Dogma,* trans. William Glen-Doepel (New York: Herder and Herder, 1969).

OSBORNE, Kenan B., *Christian Sacraments in a Post-modern World: A Theology for the Third Millennium.* (New York/Mahwah, NJ: Paulist Press 1999).

OSBORNE, Kenan B. *Ministry: Lay Ministry in the Roman Catholic Church: Its History and Theology.* (Paulist Press International, U.S. 1993).

OSBORNE, Kenan B. *The Permanent Diaconate: Its History and Place in the Sacrament of Orders.* (New York: Paulist Press 2007).

PECKLERS Keith F. *Liturgy in a Post-modern World* (New Century Theology) (New York/London: Continuum June 2003).

POSTMAN, Neil. *Building a Bridge to the Eighteenth Century: How the Past Can Improve Our Future* (New York: Alfred A. Knopf 1999).

POWER, David N. "Cult to Culture: the Mediating Role of Theology," in *Worship: Culture and Theology* (Washington, D.C.: Pastoral Press 1990).

POWER, David. *The Eucharistic Mystery*. (New York: Crossroad 1992).

POWER, David N. Foreword to *Celebrating Jesus Christ in Africa: Liturgy and Inculturation* (Maryknoll: Orbis 1998).

POWER, David. *Sacrament: The Language of God's Giving*. (New York: Crossroad, 1999).

PURNELL, Patrick, SJ. *Our Faith Story*. (London: Harper Collins, 1985).

RAHNER, Karl. "The Word and the Eucharist," *Theological Investigations* 4 (London: Burns & Oates 1968).

RAMSHAW, Gail. *Liturgical Language: Making it Metaphoric. Keeping it Inclusive* (Collegeville, MN: Liturgical Press 1996)

ROEBBEN Bert and WARREN Michael ed., *Religious Education as Practical Theology*. (Leuven: Peeters 2001).

THE ROMAN MISSAL (Rous Lench, Worcestershire: John F. Neale 1972).

RONFELDT, David. *In Search of How Societies Work: Tribes – The First and Forever Form*. (Rand Pardee Centre WR-433-RPC 2006). http://www.rand.org/pubs/working_papers/2007/RAND_WR433. pdf

RORTY, Richard. *Contingency, Irony, Solidarity*. (Cambridge: Cambridge University Press (1989).

SADIKI, L. *The Search for Arab Democracy: Discourses and Counter-Discourses* (India: C. Hurst & Co. Ltd 2004) 122.

SAID, Edward W. *Orientalism*. (London: Routledge & Kegan Paul 1978).

SCHOONENBERG, Piet. "Tegenwoordigheid," *Verbum* 31 (1964); English translation in FitzPatrick, P. J. *In Breaking of Bread,* (Cambridge: University Press 2008).

SEASOLTZ, R Kevin. *A Sense of the Sacred.* (New York/London: Continuum 2005).

SERVICE, Elman R. *Origins of the State and Civilization: The Process of Cultural Evolution.* (New York: W. W. Norton and Company 1975).

SHAPIRO Michael J. *Globalization and the Politics of Discourse.* (Durham NC: Duke University 2006). http://muse.jhu.edu/demo/social_text/ v017/17.3shapiro.html

SHEPHERD, Gregory J .ed., *Exposition of José Acosta's Historia Natural y Moral de las Indias 1590: The Emergence of an Anthropological Vision of Colonial Latin America* (Lewiston: The Edwin Mellen Press 1984).

SHORTER, Aylward. *Toward a Theology of Incultura*tion (Maryknoll: Orbis Books 1988).

SPIVAK, Gayatri Chakravorty. "Can the Subaltern Speak?" Cary Nelson and Lawrence Grossberg, eds., *Marxism and the Interpretation of Culture (Communications & Culture)* (Basingstoke: Palgrave Macmillan 1988).

STEWART, T. A. *Intellectual Capital: The New Wealth of Organizations.* (New York: Doubleday 1999).

TAILOUR, Rowland. The historye of Doctour Rowland Tailour, whiche suffred for the truth of Gods woord, vnder the tiranny of the Romayne Byshop. Anno. 1555. the. 9. day of February in *Book of Martyrs,* Book 11 p.1693 in 1570 edition. (*Foxe's Book of Martyrs Variorum Edition: Online version 1.1 – Summer 2006*).

TENNANT, Mark. *Psychology and Adult Learning.* (London: Routledge1997)

TRACY, David. *The Analogical Imagination: Christian Theology and the Culture of Pluralism.* (New York: Crossroad, 1981).

(UNITED STATES) NATIONAL CONFERENCE OF BISHOPS. *Environment and Art in Catholic Worship* (Chicago: Liturgical Training Publications 1978; 1993).

USCCB. United States Conference of Catholic Bishops. *Seeds of Promise, Seeds of Faith: Vision and Themes of the General Directory for Catechesis.* (United States Conference of Catholic Bishops, Department of Education Resource. RCL, 2001).

USCCB (Formerly NCCB/USCC). United States Conference of Catholic Bishops. *Built of Living Stones: Art, Architecture, and Worship.* (Washington: USCCB 2000).

USCCB. United States Conference of Catholic Bishops. *Co-Workers in the Vineyard of the Lord: A Resource for Guiding the Development of Lay Ecclesial Ministry.* (Washington: USCCB, 2006). http://www.usccb.org/laity/laymin/co-workers.pdf

VILLEPELET, Denis. *L'Avenir de Catéchèse.* (Paris: Les Editions de L'Atelier 2003).

VORGRIMLER, Herbert. *Sacramental Theology.* (Collegeville: The Liturgical Press 1992).

WEBER, Max, *Economy and Society: An Outline of Interpretive Sociology*, Guenther Roth and Claus Wittich, eds., (Berkeley: University of California Press, [1922, 136–137] 1978),

WESTERHOFF, John H. *Will Our Children Have Faith?* (London: Thomas More Press 2000).

WALTON, Janet. *Feminist Liturgy: A Matter of Justice.* (Collegeville, MN: Liturgical Press 2000)

YEAXLEE, B. A. *Lifelong Education.* (London: Cassell 1929).

ZIMMERMAN, Joyce. *Liturgy and Hermeneutics.* (Collegeville MN: Liturgical Press 1999).

ARTICLES

ALLEN, John L. Doubts about Dialogue: Encounter with Other Religions Runs Up Against the Vatican's Hard Doctrinal Realities. *National Catholic Reporter*, 27 August 1999.

ASHWIN, Angela. Spirituality and Corporate worship – Separate Worlds or Vitally Connected? *Worship* 75:2 (2001).

BEALL, Stephen. "Translation and Inculturation in the Catholic Church." *Adoremus* II 6 October 1996.

BOTTA, Mario. Architetture del Sacro. *Church Building* 96 (November-December 2005).

BUTORAC, Nina. The Sacramental Imagination and Catholic Literature. See http://www.alyosha.com/si/si.html 19 March 2007

CASTRILLON HOYOS, Cardinal Dario. The Fundamental Importance of Catechesis. An Address given by Cardinal Castrillon Hoyos, prefect of the Cong. for the Clergy on November 14, 1998 to those participating in a seminar on implementing the 1997 GDC. www.catholicculture.org/library/view.cfm?id=791&repos=1

CELICHOWSKI, John. Meditation and Metanoia: Using Principles of Alternative Dispute Resolution to Reform the Rite of Penance. *Worship* 76:3 (2002).

CHUPUNGCO, Anscar. Inculturation and Organic Progression of the Liturgy. *Ecclesia Orans* 7 (1990/1).

CIFERNI, Andrew D. "The Ceremonial of Bishops: Challenges and Opportunities." *Assembly* 17 (September 1991).

CURRAN, Charles. "Risks of Theology" *Pastoral Review* July 2006

DOOLEY, Catherine. Liturgical Catechesis: Mystagogy, Marriage or Misnomer? *Worship* 66.5 (1992)

GAILLARDETZ Richard R. In Service of Communion: A Trinitarian Foundation for Christian Ministry. *Worship* 67.5 (1993).

GAILLARDETZ, Richard R. North American Culture and the Liturgical Life of the Church: The Separation of the Quests for Transcendence and Community. *Worship* 68:5 (1994).

GREEN, J. Androgogy: Teaching adults. In B. Hoffman (Ed.), *Encyclopedia of Educational Technology.* (1998). http://coe.sdsu.edu/eet/Articles/andragogy/start.htm

GROOME, Thomas. Chapter Three: "What's It All About?" – Taking a Sacramental View *What Makes Us Catholic: Eight Gifts For Life.* Notes for Reading Circles In Preparation for the Marianist Universities Meetings June 7-10, 2004.

GUARDINI, Romano. "A Letter from Romano Guardini," *Herder Correspondence* 1:1 (Special issue 64).

HANSEN, Ron. Faith and Fiction, *America,* vol.178:11 (April 1998).

HEARTNEY, Eleanor. "Blood, Sex, and Blasphemy - The Catholic Imagination in Contemporary Art". *New Art Examiner.*

HOFINGER, Johannes. Evangelization by the Celebration of the Liturgical Feasts. *Worship* 10 (1955).

HORRELL, David. Converging Ideologies: Berger and Luckmann and the Pastoral Epistles. *Journal for the Study of the New Testament,* Vol. 15, No. 50 (1993).

HORRELL, David. Leadership Patterns and the Development of Ideology in Early Christianity. Sociology of Religion, Vol. 58, (1997).

IRWIN, Sarah. The Religiophoneme: Liturgy and Some Uses of Deconstruction. *Worship* 80:3 (2006).

JAGESSAR, Michael and Burns, Stephen. Fragments of a Postcolonial Perspective on Christian Worship. *Worship* 80.5 (2006).

JOHNSON, Clare V. The Children's Eucharistic Prayers: A Model of Liturgical Inculturation *Worship* 75:3 (2001).

JOHNSON, Maxwell E. Contemporary Study of Christian Initiation. *Worship* 75:1 (2001).

JUNGMANN, Josef. "The Defeat of Teutonic Ariansim and the Revolution in Religious Culture in the Early Middle Ages," in *Pastoral Liturgy* (New York: Herder and Herder 1962).

KASSAM, Tazim R. "Embracing Disability in Teaching Religion," (editorial) in *Spotlight on Teaching* 20 (May 2005).

KAVANAGH, Aidan. Unfinished and Unbegun: The Rite of Christian Initiation of Adults. *Worship* 53:4 (1979).

KEENAN, Joseph. Temples and Churches. *Worship* 68:3 (1994).

KELLEHER, Margaret Mary. Liturgy: An Ecclesial Act of Worship. *Worship* 59 (1985).

KOESTER, Anne Y. Is There Life After the Triduum? *Worship* 74.2 (2000).

LATHROP, Gordon. The Reforming Gospels: A Liturgical Theologian Looks again at Eucharistic Origins. *Worship* 83:3 (2009).

LAU, Markus. "Die *Legio X Fretensis* und der Besessene von Gerasa. Anmerkungen zur Zahlenangabe "ungefähr Zweitausend" (Mk 5:13)", *Biblica* Vol. 88 (2007).

MARLOWE, Michael. 'Against the Theory of 'Dynamic Equivalence'. (Bible Research: Internet Resources for Students of Scripture. Revised, May 2009). http://www.bible-researcher.com/dynamic-equivalence.html

MCBRIEN. Richard P. "The Church Is 'Catholic' Because It's Sacramental." *National Catholic Reporter* (January 15, 1993).

MCPARTLAND, Paul. Church and Communion. *Priest and People.* (August 2003).

MICHEL, Virgil, Infidelity in the Church, *Orate Fratres* 9 (October 1935).

MITCHELL. Nathan D., The Amen Corner *Worship* 68:2 (1994), 73:4 (1999), 73: 6 (1999), 74:1 (2000), 74:4 (2000), 74.5 (2000), 77:2 (2003), 79.2 (2005), 78:2 (2004), 80:3 (2006). 80:5 (2006).

O'CONNELL, Dan. RE in the Public Sphere. *The Furrow* July 2006.

PELLETIER, Amanda M. Catechesis and Conquest: Communion? *Worship* 80:6 (2006).

QUINN, Frank. Confirmation Reconsidered: Rite and Meaning. *Worship* 59 (1985).

RATZINGER, Joseph Cardinal. Sermon. 18 April 2005. http://www.vatican.va/gpII/documents/homily-pro-eligendo-pontifice_20050418_en.html

RONFELDT, David. *In Search of How Societies Work: Tribes – The First and Forever Form* (Rand Pardee Centre WR-433-RPC 2006).

ROSIER, Veronica. The Baptismal Catechumenate in the *General Directory for Catechesis (1997)*. *Worship* 73.2 (1999).

RUSH Orm. "Full, Conscious and Active Participation: Formation in the Sacramental Imagination". Delivered at Liturgical Symposium "Vatican Council II *Sacrosanctum Concilium* 1963-2003", Brisbane 4 December 2003.

SAID, Edward W. 'Islam Through Western Eyes,' *The Nation* April 26, 1980, first posted online January 1, 1998, accessed November 13, 2007.

SALIERS, Don. Christian Liturgy as Eschatological Art. *Arts* 11 (1990).

SANDERS, Theresa. "The Otherness of God and the Bodies of Others," *The Journal of Religion* 76:4 (1996).

SCHEPERS, Maury. An Integral Spirituality of the Paschal Mystery. *Worship* 75.2 (2001).

SEASOLTZ, R. Kevin. Artistic Images of Jesus: A Challenge to Liturgists, Religious Educators, and Theologians. *Worship* 73:1 (1999).

SERRA, Dominic E. New Observations About the Scrutinies of the Elect in Early Roman Practice *Worship* 80:6 (2006).

SHEERIN, Daniel J. *The Eucharist*, Message of the Fathers of the Church, Volume 7 (Wilmington DE: Michael Glazier 1986).

SMITH, M. K. (1996; 1999) 'Andragogy', *the encyclopaedia of informal education*, http://www.infed.org/lifelonglearning/b-andra.htm

SMITH, Mark K. 'Informal learning', *the encyclopaedia of informal education*. (1999, 2006) www.infed.org/biblio/inf-lrn.htm

SOKAL, Alan. 'Taking Evidence Seriously'. *The Guardian*. 28 February 2008. http://www.physics.nyu.edu/faculty/sokal/guardian_Feb_08.pdf

STACKHOUSE, Max. "The Theological Challenge of Globalization," *Christian Century* 106 (December 1989).

TABER, Jay. Institutional Memory as Community Safeguard. *Report: Center for World Indigenous Studies* (undated).

TURNER, Paul. Forum: Confusion over Confirmation. *Worship* 71.6 (1997).

TURNER, Paul. The Origins of Confirmation: An Analysis of Aidan Kavanagh's Hypothesis. *Worship*, 65:4 (1991).

VICKERY G. & WURZBURG G., Flexible firms, skills and employment, *OECD Observer*, (1996) no. 202.

VILLEPELET, Denis. « Catéchèse en mutation I : Les défis actuels de la tâche catéchétique en France ». *Catéchèse : Revue de pastora* Villepelet, Denis. « Catéchèse en mutation I : Les défis actuels de la tâche catéchétique en France ». *Catéchèse : Revue de pastorale et de formation*. 172 3/2003.*le et de formation*. 172 3/2003.

VOSKO, Richard S. A House for the Church: Structures for Public Worship in a New Millennium. *Worship* 74.3 (2000).

WALKER, Paul. Leeds Cathedral Reordering. *Church Building* 104 (March -April 2007).

WALSH, Christopher J. Minding Our Language: Issues of Liturgical Language Arising in Revision. *Worship* 74.6 (2000).

WEDIG, Mark E. Evangelization, Inculturation and the RCIA. *Worship* 76:6.

WESTERHOFF, John H. III. *Will Our Children Have Faith?* (New York: Morehouse Publishing 2002).

WINKLER, G. Confirmation or Chrismation? A Study in Comparative Liturgy. *Worship* 58 (1984).

WINDSCHUTTLE, Keith. Edward Said's "Orientalism" revisited. *The New Criterion* (January 17, 1999).

DOCUMENTS OF THE MAGISTERIUM

AA: Second Vatican Council, Decree on the Apostolate of the Laity, *Apostolicam Actuositatem* (18 November, 1965).

ACCC: International Council for Catechesis. *Adult Catechesis in the Christian Community: Some Principles and Guidelines.* (Vatican: Libreria Editrice Vaticana 1990).

AG: Second Vatican Council, Decree on Missionary Activity in the Church *Ad Gentes* (7 December 1965).

CD: Second Vatican Council, Decree on the Pastoral Office of Bishops in the Church *Christus Dominus* (28 October 1965).

CCC: *Catechism of the Catholic Church* (11 October 1992).

CCC: *Catechism of the Catholic Church*, (London: Continuum 2002).

CIC: *Codex Iuris Canonici* (25 January 1983).

ChL: John Paul II, Post-synodal Apostolic Exhortation, *Christifideles Laici* (30 December 1988).

COINCATI: International Council for Catechesis, *Adult Catechesis in the Christian Community*, (Libreria Editrice Vaticana, 1990).

CLP: On The Translation Of Liturgical Texts For Celebrations With A Congregation *Comme le prévoit*. Consilium for Implementing the Constitution on the Sacred Liturgy (1969).

CT: John Paul II, Apostolic Exhortation. Catechesis in Our Time. *Catechesi Tradendae* (16 October 1979).

DCG (1971): Sacred Congregation for the Clergy, General Catechetical Directory, *Ad normam decreti* (11 April 1971).

DJ (2000); Declaration *"Dominus Jesus"* On the Unicity and Salvific Universality of Jesus Christ and the Church. Congregation for the Doctrine of the Faith. (6 August 2005)

DV: Second Vatican Council, Dogmatic Constitution on Divine Revelation *Dei Verbum* (18 November 1965).

EA: John Paul II, Post-synodal Apostolic Exhortation *Ecclesia in Africa* (14 September 1995).

EN: Paul VI, Apostolic Exhortation *Evangelii Nuntiandi* (8 December 1975).

EV: John Paul II, Encyclical Letter, *Evangelium Vitae* (25 March 1995).

FC: John Paul II, Post-synodal Apostolic Exhortation *Familaris Consortio* (22 November 1981).

GDC: Sacred Congregation for the Clergy. General Directory for Catechesis. (11 August 1997).

GE: Second Vatican Council, Declaration on Education, *Gravissimum Educationis* (28 October 1965).

GS: Second Vatican Council, Pastoral Constitution: The Church in the Modern World. *Gaudium et Spes* (7 December 1965).

LA: On the Use of Vernacular Languages in the Publication of the Books of the Roman Liturgy *Liturgiam Authenticam* (LA) *Fifth Instruction*

"For the Right Implementation of the Constitution on the Sacred Liturgy of the Second Vatican Council" (Sacrosanctum Concilium, art. 36). Congregation for Divine Worship and the Discipline of the Sacraments (28 March 2001).

LE: John Paul II, Encyclical Letter: *Laborem Exercens* (14 September 1981).

LG: Second Vatican Council, Dogmatic Constitution on the Church *Lumen Gentium* (21 November 1964).

NA: Second Vatican Council, Decree on the relationship of the Church with non-Christian Religions, *Nostra Aetate* (28 October 1965).

NMI: Pope John Paul II. Apostolic Letter: At the beginning of the new millennium. *Novo Millennio Ineunte.* (6 January 2001).

OCF: Order of Christian Funerals (London: Geoffrey Chapman 1990).

ODC: Congregation for Divine Worship and the Discipline of the Sacraments. Order for the dedication of a church an altar. *Ordo dedicationis ecclesiae et altaris.* (1989).

PB: Sacred Congregation for Divine Worship. Directory for Masses With Children. *Pueros Baptizatos* (November 1, 1973).

PO: Second Vatican Council, Decree on Priestly Life and Ministry *Presbyterorum Ordinis* (7 December 1965).

PP: Paul VI, Encyclical Letter *Populorum Progressio* (26 March 1967).

RH: John Paul II, Encyclical Letter *Redemptor Hominis* (4 March 1979).

RCIA: Rite of Christian Initiation of Adults. *Ordo Initiationis Christianae Adultorum,* (RCIA) (1972).

RM: John Paul II, Encyclical Letter *Redemptoris Missio* (7 December 1990).

SC: Second Vatican Council, Constitution on the Sacred Liturgy *Sacrosanctum Concilium* (4 December 1963).

SRS: John Paul II, Encyclical letter *Sollicitudo Rei Socialis* (30 December 1987).

TMA: John Paul II, Apostolic Exhortation, *Tertio Millennio Adveniente* (10 November 1994).

TPAC: Pontifical Council for Culture. "Toward a Pastoral Approach to Culture" (23 May 1999).

UR: Second Vatican Council, Decree on Ecumenism *Unitatis Redintegratio* (21 November 1964).

UUS: John Paul II, Encyclical Letter *Ut Unum Sint* (25 May 1995).

VL: Congregation for Divine Worship and the Discipline of the Sacraments. Inculturation and the Roman Liturgy *Varietates Legitimae* (VL) *Fourth Instruction for the Right Application of the Conciliar Constitution on the Liturgy (Nos. 37-40)* (29 March 1994).

VS: John Paul II, Encyclical Letter *Veritatis Splendor* (6 August 1993).

FATHERS OF THE CHURCH

St Andrew of Crete. *Addresses.*

St Augustine. *Sermones.*

St. Basil the Great. *Homilies.*

Bede the Venerable. *History of the English Church and People.*

Eusebius. *Demonstratio evangelica.*

Origen. *Homily on Exodus.*

St. Gregory of Nyssa. *Accurate Exposition of the Canticle of Canticles.*

St. Ignatius of Antioch. *Letter to the Magnesians.*

St Justin. *Dialogus cum Tryphone.*

St. Maximus of Turin. *Sermons.*

Melito of Sardis. *Peri Pascha ("Concerning the Passover").*

Notes

INTRODUCTION

1   Eliot, T. S. *Collected Poems 1909-1962*. (New York: Harcourt, Brace & World 1970).

2   GDC: Sacred Congregation for the Clergy. General Directory for Catechesis. (11 August 1997).

3   GS: Second Vatican Council. Pastoral Constitution: The Church in the Modern World. *Gaudium et Spes*. (1965) 62.

4   See http://www.ihabhassan.com/postmodernism_to_postmodernity.htm

5   John Paul II, Apostolic Exhortation. Catechesis in Our Time *Catechesi Tradendae*. (16 October 1979).

CHAPTER 1   MODERNITY

6   Gaillardetz Richard R. In Service of Communion: A Trinitarian Foundation for Christian Ministry. *Worship* 67.5 (1993) 426.

7   Berger, Peter L., Luckmann, Thomas. *The Social Construction of Reality: A Treatise in the Sociology of Knowledge* (London: Penguin Social Sciences 1991).

8   For a useful Glossary of Terms see http://www.sagepub.com/upm-data/13300_Glossary.pdf

9   Ibid., 65-70.

10   Ibid., 71-78.

11   Ibid., 79-84.

12   Ibid., 130.

13   Ibid., 132.

14   Ibid., 134.

15   Ibid., 134.

16   Ibid., 139.

17   Ibid., 140.

18   Ibid., 143.

19   Ibid., 154.

20   Ibid., 163.

21   Ibid., 173.

22   Ibid., 174.

23   Ibid., 179.

24   Horrell, David. Converging Ideologies: Berger and Luckmann and the Pastoral Epistles. *Journal for the Study of the New Testament*, Vol. 15, No. 50 (1993) 85-103.

25   Horrell, David. Leadership Patterns and the Development of Ideology in Early Christianity. Sociology of Religion, Vol. 58, (1997).

CHAPTER 2   POST-MODERNITY

26   Professor Zygmunt Bauman interviewed by Tony Robertson in *Network Newsletter of the British Sociological Association* Number 83 October 2002 1-3. http://www.britsoc.co.uk/Library/BSANetwork83.pdf

27   See the biography of Zygmunt Bauman at *www.magnespress.co.il/website_en/index.asp?action=author_page&aet_id=1464*

28   See Bauman, Zygmunt, *Liquid Modernity* (Cambridge: Polity Press 2000).

29   Bauman, Zygmunt. 'A Sociological Theory of Post-modernity' in *The Postmodern Reader* ed. Drolet, Michael. (London: Routledge 2003) Chapter 18, pp. 238 ff.

30   Ibid.

31   Ibid.

32   Ibid.

33   Ibid.

34   Ibid.

35   Professor Zygmunt Bauman interviewed by Tony Robertson in Network Newsletter of the British Sociological Association Number 83 October 2002 1-3. http://www.britsoc.co.uk/Library/BSANetwork83.pdf

36   Bauman, Zygmunt. *Community: Seeking Safety in an Insecure World* (Themes for the 21st Century Series) (Cambridge: Polity Press 2000).

37   Ibid.

CHAPTER 3   CHALLENGES

[38]   Shapiro, Michael J. *Globalization and the Politics of Discourse.* (Durham NC: Duke University 2006) 111-127. http://muse.jhu. edu/demo/social_text/v017/17.3shapiro.html

[39]   Kellner, Douglas. *Globalization and the Postmodern Turn.* Graduate School of Education & Information Studies. (Los Angeles: University of California 1998) 8. 28 Mar 09. http://www.gseis. ucla.edu/faculty/kellner/essays/globalizationpostmodernturn. pdf

[40]   Stackhouse, Max. "The Theological Challenge of Globalization," *Christian Century* 106 (December 1989): 468.

[41]   O'Meara, Thomas F. *Foreword to Karl Rahner and Karl Lehmann, Kerygma and Dogma,* trans. William Glen-Doepel (New York: Herder and Herder, 1969), 8.

[42]   This latter repression has a long tradition. During Christianity's earliest encounters with Islam in the ancient world and continuing through the Renaissance, Christian writers avoided using religious markers for Muslims and instead referred to them in ethnic terms: as Saracens, Moors, Tatars, among others. See Lewis, Bernard. *Islam and the West.* (New York: Oxford University Press, 1993) 7.

[43]   Bottery, Mike. "Education and Globalisation: Redefining the Role of the Educational Professional". *Educational Review* 58.1 February 2006. 95-113.

[44]   Ibid., 98.

[45]   Rorty, Richard. *Contingency, Irony, Solidarity.* (Cambridge: Cambridge University Press 1989) 73-74.

[46]   This means that, in order to deal with rights and duties in multiple governance levels if residual and post-national concepts of European citizenship are found wanting, European citizenship should be nested in various sites: regional, state and supra-state

forms of citizenship would function in complementary ways ,
while the associated norms, rules and institutions would be subject
to constant revision and further development on all governance
levels. The concept of nested citizenship may help to overcome
the fruitless dichotomy of Euro-optimism and Euro-pessimism
concerning social policy and citizenship.

[47] See Faist, Thomas. Social Citizenship in the European Union:
Nested Membership. *Journal of Common Market Studies.* (Oxford:
Blackwell Publishers 2001).

[48] Margaret Thatcher in an interview for *Women's Own* published
31 October 1987 http://www.margaretthatcher.org/speeches/
displaydocument.asp?docid=106689

[49] July 18th 2003 http://www.cafod.org.uk/events/
popepaullecture2003report.shtml

[50] See Stewart, T. A. *Intellectual Capital: The New Wealth of Organizations.*
(New York: Doubleday 1999).

[51] See Drucker, P. *The Age of Discontinuity; Guidelines to Our Changing
Society.* (New York: Harper and Row 1969) Chapter 12.

[52] Stewart (1999) 67.

[53] Vickery G. & Wurzburg G., 'Flexible firms, skills and employment',
OECD Observer, 1996 n° 202, 17-21.

[54] Stewart (1999) 189.

[55] Miller, Vincent J. *Consuming Religion: Christian Faith and Practice in a
Consumer Culture.* (New York: Continuum 2004) 228.

[56] John Paul II, Encyclical Letter: *Veritatis Splendor.* (6 August
1993).

[57] Stafford, Tim. "The Third Coming of George Barna." *Christianity
Today* August 2 2002 http://www.christianitytoday.com/ct/
archives/august2002.html 9 November 2007.

[58] Ibid.

[59] Miller (2004), 228.

[60] Mitchell, Nathan D. The Amen Corner. *Worship* 79.2 (2005), 177.

[61] Ibid. 177.

[62] Miller (2004), 30-31

[63] Mitchell (2005), 179.

CHAPTER 4   OPPORTUNITIES

[64] Derrida, Jacques. Letter to a Japanese Friend. *Derrida and Différance*, ed. David Wood and Robert Bernasconi (Warwick: Parousia 1985) 3.

[65] Johnson, Barbara. *The Critical Difference*. (Baltimore: John Hopkins University Press 1981).

[66] See article on Nihilism. http://en.wikipedia.org/wiki/Nihilism 20 June 2009

[67] Sokal, Alan. 'Taking Evidence Seriously'. *The Guardian*. 28 February 2008. http://www.physics.nyu.edu/faculty/sokal/guardian_Feb_08.pdf

[68] Ratzinger, Joseph Cardinal. Sermon. 18 April 2005. http://www.vatican.va/gpII/documents/homily-pro-eligendo-pontifice_20050418_en.html

[69] Derrida, Jacques. "Deconstruction and the Other," in Richard Kearney, *Dialogues with Contemporary Continental thinkers: The Phenomenological Heritage* (Manchester: Manchester University Press, 1984) 123-124.

[70] Irwin, Sarah. The Religiophoneme: Liturgy and Some Uses of Deconstruction. *Worship* 80:3 (2006) 237.

71   Zimmerman, Joyce. *Liturgy and Hermeneutics.* (Collegeville MN: Liturgical Press1999) 12.

72   See Kelleher, Margaret Mary. Liturgy: An Ecclesial Act of Worship. *Worship* 59 (1985) 482.

73   Ibid., 248.

74   Saliers, Don. Christian Liturgy as Eschatological Art. *Arts* 11 (1990) 19.

75   Ibid., 249.

76   Ibid., 250.

77   Ibid., 252.

78   Ibid., 252.

79   Said, Edward W. *Orientalism.* (London: Routledge & Kegan Paul 1978).

80   Windschuttle, Keith. Edward Said's "Orientalism" revisited. *The New Criterion* January 17, 1999.

81   Said, Edward W. Islam Through Western Eyes. *The Nation* April 26, 1980, first posted online January 1, 1998, accessed November 13, 2007.

82   Sadiki, L. *The Search for Arab Democracy: Discourses and Counter-Discourses* (India: C. Hurst & Co. Ltd 2004) 122.

83   Pelletier, Amanda M. Catechesis and Conquest: Communion? *Worship* 80:6 (2006).

84   Shepherd, Gregory J .ed., *Exposition of José Acosta's Historia Natural y Moral de las Indias 1590: The Emergence of an Anthropological Vision of Colonial Latin America* (Lewiston: The Edwin Mellen Press 1984).

85   Pelletier, 505-506.

86   Ibid., 510.

87 Jagessar, Michael and Burns, Stephen. Fragments of a Postcolonial Perspective on Christian Worship. *Worship* 80.5 (2006) 428-452.

88 Beall, Stephen. "Translation and Inculturation in the Catholic Church." *Adoremus* II 6 October 1996. http://www.adoremus. org/1096-Beall.html

89 John Paul II, Encyclical Letter *Redemptoris Missio* (RM). (7 December 1990).

90 For citations see Faith and Cultures in Ethiopia. A Symposium - How to Evangelize Cultures and Inculturate Faith. February 5th to 9th 1996 http://www.vatican.va/roman_curia/pontifical_ councils/cultr/documents/rc_pc_cultr_01061996_doc_ii-1996- ple_en.html See also: Shorter, Aylward. *Toward a Theology of Inculturation*. (Maryknoll, NY, Orbis Books 1988).

91 Jagessar, Michael and Burns, Stephen. Fragments of a Postcolonial Perspective on Christian Worship. *Worship* 80.5 (2006) 428-452

92 Brueggemann, Walther. *Texts under Negotiation: The Bible and Postmodern Imagination*. (Minneapolis: Fortress Press 1993) 19-20.

93 SC 37-40.

94 Ibid.

95 Chupungco, Anscar. "The Theological Principle of Adaptation," Dwight Vogel. Ed., *Primary Sources of Liturgical Theology: A Reader*. (Collegeville, MN: Liturgical Press 2000) 252.

96 See footnote 28.

97 Jagessar and Burns 440.

98 Ibid., 441.

99 Ramshaw, Gail. *Liturgical Language: Making it Metaphoric. Keeping it Inclusive*. (Collegeville, MN: Liturgical Press 1996) 29.

100 Ibid., 30.

101 Said 3.

[102]   Ramshaw 31.

[103]   Kassam, Tazim R "Embracing Disability in Teaching Religion," (editorial) in *Spotlight on Teaching* 20 (May 2005) i.

[104]   Walton, Janet. *Feminist Liturgy: A Matter of Justice.* (Collegeville, MN: Liturgical Press 2000) 37-38.

[105]   Spivak, Gayatri Chakravorty. "Can the Subaltern Speak?" Cary Nelson and Lawrence Grossberg, eds., *Marxism and the Interpretation of Culture (Communications & Culture)* (Basingstoke: Palgrave Macmillan 1988) 271-313, 306.

CHAPTER 5   DEVELOPMENTS

[106]   Ronfeldt, David. *In Search of How Societies Work: Tribes – The First and Forever Form* (Rand Pardee Centre WR-433-RPC 2006). http://www.rand.org/pubs/working_papers/2007/RAND_WR433.pdf

[107]   Ibid., 8.

[108]   Drucker, Peter F. *Managing for the Future.* (Oxford: Butterworth-Heinemann 1993) 171.

[109]   For a detailed description of the framework, see Ronfeldt 16.

[110]   Service, Elman R. *Origins of the State and Civilization: The Process of Cultural Evolution.* (New York: W. W. Norton and Company, 1975) 314-322.

[111]   Ronfeldt 52.

[112]   Weber, Max, *Economy and Society: An Outline of Interpretive Sociology,* Guenther Roth and Claus Wittich, eds., (Berkeley: University of California Press, [1922, 136–137] 1978), 40– 43.

[113]   Taber, Jay. Institutional Memory as Community Safeguard. *Report: Center for World Indigenous Studies* (undated) http://cwis.org/

fwj/71/Institutional%20Memory%20as%20Community%20 Safeguard.htm

114   Ibid.

115   Ibid.

116   Ibid.

117   See   http://lawdepartmentmanagement.typepad.com/law_ department_management/knowledge_management_in_law_ departments/index.html

118   Curran, Charles. "Risks of Theology." *Pastoral Review* (July 2006).

119   Ibid.

CHAPTER 6   INCULTURATION

120   Inculturation and the Roman Liturgy *Varietates Legitimae* (VL) *Fourth Instruction for the Right Application of the Conciliar Constitution on the Liturgy (Nos. 37-40)* Congregation for Divine Worship and the Discipline of the Sacraments (29 March 1994) 4.

121   John Paul II, Encyclical Letter *Redemptoris Missio* (7 December 1990) 10.

122   See VL 5 for references in this paragraph to preceding documents.

123   Mitchell, Nathan D. The Amen Corner. *Worship* 77:2 (2003) 171-181.

124   Working Document, 45; ibid.174.

125   The English text cited by John L. Allen, "Doubts about Dialogue: Encounter with Other Religions Runs Up Against the Vatican's Hard Doctrinal Realities," National Catholic Reporter, 27 August

1999. The subject-matter of the final sentence in this quotation reappears the following year in the CDF's declaration Dominus Jesus.

126 Declaration *Dominus Jesus* On the Unicity and Salvific Universality of Jesus Christ and the Church. Congregation for the Doctrine of the Faith. (6 August 2000), 4.

127 See "Toward a Pastoral Approach to Culture," 23 May 1999; English translation in *Origins* 29 (17 June 1999) 65-84.

128 Ibid., 76 (Paragraph 22).

129 Mitchell's (see note 123) footnote is offered here in full for the benefit of those who wish to know more of Modernism: "Readers will recall that 'Modernism' is a rather fluid, catch-all term for a variety of initiatives launched late in the nineteenth century by European Catholic scholars who sought to reconcile Christian faith with new perspectives in science and philosophy, especially through work in the fields of biblical criticism, church history, the philosophy of religion; and the history of doctrine. Many of its tenets and some of its personalities were condemned early in the twentieth century during the pontificate of St Pius X, especially in *Lamentabili*, a decree of the Holy Office listing the *"Errores Modernistarum"* (3 July 1907) and in the encyclical *Pascendi* (8 September 1907). The 'oath against modernism,' prescribed by Pius X in 1910, had to be taken by all candidates for ordination and was required annually, as well, from all seminary and theological faculties. Among many other things, those who took the oath rejected 'the false invention of the evolution of dogmas' and promised to adhere with all their hearts 'to all the condemnations, declarations, and prescriptions contained in the encyclical *Pascendi* and in the decree *Lamentabili.*' [For excerpts from both *Lamentabili* and *Pascendi*, see DS 3401-3466; 3475-3500; an English text of the oath against modernism, see J. Neuner, H. Roos, and K. Rahner, *The Teaching of the Catholic Church*, trans. "G.S.," (New York: Alba House 1967) 41-44.]"

130   On the Use of Vernacular Languages in the Publication of the Books of the Roman Liturgy *Liturgiam Authenticam* (LA) *"Fifth Instruction 'For the Right Implementation of the Constitution on the Sacred Liturgy of the Second Vatican Council'"* (*Sacrosanctum Concilium*, art. 36). Congregation for Divine Worship and the Discipline of the Sacraments (28 March 2001).

131   "Toward a Pastoral Approach to Culture," 2; *Origins* 29 (1999) 67.

132   Lynch, William F. *Christ and Apollo: The Dimensions of the Literary Imagination.* (New York: New American Library 1960) 118.

133   See "The Waste Land" (1922) in T. S. Eliot, Collected Poems 1909-1962 (New York: Harcourt, Brace & World 1970) 53.

134   Mitchell 180.

135   See Jameson, Fredric. "Postmodernism and Consumer Society," in Foster, Hal, ed., *Postmodern Culture* (London: Bay Press 1985) 114.

136   Mitchell, Nathan D. The Amen Corner *Worship* 74:1 (2000) 59-68.

137   Ibid., 61.

138   Fingarette, Herbert. *Confucius -The Secular as Sacred* (New York: Harper Torchbooks 1972) 116-17.

139   Seasoltz, R. Kevin. Artistic Images of Jesus: A Challenge to Liturgists, Religious Educators, and Theologians. *Worship* 73:1 (1999) 12-42.

140   Ibid., 14.

141   Ibid.

142   Walsh, Christopher J. Minding Our Language: Issues of Liturgical Language Arising in Revision. *Worship* 74.6 (2000) 482 – 503.

143   Ibid., 484.

[144]   *Comme le prévoit* – On The Translation Of Liturgical Texts For Celebrations With A Congregation. Consilium for Implementing the Constitution on the Sacred Liturgy 1969. http://www.ewtn.com/library/CURIA/CONSLEPR.HTM

[145]   Ibid., 498.

[146]   Ibid., 502

[147]   Ibid.

[148]   Ibid., 503.

[149]   Bede the Venerable, *History of the English Church and People*, chapter 1.27, unpublished translation by N. Mitchell, quoted in Ostdiek, G. Principles of Translation in the Revised Sacramentary in *Liturgy for the New Millennium: a Commentary on the Revised Sacramentary*, ed. Francis, M.R. and Pecklars, K. F. (Collegeville MN: The Liturgical Press 2000) 33.

[150]   Mitchell, Nathan D. The Amen Corner. *Worship* 74.5 (2000) 468-477.

[151]   Ibid., 477.

CHAPTER 7   EVANGELISATION

[152]   Paul VI, Apostolic Exhortation *Evangelii Nuntiandi*. (8 December 1975).

[153]   Conférence des Évêques de France. *Proposer la foi dans la société actuelle, III. Lettres aux catholiques de France.* (Paris : Les Editions du Cerf 1996).

[154]   See http://en.wikipedia.org/wiki/D._S._Amalorpavadass

[155]   See http://www.sedos.org/english/amaladoss.htm

[156] John Paul II. Post-Synodal Apostolic Exhortation *Ecclesia In Asia*. (6 November 1999).

[157] Freire, Paulo. *Pedagogy of the Oppressed.* (London: Continuum 2001).

[158] Freire, Paulo. Education, Liberation and the Church. *Theological Perspectives on Christian Education. A Reader on Theology and Christian Education.* Ed. Jeff Astley, Leslie J. Francis and Colin Crowder (Grand Rapids, Michigan: Gracewing 1996). pp169-186

[159] Ibid., 178.

[160] See Moltmann, Jurgen. *Religion, Revolution and the Future.* (New York, Charles Scribner's Sons, 1969), 5-6.

[161] Freire 1996, 181.

[162] Ibid., 185.

[163] Groome, Thomas H. *Christian Religious Education: Sharing Our Story and Vision.* (San Francisco: Jossey Bass 1999).

[164] O'Connell, Dan. RE in the Public Sphere. *The Furrow* July 2006.

CHAPTER 8   LIFELONG LEARNING

[165] Yeaxlee, B. A. *Lifelong Education,* (London: Cassell 1929).

[166] Ministry of Reconstruction (1919) *Final Report of the Adult Education Committee,* London: HMSO. 410 pages. Republished by University of Nottingham Department of Adult Education. Abridged version with an introduction by R. D. Waller published (1956) as *A Design for Democracy,* London: Max Parrish. 22.

[167] Fauré, E. *Learning to be.* (Paris: UNESCO 1972).

168   Bentley, T. *Learning beyond the Classroom: Education for a changing world*, (London: Routledge 1998), reported in *The Economist*, October 9, 1999, page 42.

169   Catholic Education Service. *The Catholic Partnership for Lifelong Learning*. (Chelmsford: Matthew James. 1999).

170   Catholic Education Service. *The Common Good in Education*. (London: CES 1997).

171   Introduction: Main Findings 5, p.6.

172   Catholic Bishops' Conference of England and Wales. *Religious Education Curriculum Directory*. (Chelmsford: Matthew James. 1996).

173   For details of the qualification see the EDI website http://www.lccieb.com/documents/Way%20of%20Faith%20L3%20Horizons%20Specification%20-%20website.pdf

174   See Raggatt *et al* 1996: 1, quoted in Smith, M. K. (1996, 2001) 'Lifelong learning', *the encyclopedia of informal education*. http://www.infed.org/lifelonglearning/b-life.htm.

175   See Coffield (1999) quoted in Smith(1996, 2001).

176   Leadbeater, Charles. *Living on Thin Air. The new economy*. (London: Penguin 2000), 111-112.

177   See Coombs, P. H. and Ahmed, M. *Attacking Rural Poverty. How non-formal education can help*. (Baltimore: John Hopkins University Press 1974) 8.

178   Eraut, M. Non-formal learning, implicit learning and tacit knowledge in professional work, in Coffield F. *The Necessity of Informal Learning*. (Bristol: The Policy Press 2000) 12.

179   Tennant, Mark. *Psychology and Adult Learning*. (London: Routledge1997) 77.

180   Ibid., 170.

181   See Smith, Mark K. Informal learning, *the encyclopaedia of informal education*. (1999, 2006) www.infed.org/biblio/inf-lrn.htm

182   For a detailed history of the term, see: Smith, M. K. (1996; 1999) Andragogy, *the encyclopaedia of informal education*. http://www.infed.org/lifelonglearning/b-andra.htm

183   See Knowles, Malcolm. *History, philosophy, and nature of adult education*. (Fort Lauderdale: Nova University, Center for Higher Education 1980).

184   Ibid., 44-45.

185   See Smith (1996, 2000).

186   See Green, J. Androgogy: Teaching adults. In B. Hoffman (Ed.), *Encyclopedia of Educational Technology*. (1998). http://coe.sdsu.edu/eet/Articles/andragogy/start.htm.

187   Jarvis, P. *The Sociology of Adult and Continuing Education*, (Beckenham: Croom Helm 1985). See Smith (1996, 2000). See Green (1998).

188   Freire, Paulo. *Pedagogy of the Oppressed*. (London: Continuum 2001).

189   For a detailed critique of Knowles' work see Smith, M. K. (1996; 1999) 'Andragogy', *the encyclopaedia of informal education*, http://www.infed.org/lifelonglearning/b-andra.htm

190   See Kliebart, H. M. *The Struggle for the American Curriculum 1893-1958,* (New York: Routledge 1987).

191   Kidd, J. R. *How Adults Learn* (Englewood Cliffs, N.J.: Prentice Hall Regents 1978) 17.

192   GE: Second Vatican Council, Declaration on Education, *Gravissimum Educationis*. (28 October 1965) Introduction 1.

193   Ibid., 2.

194   GDC: Sacred Congregation for the Clergy. General Directory for Catechesis. (11 August 1997).

CHAPTER 9   COMMUNITY

[195]   Ashwin, Angela. Spirituality and Corporate Worship – Separate Worlds or Vitally Connected. *Worship* 75:2 (2001) 106-129; here 108.

[196]   Beauduin, Lambert. *Liturgy the Life of the Church,* trans. Virgil Michel (Collegeville: The Liturgical Press 1926) 13. First published in French in 1914.

[197]   Ibid., 70.

[198]   Guardini, Romano. *The Spirit of the Liturgy,* trans. Ada Lane (New York: Crossroad Publishing Company 1998) 50. First published in German in 1918.

[199]   McPartland, Paul. Church and Communion. *Priest and People.* (August 2003).

[200]   Bishops' Conference of England and Wales. *The Sign We Give: Report from the Working Party on Collaborative Ministry.* (Chelmsford: Matthew James Publishing 1995).

[201]   Ibid., 35.

[202]   Pope John Paul II. Apostolic Letter: At the beginning of the new millennium. *Novo Millennio Ineunte.* (6 January 2001).

[203]   Lathrop, Gordon. The Reforming Gospels: A Liturgical Theologian Looks again at Eucharistic Origins. *Worship* 83:3 (2009), 194-212; here 211.

[204]   Michel, Virgil, Infidelity in the Church, *Orate Fratres* 9 (October 1935): 495.

[205]   Boys, Mary. *Maps and visions: educating in faith.* (Lima, Ohio: Academic Renewal Press 1989) 89.

[206]   Ibid., 120.

207   Hofinger, Johannes. Evangelization by the Celebration of the Liturgical Feasts. *Worship* 10 (1955) 249. 243-60.

208   Hofinger, Johannes. *The art of teaching Christian doctrine.* (Notre Dame: University of Notre Dame Press 1957) 132.

209   Gaillardetz, Richard R. North American Culture and the Liturgical Life of the Church: The Separation of the Quests for Transcendence and Community. *Worship* 68:5 (September 1994) 403-416.

210   Ibid., 405.

211   Ibid., 406.

212   Ibid.

213   Ibid., 407.

214   Rasmussen, Larry. *Moral fragments & Moral Community: A Proposal for Church in Society.* (Minneapolis: Fortress 1993).

215   Ibid., 408.

216   Ibid., 410.

217   Ibid.

218   Ibid., 413.

219   Ibid., 415.

220   Mitchell, Nathan. The Amen Corner *Worship* 68:2 (1994) 167.

CHAPTER 10   THE PASCHAL MYSTERY

221   Bonhoeffer, Dietrich. *Letters and Papers from Prison*, (first English translation 1953 by SCM Press). This edition translated by Reginald H. Fuller and Frank Clark from *Widerstand und Ergebung: Briefe und Aufzeichnungen aus der Haft*. (Munich: Christian Kaiser Verlag 1970. Touchstone 1997).

222   The *Sermons* of St Maximus of Turin. Sermon 53,2,4.

223   Boulding, Maria. *The Coming of God.* (London: SPCK 1982).

224   *Letter to the Magnesians* 9, 1 (SC 10:102-5).

225   St Justin, *Dialogus cum Tryphone* 40.

226   Melito of Sardis, *Peri Pascha ("Concerning the Passover")* 11 and 15.

227   Eusebius, *Demonstratio evangelica* I, 10 (PG 22:92).

228   *Ibid.*, V, 3 (PG 22:368).

229   Mohrman, C. *"Sacramentum* dans les plus anciens texts chrétiens," in her *Etudes sur le latin des chrétiens* 1 (Storia e letteratura 65; Rome: Edizioni di storia e letteratura. 1958), 233-44.

230   Martimort, A.G. *The Church at Prayer, Vol 1 Principles of the Liturgy.* (London Geoffrey Chapman 1983) 257.

231   Fourth Eucharistic Prayer in *The Roman Missal* (Rous Lench, Worcestershire: John F. Neale 1972).

232   SC 11, 14, 19, 21, 27, 30, 41, 50, 79, 113, 114, 121, 124.

233   Irwin, Kevin. *Models of the Eucharist.* (New York/Mahwah NJ, Paulist Press. 2005) 143.

234   SC 102-4.

235   Casel, Odo. *Das christliche Kultmysterium*, 4th revised and expanded ed. by B. Neunheuser (Regensberg: Pustet, 1960), 29; English

translation: *The Mystery of Christian Worship* (Westminster, Md.: Newman, 1962), 12.

[236] Martimort, A.G. *The Church at Prayer, Vol 1 Principles of the Liturgy* (London Geoffrey Chapman 1983) 265.

[237] Schepers, Maury. An Integral Spirituality of the Paschal Mystery. *Worship* 75.2 (2001) 99.

[238] Ibid., 101.

[239] Ibid., 106.

[240] Mitchell, Nathan D. Mystery and Manners: Eucharist in Post-modern Theology. *Worship* 79:2 (2005) 130-151.

[241] Ibid., 136-139.

[242] See Luke 10:21-22: "At that same hour Jesus rejoiced in the Holy Spirit and said, 'I thank you, Father, Lord of heaven and earth, because you have hidden these things from the wise and the intelligent and have revealed them to infants; yes, Father, for such was your gracious will. All things have been handed over to me by my Father; and no one knows who the Son is except the Father, or who the Father is except the Son and anyone to whom the Son chooses to reveal him.'"

[243] Marion, Jean-Luc. "The Gift of a Presence," in *Prolegomena to Charity*, trans. Stephen Lewis (New York: Fordham University Press 2002) 151-152.

[244] Mitchell (2005) 149-150.

[245] From the *Addresses* of St Andrew of Crete. Or 9.

CHAPTER 11   LITURGY

[246] Second Vatican Council, Dogmatic Constitution on Divine Revelation *Dei Verbum* (18 November 1965)

247   Rahner, Karl. "The Word and the Eucharist," *Theological Investigations* 4 (London: Burns & Oates 1968) 253-86.

248   Vorgrimler, Herbert, *Sacramental   Theology.* (Collegeville: The Liturgical Press 1992) 8-9.

249   Mitchell, Nathan D. The Amen Corner. Worship 73.6 (1999) 545-555.

250   Hebblethwaite, Peter. *Paul VI: The First Modern Pope* (New York: Paulist Press 1993) 305. For further documentation and detail see Aimé Georges Martimort, « Le role de Paul VI dans la réforme liturgique, » in *Le Role de G. B. Montini-Paul VI dans la Réforme Liturgique* [Brescia: Istituto Paolo VI 1987] 59-73.

251   Hebblethwaite, 376; see Martimort, 62-63 for discussion of this incident and for a comparison of the two texts of the *motu proprio.*

252   Mitchell (1999) 548.

253   Pecklers Keith F. *Liturgy in a Post-modern World* (New Century Theology) (New York/London: Continuum June 2003).

254   Congregation for Divine Worship and the Discipline of the Sacraments. Inculturation and the Roman Liturgy *Varietates Legitimae* (VL) *Fourth Instruction for the Right Application of the Conciliar Constitution on the Liturgy* (Nos. 37-40) (29 March 1994).

255   Sacred Congregation for Divine Worship. Directory for Masses With Children *Pueros Baptizatos* (November 1, 1973). First published in England as: Directory on children's masses, with an appendix on the Eucharistic Prayers (London; CTS 1974).

256   Johnson, Clare V. The Children's Eucharistic Prayers: A Model of Liturgical Inculturation. *Worship* 75:3 (2001) 209-227.

257   Ibid., 213, note 14.

258   Ibid., 217.

259   Ibid., 226.

²⁶⁰ See Shorter, Aylward. *Toward a Theology of Inculturation* (Maryknoll: Orbis Books 1988).

²⁶¹ Chupungco, Anscar J. *Liturgical Inculturation: Sacramentals, Religiosity and Catechesis* (Collegeville: The Liturgical Press 1992) 30.

²⁶² Ibid., 32.

²⁶³ Ibid., 35.

²⁶⁴ Ibid., 37.

²⁶⁵ See Nida, Eugene. *Message and Mission.* (New York: Harper & Brothers 1960).

²⁶⁶ Ibid., 221.

²⁶⁷ Nida, Eugene. *Theory and Practice of Translation.* (Leiden: Brill 1969) 31-2.

²⁶⁸ Marlowe, Michael. Against the Theory of 'Dynamic Equivalence'. (Bible Research. Internet Resources for Students of Scripture. Revised, May 2009). http://www.bible-researcher.com/dynamic-equivalence.html

²⁶⁹ Chupungco, Anscar J. Inculturation and Organic Progression of the Liturgy. *Ecclesia Orans 7* (1990/1) 7-21.

²⁷⁰ Antonio, David William. *An Inculturation Model of the Catholic Marriage Ritual.* (Collegeville: Liturgical Press 2002).

²⁷¹ Chupungco (1992) 53.

²⁷² Ibid., 53-54.

CHAPTER 12 INITIATION

²⁷³ First published in England: *Rite Of Christian Initiation Of Adults.* (London: Catholic Truth Society 1976). Revised edition: ICEL.

Rite Of Christian Initiation Of Adults. (London: Geoffrey Chapman 1985).

274   Bugnini, Annibale. *The Reform of the Liturgy 1948-1975* (Collegeville MN: The Liturgical Press 1990) chapter 35. For a detailed discussion of the process see Bugnini cp 35.

275   Bugnini 586.

276   *Visio Baronti Monachi Longoretensis* (679). See Lucey-Roper, Michelle M. *The Visio Baronti in its early medieval context.* (Oxford: University of Oxford 2000).

277   Norberg, Dag. Medieval Latin After the Year 1000. *Manuel pratique de latin médiéval* (Paris, 1980), English translation by R.H.Johnson. http://www.orbilat.com/Languages/Latin_Medieval/Dag_Norberg/07.html

278   Bugnini (1990) 591.

279   Serra, Dominic E. New Observations About the Scrutinies of the Elect in Early Roman Practice *Worship* 80:6 (2006) 511-527.

280   See Power, David N. "Cult to Culture: the Mediating Role of Theology," in *Worship: Culture and Theology* (Washington, D.C.: Pastoral Press 1990) 3-24.

281   See Jungmann, Josef. "The Defeat of Teutonic Ariansim and the Revolution in Religious Culture in the Early Middle Ages," in *Pastoral Liturgy* (New York: Herder and Herder 1962) 1-101.

282   Chupungco, Anscar J. *Liturgies of the Future: The Process and Methods of Inculturation.* (New York: Paulist 1989) 3-55.

283   See Wedig, Mark E. Evangelization, Inculturation and the RCIA. *Worship* 76:6 (2002) 503-520.

284   Second Vatican Council, Decree on missionary activity in the Church *Ad Gentes* (7 December 1965) 23.

285   Chupungco, Anscar J. *Liturgical Inculturation: Sacramentals, Religiosity and Catechesis.* (Collegeville: The Liturgical Press 1992) 30.

286   See Chapter 11.

287   Chupungco, Anscar J. "Baptism, Marriage and Funeral Rites: Principles and Criteria for Inculturation," in *Baptism, Rites of Passage and Culture*, edited by Stauffer, S. Anita (Geneva: Lutheran World Federation 1998) 51.

288   Kavanagh, Aidan. *The Shape of Baptism: The Rite of Christian Initiation.* (Collegeville: The Liturgical Press 1978/1991) 102-106.

289   Power, David N. Foreword to *Celebrating Jesus Christ in Africa: Liturgy and Inculturation.* (Maryknoll: Orbis 1998) ix.

290   Borgmann, Albert. *Crossing the Postmodern Divide.* (Chicago: University of Chicago Press 1992) 6.

291   Ibid., 110-147.

292   Ibid., 106.

293   Ibid., 110-116.

294   Cf. Haughton, Rosemary. *Images for change: The Transformation of Society.* (New York: Paulist 1997) 45-84.

295   Borgmann, 123.

296   Koester, Anne Y. Is There Life After the Triduum? *Worship* 74.2 (2000).

297   Dujarier, Michael. *The Rites of Christian Initiation* (New York: Wm H Sadlier, Inc 1979) 208.

298   Morris, Thomas H. *The RCIA: Transforming the Church – A Resource for Pastoral Implementation.* (New York: Paulist Press 1997) 212.

299   RCIA 248.

300   RCIA 4.

301   RCIA 246.

CHAPTER 13   IMAGINATION

302   These remarks followed Stephen Schloesser's presentation "Inventing the Catholic Novel," and were given as part of a panel discussion on "The Catholic Imagination: Faith and Modernism" at Santa Clara University's conference Jesuit Humanism: Faith, Justice, and Empiricism in the Liberal Arts, May 5, 2001 http://www.scu.edu/ignatiancenter/bannan/publications/explore/spring02/pollutedprotagonists.cfm 19 March 2007

303   McBrien. Richard P. "The Church Is 'Catholic' Because It's Sacramental." *National Catholic Reporter* (January 15, 1993), 26

304   Ibid.

305   Greeley, Andrew M. *The Catholic Imagination.* (Berkeley: University of California Press, 2000), 1.

306   Ibid., 168

307   See note 2.

308   Hilkert. Mary Catherine. *Naming Grace: Preaching and the Sacramental Imagination.* (New York: Continuum 1997).

309   See Tracy, David. *The Analogical Imagination: Christian Theology and the Culture of Pluralism.* (New York: Crossroad 1981).

310   In a review of Hilkert's *Naming Grace: Preaching and the Sacramental Imagination* by Linda Lee Nelson in *Christian Century*, March 4, 1998.   http://findarticles.com/p/articles/mi_m1058/is_n7_v115/ai_20412573/?tag=content;col1

311   Mitchell. Nathan D. The Amen Corner. *Worship* 74:4 (2000) 370-379, here 371.

312   Hansen, Ron. Faith and Fiction, *America,* vol.178:11 (April 1998) 8-16, here 10.

313   Mitchell, 374-375.

314   Butorac, Nina. The Sacramental Imagination and Catholic Literature. See http://www.alyosha.com/si/si.html 19 March 2007

315   Greeley, Andrew. *The Catholic Myth*. (New York; Macmillan Publishing Company, 1990) 34.

316   Ibid 45

317   Ibid 45

318   CCC 1131

319   Heartney, Eleanor. "Blood, Sex, and Blasphemy - The Catholic Imagination in Contemporary Art". *New Art Examiner.*

320   *On the Way to Life: Contemporary Culture and Theological Development as a Framework for Catholic Education, Catechesis and Formation.* A Study by The Heythrop Institute for Religion, Ethics and Public Life. (London: C.E.S. 2005).

321   OTWTL 63.

322   Ibid., 63.

323   Ibid., 65.

324   http://www2.ces.web.baigent.net/standard.asp?id=513

325   Groome, Thomas. Chapter Three: "What's It All About?" – Taking a Sacramental View *What Makes Us Catholic: Eight Gifts For Life*. Notes for Reading Circles In Preparation for the Marianist Universities Meetings June 7-10, 2004.

326   Rush Orm. "Full, Conscious and Active Participation: Formation in the Sacramental Imagination". Delivered at Liturgical Symposium "Vatican Council II *Sacrosanctum Concilium* 1963-200", Brisbane 4 December 2003. http://dlibrary.acu.edu.au/research/theology/ejournal/aejt_2/Liturgy.htm

CHAPTER 14   SACRAMENTS

[327]   For details see Turner, Paul. Forum: Confusion over Confirmation. *Worship* 71.6 (1997) 538.

[328]   Ibid., 539.

[329]   Ibid., 540.

[330]   Ibid., 541.

[331]   Ibid., 543.

[332]   Turner, Paul. "The Origins of Confirmation: An Analysis of Aidan Kavanagh's Hypothesis." *Worship*, 65:4 (1991) 326-36.

[333]   For a detailed treatment of this issue see Johnson, Maxwell E. Contemporary Study of Christian Initiation. *Worship* 75:1 (2001) 25-26.

[334]   Winkler, G. "Confirmation or Chrismation? A Study in Comparative Liturgy," *Worship* 58 (1984) 2-17.

[335]   Johnson 29.

[336]   For a more detailed reflection on the 1971 revision see Quinn, Frank. "Confirmation Reconsidered: Rite and Meaning. *Worship* 59 (1985) 354-70.

[337]   Quinn 29.

[338]   See Austin, G. *Anointing with the Spirit.* (Collegeville: Pueblo 1985) 155.

[339]   Humfrey, Peter. *Confirmation : A Community Preparation.* (London: Geoffrey Chapman 1985) 5-6.

[340]   Ibid. 31.

341   Order of Christian Marriage. (London: Pastoral Liturgy Committee, Bishops' Conference of England and Wales 1992) no 602.

342   International Commission on English in the Liturgy. *The Rite of Penance*. (London: J F Neale 1974)

343   Irish Bishops Conference. Rite of Penance (Dublin: Veritas 1976) 31.

344   Celichowski, John. Meditation and Metanoia: Using Principles of Alternative Dispute Resolution to Reform the Rite of Penance. *Worship* 76:3 (2002) 244-267.

345   Challeen, Dennis. *Making It Right: A Common Sense Approach to Criminal Justice* (New York: Melius & Peterson 1986), quoted in Gorringe, Timothy. *God's Just Vengeance* (New York: Cambridge University Press 1996) 250.

346   Order of Christian Funerals (London Geoffrey Chapman 1990).

347   OCF 8.

CHAPTER 15   PRESENCE

348   Lau, Markus. "Die *Legio X Fretensis* und der Besessene von Gerasa. Anmerkungen zur Zahlenangabe "ungefähr Zweitausend" (Mk 5:13)", *Biblica* Vol. 88 (2007) 351-364.

349   Josephus, Titus Flavius. *The Jewish War* 2, 499-506).

350   SC 7.

351   Mitchell, Nathan. The Amen Corner. *Worship* 80:3 (2006) 252-265.

352   Murphy-O'Connor, Jerome. Commentary on I Corinthians, 11:17-34 in Brown, Raymond E. et al., eds., *The New Jerome Biblical*

Commentary (Englewood Cliffs NJ: Prentice-Hall 1990) 49:56, p. 809.

Casel, Odo. "The Mystery of Worship," an excerpt from *The Mystery of Christian Worship and Other Writings*, in Vogel, Dwight W. ed., *Primary Sources of Liturgical Theology: A Reader* (Collegeville, MN: Liturgical Press 2000) 29; emphasis added.

Casel, Odo. *Das Christliche Kultmysterium*, 3rd ed. (Regensburg: Pustet 1948) 102; cited in Hall, *We Have the Mind of Christ*, 11.

Marion, Jean-Luc, "The Gift of a Presence," in *Prolegomena to Charity*, trans. Stephen Lewis (New York: Fordham University Press 2002) 124.

Schoonenberg. Piet. "Tegenwoordigheid," *Verbum* 31 (1964) 395-415; here, 396; English translation in FitzPatrick, P. J. *In Breaking of Bread*, (Cambridge: University Press 2008) 59.

Catechism of the Catholic Church. (London: Continuum 2002) 1396.

Hall, M. Jerome. *We Have the Mind of Christ: The Holy Spirit and Liturgical Memory in the Thought of Edward J. Kilmartin.* (Collegeville: Liturgical Press 2001) 42.

Ibid., 43.

Ibid.

Ibid.

Hall, 120.

Ibid.

Marion, Jean-Luc. "The Present and the Gift," in *God Without Being*, trans. Thomas A. Carlson (Chicago: University of Chicago Press 1991) 161-82.

Ibid., 164.

Ibid.

367 Sanders, Theresa. The Otherness of God and the Bodies of Others. *The Journal of Religion* 76:4 (1996) 572-87; here, 576. The phrase "brandished like a banner [in] processions" is Marion's; see "The Present and the Gift," 164.

368 Marion 166.

369 Ibid., 178.

370 Mitchell, Nathan. The Amen Corner. *Worship* 80:5 (2006) 453-466.

371 See Chauvet, Louis-Marie. *Symbol and Sacrament. A Sacramental Reinterpretation of Christian Existence*, trans. Patrick Madigan and Madeleine Beaumont (Collegeville MN: Liturgical Press/A Pueblo Book 1995) 275-276.

372 Marion, Jean-Luc. *Prolegomena to Charity*, trans. Stephen Lewis (New York: Fordham University Press 2000) 124-152, here 124.

373 Ibid.

374 Ibid., 127.

375 Origen, *Homily on Exodus* 13.3; English translation in Sheerin, Daniel J. *The Eucharist*, (Message of the Fathers of the Church, Volume 7; Wilmington, DE: Michael Glazier 1986) 178.

376 Power, David. *Sacrament: The Language of God's Giving*. (New York: Crossroad, 1999).

377 Fourth Eucharistic Prayer in *The Roman Missal* (Rous Lench, Worcestershire: John F. Neale 1972).

378 Power, David. *The Eucharistic Mystery*. (New York: Crossroad 1992) 288.

379 Mitchell, Nathan. The Amen Corner. *Worship* 80:5 (2006) 562.

[380] Denzinger, H. and Schönmetzer A. *Enchiridion Symbolorum Definitionum Et Declarationum De Rebus Fidei Et Morum.* (DS) (New York: Herder 1957) 1651.

[381] DS 1636; 1651.

[382] *Catechism of the Catholic Church (CCC)* 1374.

[383] Mitchell, Nathan. The Amen Corner. *Worship* 80:5 (2006) 565.

CHAPTER 16   CATECHESIS

[384] Foxe, John. The historye of Doctour Rowland Tailour, whiche suffred for the truth of Gods woord, vnder the tiranny of the Romayne Byshop. Anno. 1555. the. 9. day of February in *Book of Martyrs,* Book 11 p.1693 in 1570 edition. (*Foxe's Book of Martyrs Variorum Edition: Online version 1.1 – Summer 2006*). http://www.hrionline.ac.uk/johnfoxe/

[385] Castrillon Hoyos, Cardinal Dario. The Fundamental Importance of Catechesis. An Address given by Cardinal Castrillon Hoyos, prefect of the Cong. for the Clergy on November 14, 1998 to those participating in a seminar on implementing the 1997 GDC. www.catholicculture.org/library/view.cfm?id=791&repos=1

[386] International Council for Catechesis. *Adult Catechesis in the Christian Community: Some Principles and Guidelines* (ACCC). (Vatican: Libreria Editrice Vaticana 1990).

[387] RCIA 75.

[388] Villepelet, Denis. « Catéchèse en mutation I : Les défis actuels de la tâche catéchétique en France ». *Catéchèse : Revue de pastorale et de formation.* 172 3/2003.21-47.

389   Catechetical Commission of the Ukrainian Catholic Church. *Catechetical Directory of the Ukrainian Catholic Church*. (Lviv: Svichado 2000).

390   CT 23.

391   St. Gregory of Nyssa. *Accurate Exposition of the Canticle of Canticles*, 8.

392   St. Basil the Great, *Homilies*, 8.

393   See Westerhoff, John H. III. *Will Our Children Have Faith?* (New York: Morehouse Publishing 2002).

394   Chupungco, Anscar. *Liturgical Inculturation: Sacramentals, Religiosity and Catechesis*. (Collegeville, MN: The Liturgical Press 1992) 134.

395   SC 10.

396   Kottak, Conrad Phillip. *Windows on Humanity*. (New York: McGraw Hill 2005) 209.

397   *Ordo dedicationis ecclesiae et altaris*, 4, 3.

398   Chupungco, 170.

399   GDC 59, 90.

400   Rosier, Veronica. The Baptismal Catechumenate in the *General Directory for Catechesis (1997)*. *Worship* 73.2 (1999) 98-124.

401   Dooley, Catherine. Liturgical Catechesis: Mystagogy, Marriage or Misnomer? *Worship* 66.5 (1992) 386.

402   Morris, Thomas H . *The RCIA: Transforming the Church, A Resource for Pastoral Implementation* (Mahwah, N.J.: Paulist 1997) 2, 48-50. For a full discussion of model see Rosier's article especially 101-115.

403   Rosier 114.

404   Ibid., 117

384

[405] *Catechism of the Catholic Church*, (London: Continuum 2002) 1210-1690.

[406] *Ad gentes* 14; RCIA 1, 8; *Catechesi tradendae* 5.

[407] Rosier, 123.

[408] Lewinski, Ron. "Recovering Christian Mystagogy for Contemporary Churches," in *Before and After Baptism*, ed. James A. Wilde (Chicago: Liturgy Training Publications 1988) 91.

CHAPTER 17   MINISTRY

[409] Second Vatican Council. *Decree on the Apostolate of the Laity (Apostolicam Actuositatem)* (AA) 10, in *The Documents of Vatican II*, edited by Walter M. Abbott (London: Geoffrey Chapman 1967).

[410] .Mitchell, Nathan D, The Amen Corner *Worship* 78:2 (2004) 165-175.

[411] Ibid., 166.

[412] Ibid.

[413] Ibid., 167.

[414] Hahnenberg, Edward P. *Ministry: A Relational Approach* (New York: Crossroad Publishing Company 2003) 175.

[415] Ibid.

[416] Kavanagh, Aidan. Unfinished and Unbegun: The Rite of Christian Initiation of Adults. *Worship* 53:4 (1979) 335-36.

[417] Gaillardetz Richard R. In Service of Communion: A Trinitarian Foundation for Christian Ministry. *Worship* 67.5 (1993) 418-433, here 418.

[418] Ibid., 428.

419   Ibid. 430.

420   Nouwen, Henri J. M. *The Wounded Healer.* (Garden City: Image Books 1972).

421   Gaillardetz, 431.

422   Ibid., 432.

423   Osborne, Kenan B., *The Permanent Diaconate: Its History and Place in the Sacrament of Orders.* (New York: Paulist Press 2007).

424   Ibid. 140.

425   Collins, John N., *Deacons and the Church: Making Connections Between Old and New.* (Leominster; Gracewing 2008).

426   Cummings, Owen. *Deacons and the Church.* (Mahwah NJ: Paulist Press 2004).

427   USCCB. *Co-Workers in the Vineyard of the Lord: A Resource for Guiding the Development of Lay Ecclesial Ministry.* (Washington: USCCB, 2006), 15.

428   Ibid., 5.

429   Diocese of Arundel & Brighton. *Preparing Together; A Reflection and Discussion Programme Offered to Parish Communities in November 2002.* Diocese of Arundel & Brighton Pastoral Service. www.dabnet.org/docs.httm

CHAPTER 18   SACRED SPACE

430   National Conference of Bishops [United States]. *Environment and Art in Catholic Worship* (Chicago: Liturgical Training Publications 1978; 1993).

United States Conference of Catholic Bishops (USCCB). *Built of Living Stones: Art, Architecture, and Worship.* (Washington: USCCB 2000). *http://www.nccbuscc.org/liturgy/livingstonesind.shtml*

431   Canadian Conference of Catholic Bishops. *Our Place in Worship.* (Ottawa, ON: Publications Service CCCB 1999).

432   Catholic Bishops' Conference of England and Wales. *The Parish Church: principles of liturgical design and reordering.* (London: Catholic Truth Service, 1984).

Catholic Bishops' Conference of England and Wales. *Consecrated for Worship. A Directory on Church Building.* (London: Catholic Truth Society 2006). Full text and resources can be accessed at www. liturgyoffice.org.uk/Resources/CFW

433   Keenan, Joseph. Temples and Churches. *Worship* 68:3 (1994) 222-231; here 222.

434   Ibid., 223-226. For a detailed discussion of buildings and rites in the first four centuries see Dujarier, Michel. *A History of the Catechumenate: The First Six Centuries.* (New York: William H Sadlier 1979).

435   Ibid., 228.

436   Ibid., 231.

437   Canadian Conference of Catholic Bishops, *Our Place of Worship* (Ottawa, ON: Publications Service CCCB 1999) 17; 13. Cf. SC 124.

438   NCCB/USCC (Now USCCB) *Built of Living Stones: Art, Architecture, and Worship.* (November 16, 2000) 17.

439   Ibid., 11.

440   Ibid., 48.

441   "A Letter from Romano Guardini," *Herder Correspondence* 1:1 (Special issue 64) 24-26; here, 25.

442   Ciferni, Andrew D. "The Ceremonial of Bishops: Challenges and Opportunities." *Assembly* 17 (September 1991) 532.

443 International Committee on English in the Liturgy (ICEL). General Instruction of the Roman Missal (*Institutio Generalis Missalis Romani. 2002*) (London: Catholic Truth Society 2005).

444 Ciferni, 532.

445 *Our Place of Worship*, 26.

446 CFW 209.

447 Mitchell, Nathan D. The Amen Corner. *Worship* 73.4 (1999) 359-368; here 360.

448 Ibid., 363.

449 Vosko, Richard S. A House for the Church: Structures for Public Worship in a New Millennium. *Worship* 74.3 (2000) 194-212; here 195.

450 Postman, Neil. *Building a Bridge to the Eighteenth Century: How the Past Can Improve Our Future* (New York: Alfred A. Knopf 1999) 10.

451 Vosko, 196.

452 Postman, 109 ff.

453 Ibid., 198.

454 Ibid., 199.

455 Ibid., 209.

456 Ibid., 201.

457 Merton, Thomas. *Sign of Jonas*. (New York: Harcourt and Brace 1979) 87.

458 Botta, Mario. Architetture del Sacro. *Church Building* 96 (November-December 2005) 12-15.

459 See the brilliant animated tour at http://www.ndarche.org/

460   Walker, Paul. Leeds Cathedral Reordering. *Church Building* 104 (March -April 2007) 34-37. For a visual guide see http:// www.dioceseofleeds.org.uk/cathedral/cathedral_tour/view_ cathedral.php

461   For the complete interpretation by the architect Franck Hammoutène see http://catholiques.aladefense.cef.fr/IMG/ pdf/Guide_de_visite.pdf

462   Catholic Bishops' Conference of England and Wales. *Consecrated for Worship. A Directory on Church Building.* (London: Catholic Truth Society 2006).

463   Second Vatican Council, Dogmatic Constitution on the Church *Lumen Gentium* (21 November 1964) 8.

Lightning Source UK Ltd.
Milton Keynes UK
23 November 2010

163324UK00001B/32/P